Social Theory and Modernity

For Gio and Elliot

Social Theory and Modernity

Nigel Dodd

Polity Press

First published in 1999 by Polity Press
in association with Blackwell Publishers Ltd.

Editorial office:
Polity Press
65 Bridge Street
Cambridge CB2 1UR, UK

Marketing and production:
Blackwell Publishers Ltd
108 Cowley Road
Oxford OX4 1JF, UK

Published in the USA by
Blackwell Publishers Inc.
Commerce Place
350 Main Street
Malden, MA 02148, USA

ISBN 0-7456-1313-6
ISBN 0-7456-1314-4 (pbk)

A catalogue record for this book is available from the British Library.

Library of Congress Cataloging-in-Publication Data

Dodd, Nigel, 1965–
    Social theory and modernity / Nigel Dodd.
        p.   cm.
    Includes bibliographical references.
    ISBN 0-7456-1313-6 (plpc : alk. paper). —— ISBN 0-7456-1314-4 (pbk. : alk. paper)
    1. Sociology—History—19th century.   2. Sociology—History—20th century.   I. Title.
    HM445.D63   1999
    301'.09—dc21
                                                        99-25388
                                                        CIP

Typeset in 10.5 on 12 pt Palatino
by Ace Filmsetting Ltd, Frome, Somerset
Printed in Great Britain by MPG Books, Bodmin, Cornwall

This book is printed on acid-free paper.

Contents

Acknowledgements

The arguments of this book have been developed over several years in which I have been involved in teaching social theory to undergraduates and postgraduates, and in investigating how theoretical ideas can facilitate research in the context of the sociology of economic life. I would like to thank: Tony Giddens for commissioning the book and offering valuable advice on its content; an anonymous referee for providing constructive and useful comments; Bridget Hutter for superbly detailed and critical comments on an earlier draft which made a significant difference to the structure of the book – and for being an incomparable colleague and friend; and Giovanna Pontieri, for reading and commenting on successive drafts with great clarity and insight – and for her extreme patience and good humour. Unfortunately, the errors are all mine.

Introduction: Modern and Postmodern Social Theory

According to its postmodern critics, the project of modernity has disintegrated. The concepts, categories and modes of explanation of modern social theory must therefore be set aside. Not only were they conceived for a society that no longer exists. They are symptomatic of, even partly responsible for, the failure of that society. The project of modernity was an idealization of society which sought to build on Enlightenment thought. It focused on universal values, and drew nourishment from the belief that history is a process of advancement towards the realization of those values. Modern social theory was a means not only of explaining, but primarily of justifying those values and that belief. It consisted of a generalized model of society which, through its concepts and categories, symbolized the ideals of modernity. And in its modes of explanation, modern social theory epitomized the belief in history as progress. It is this relationship, between the project of modernity and the social theories which were deployed in its name, that informs the argument and organization of this book.

This book has two basic aims. First, to provide a brief but critical account of the work of fifteen major social theorists. And second, to develop a very tentative argument about how some of the questions, problems and dilemmas that arise from that account might be addressed. My starting-point is this. The postmodern critique of modern social theory and the project of modernity raises questions to which, as yet, we have no satisfactory answers. But the debate between modernists and postmodernists is not, fundamentally, about competing descriptions of social reality. The questions raised by the debate concern rival theoretical territories and conflicting normative ideals. Such questions include: Is social theory objective or subjective? Does it embrace universalism or pluralism? Should it employ a concept of reason which governs and justifies belief, or which merely empathizes with and interprets it? Is it part of a formal dialogue, or of an informal conversation? And should it begin at the level of society and the social system, or with the individual? One significant question which rarely seems to arise in the debate – or which, at best, is an area in which not much appears to be at stake – concerns the relationship between theoretical concepts and modes of explanation on the one hand, and empirical research on the other. One need hardly be surprised by this. But it is important that we are aware of it. It will be a significant theme as the discussion in this book proceeds.

Clarity of concepts and categories seems often to be something of a novelty in the literature on modernity and postmodernity, so let me begin by trying to define the ideas, arguments and terms of debate that are used in the following chapters. I have already suggested that the debate between modernists and postmodernists addresses two major sets of questions. The first is about social theory, the second about conflicting normative projects. By theory, I refer to a system of interrelated concepts, categories and modes of explanation that are, at the very least, designed to make sense of the world around us. Functionalism is a theory, as is Marxism. Modernity and postmodernity are not theories. These terms are often used to refer to, and therefore as interchangeable with, the ideas of modern society and postmodern society, respectively. Without implying criticism of this usage, I shall not adopt it. For the sake of clarity, I shall employ the words modernity and postmodernity only as generic terms which refer to normative projects. A normative project can be defined as a system of thought and belief which is concerned in some way with improving society. It is normative because values and ideals are not only implied but in question. It is a project because there is an implicit, but more often explicit and systematic, involvement with the way in which society reproduces itself over time.

The separation of a social theory from a normative project is heuristic, that is, something which enables us more closely to investigate a state of affairs, but which does not exhaustively describe it. I am using it primarily to draw out a distinction which is sometimes only insinuated by, and therefore must be read into, the social theories discussed in this book. For that reason, the distinction will occasionally break down, as in the case of Foucault. But that is the point of using the distinction in the first place. Because it is heuristic, it is not meant to describe a state of affairs in an exact way. It is a tool of understanding, intended to clarify similarities and differences which, quite often, are not very clear at all. When the distinction begins to break down – or alternatively, when it appears to fit – we might learn something.

As indicated above, I shall not be using the terms modernity and postmodernity to denote particular societies or periods of history, but the normative projects that are associated with them. When modern or postmodern society is referred to, I shall do so literally. Chronologically, modern society is in some ways much easier to define than postmodern society, although common usage of the term modern to mean contemporary can create confusion. When modern society is taken to mean a specific historical period or age, one might provide a different account of when it began – and, perhaps, when it ended – depending on whether it is defined primarily in cultural, political or economic terms. Because he seeks to combine these terms, I shall use Giddens's definition of modern society: 'those modes of social life or organization emerging in Europe from around the seventeenth century, and which subsequently became worldwide in their influence' (1990: 1).

As I have already said, postmodern society is more difficult to pin down in a precise way, and for many theorists this is either part of the problem or the source of its attraction. No single definition is entirely satisfying. As I shall discuss in chapter 6, postmodern society is closely associated with post-industrialism, which we can trace back to the early 1960s in the United States and to the late 1960s in Europe; to the information society, which came a little later; and to consumer society, which according to some commentators came later still. There are further complications. The notion of postmodernism is often used to refer to questions which arise in relation to epistemology, aesthetics and culture. But again, usage is uneven. Although there are some strong links between these different treatments of postmodernism, there are also some rather alarming inconsistencies. I shall discuss these in chapters 6 and 7 only in so far as they have some bearing on postmodern social theory. But for the time being, and to remain consistent with the definition of modern society, I propose to define postmodern society as those modes of *re*organization of social institutions and social life which began to emerge during the late 1960s, and which primarily consist of a growth in information technology, global communications media and the service sector; an expansion of exchange relations in consumerism and financial markets; and increasing cultural pluralism.

I have suggested that the debate between modernists and postmodernists is primarily addressed to competing versions of social theory, and rival normative projects, rather than to different descriptions of reality. The organization of this book has been taken directly from this distinction. Each chapter will contain three sections. In the first section, I shall try to explain the theoretical concepts, categories and modes of explanation that are used by the theorist under discussion. In the second, I shall focus on their normative arguments: either directly, as they have formulated them, or indirectly in so far as they are implied by the theories themselves. The balance between these two sections will vary in proportion to the relative prominence of theoretical and normative arguments in the work of each major theorist. But as I have already indicated, this is something from which we can learn.

The discussion in the first two sections of each chapter will be devoted entirely to exposition, that is to providing an account of the main concepts and arguments of each theorist. Because entire volumes have already been devoted to explaining, interpreting and criticizing the work of many of the theorists discussed, I shall – wherever relevant – indicate where a more detailed account of the arguments can be found, both in original texts and in commentaries. If a representative selection of writings exists for the theorist in question, I shall cite it. If my own interpretation of a particular concept or argument may be debatable, I shall as far as possible indicate where an alternative may be found. But the exposition will, of necessity, be selective.

In the third section of each chapter, I shall examine in a critical way the relationship between theoretical and normative arguments within the theories under scrutiny. The major premise of the critical discussion in each case will be that this relationship is problematic: that there is tension, and sometimes contradiction, between the theoretical concepts and arguments of each theorist, and the manner in which they interconnect with, or are implicated by, a normative project or a broader-based set of normative arguments. That tension exists for the following reason. A theory is designed to make sense of the world in some way. It has an implicit, or sometimes explicit, connection with discovering more about that world, or with revising what we thought we knew about it. It seeks to represent the world in some fashion, and may claim to do so either from outside society (objectively), or from within society (subjectively). A project, on the other hand, aims to improve the world, and therefore tends to adopt a normative position within or in relation to it. But that does not automatically mean that it is subjective. In several instances among the theorists discussed in this book, the distinction between objectivity and subjectivity is brought into question. I do not mean to suggest, either, that theoretical and normative arguments are necessarily incompatible. Marx, among others, argues that they are inseparable. But what I am saying is that the relationship between them is usually problematic. Indeed, it raises questions and difficulties that reach into the heart of the debate between modernists and postmodernists. For that reason, the critical discussion in each chapter will be uncompromising. It will be concerned with critique, with putting the case against the theorist in question. But at the same time, I shall be seeking to draw out particular concepts and arguments which, it will be suggested, point up a way forward from the apparent impasse between modern and postmodern social theory.

So what is the impasse? I want to suggest that the terms of reference in which the debate between modernists and postmodernists has taken place come down to competing interpretations of reason: as an epistemological and methodological framework for social theory; and as a force for change and improvement in society. For some theorists, reason is equivalent to the gaining of certain knowledge through systematic deduction. For others, it means rigorous and methodical doubt. For others still, reason is no different from other cultural outlooks. In each of these accounts of the meaning and significance of reason, different stresses and strains arise when we come to discuss its role and importance for social theory. In the debate between modernists and postmodernists, reason is both our guide and our central source of difficulty. But in a very basic way, the following heuristic distinctions can be drawn. Within the terms of modern social theory, reason tends to be conceptualized as an epistemological foundation for social theory, and as a framework for the project of modernity which transcends culture. In postmodern social theory, reason can be viewed as equivalent to culture, as bolstered by power, and therefore not as a foundation for but as a distortion of attempts by theorists to make sense of the world. Now these distinctions do not necessarily mean that the modern and postmodern theorists discussed actually define and apply reason in this exact way. But such distinctions can help us to understand the terms of reference in which their arguments are expressed. For example, the theorists of the Frankfurt School are explicitly opposed to a foundationalist concept of reason. But on no account could their arguments be cast as postmodernist: they are working within that foundationalist framework, albeit principally in order to disrupt and undermine it. Much the same might be said of Foucault.

From the interpretation of reason, further distinctions follow. These concern what I shall call the epistemology and method of social theory, its core explanatory and normative concepts, and its ultimate objective. In each case, I shall retain the heuristic division between theoretical and normative arguments. By epistemology and method, I mean the way in which a theorist has approached the following questions: How can knowledge, and by extension theory, be verified? And how should a political community constitute itself in order to realize the 'good society'? In theoretical terms, the modernists conceptualize theory as objective, while the postmodernists tend to argue that it is subjective. Distinctive interpretations of our use of reason are implicit in this. Another, and perhaps less controversial way of saying this might be that for the modernists, social theory should have a privileged claim on our credibility (even the Frankfurt theorists and Foucault advance such a claim); while for the postmodernists, social theory provides only an interpretation of the world. When it comes to the passage towards a good society, the modernists tend to focus on rational dialogue, the postmodernists on conversation or playful contestation. The Frankfurt theorists and Foucault fit into neither category, preferring instead to base their normative arguments on some prior notion of the individual or the species-being. But once again, something can be learned from this about where their normative arguments are heading.

By core explanatory concept, I am referring to the central theme around which the theoretical and normative arguments of modern and postmodern social theorists can be said to cohere. In modern social theory, theoretical accounts of the origins, emergence and development of modern society focus on the concept of differentiation, or the specialization of functions in society. This is a form of rationalization, and establishes a clear connection between reason and instrumental efficiency. It is also, as theorists such as Simmel and Weber suggest, a potential drag on the development of modern culture. For the postmodernists, by contrast, the exhaustion or limitations of modern society are characterized by a process of de-differentiation or contextualization, where the boundaries between various dimensions of society – and even the boundary between reality and our representation of it – begin to wear away and break down. In some cases, the process of erosion is attributed to a loss of faith in the privilege of reason, or to some sense that its connection with efficiency has dispiriting consequences for culture. In normative terms, the modernists tend to focus on the concepts of justification and legislation, and suggest that reason can be used to justify our beliefs and legislate our public (and even private) affairs. Postmodernists, by contrast, prioritize empathy and interpretation: either by reconceptualizing reason as Bauman does, or by rejecting its relevance for the good society altogether, as in the case of Lyotard.

And so we come to the aims and objectives of modern and postmodern social theory. By this, I mean the intended outcome, or result, of theoretical argument and normative discussion. Once again, it should be emphasized that the following distinctions are heuristic. If modern social theory has a core theoretical aim, it is to provide a general and representative model of society: a model which depicts society from above, explains the relationship between its major institutions and dimensions, and provides an account of its development. It is an aim which both reflects and derives from the privileged status and systematic use of reason. Again, Foucault emerges as the problematic case. But he works specifically against this objective in order to subvert it, emphasizing the particular and non-rational in his historical accounts of madness, the clinic, and discipline. What he does not suggest is that society can be depicted through mirroring or mimesis, that is, by a theoretical imitation or reflection of society. This latter approach tends to be taken up by the postmodernists, some of whom automatically associate the fragmentation of society with a fragmentation of social theory. In normative terms, the project of modernity is primarily concerned with the achievement of synthesis or universal consensus. In the work of the Frankfurt theorists and Foucault, that synthesis focuses on, respectively, the relationship between the individual and nature, and between the individual and his or her self. If there is an identifiable project associated with the concept of postmodernity, it is concerned above all with pluralism rather than universalism, and with sustaining difference rather than achieving synthesis. The interpretation of reason is important to this distinction. If reason transcends culture, it can be used not only as a basis on which to model society, but also as a basis on which to realize the good society by adjudicating between competing perspectives and beliefs. If reason is part of or tainted by culture, it cannot claim to do so: indeed we lack any means of adjudication and must therefore not only live with but embrace pluralism.

The primary aim of the discussion in the following chapters is to explore how these categories and distinctions are interpreted, adopted, rejected or evaded by modern and postmodern social theorists. But there is another aim, which will come into focus more clearly as the argument develops. I want to ask whether the concepts and categories of modern or postmodern arguments as social theories on the one hand, and modernity or postmodernity as normative projects on the other, necessarily imply or support each other. For example, I shall investigate the extent to which a particular theoretical concept necessarily entails a specific normative argument; or whether a single theoretical objective must automatically translate into a certain normative goal. This is important to the debate between modernists and postmodernists because, as our discussion will reveal, the terms of that debate frequently suggest that those conditions are indispensable. As I maintained earlier on in this introduction, the postmodern rejection of the project of modernity tends to be directly associated with a dismissal of the theoretical aims, scope and explanatory range to which modern social theorists tend to aspire. For example, Giddens and Bauman argue that there is an inextricable relationship between a theory of the social system which seeks to model society from above, and the normative project of managing society through a high-level intelligence such as the state. In a similar way, Lyotard's rejection of the goal of universal consensus in the project of modernity as conceived by Habermas is closely linked to the argument that the narrative account of the development of modern society which is provided by Habermas's theory is untenable. Throw out the project, they appear to be saying, and the theory must go too.

I shall place that line of reasoning under scrutiny in this book. I shall argue that in the debate between modern and postmodern social theory, there is an absence of clarity concerning the exact grounds on which a particular theoretical approach or normative argument is rejected, or sometimes even adopted. In some cases, the two are conflated. I want to ask whether that conflation is necessary, and whether it is justified. If postmodern society is pluralistic, does it necessarily follow that social theory must be fragmented and subjective? Is the mission to discover and explain more about society through the rigorous use of theoretical concepts incompatible with a belief that society is pluralistic, fragmentary and ever-changing? The theorists whose arguments are discussed and evaluated in this book provide wide-ranging and often revealing answers to these questions. My aim is to draw out and emphasize these answers: to scrutinize and compare them; and to ask what they tell us about a way forward out of the apparent impasse between modern and postmodern social theory. But that aim is informed by one central conviction: that social theory should play a more central role than it does within the discipline of sociology; that it should sensitize and facilitate social research; and that it should help us to make better sense of, not obscure, the world around us. That conviction is informed by a conclusion that may as well be stated here. Social theory – in its modern and postmodern guises – is failing us. This book offers a constructive account of that failure.

Part I
Classical Social Theory

1

Modernity and Society: Marx and Durkheim

In this chapter, I shall discuss core themes within the work of Marx and Durkheim which continue to be relevant to the debate between modern and postmodern theorists.[1] Marx's analysis of capitalist political economy defines the so-called production paradigm, based on manufacturing, against which postmodernists allege that we have moved into a new era of exchange and circulation: not of commodities, but of signs. They describe an information-rich world in which it is increasingly difficult to distinguish between reality and its representation in the mass media. This inversion of Marx's basic approach to the relationship between production and exchange raises far-reaching questions about social class, culture and self-identity. In postmodern social theory, the notion of a feasible alternative to capitalism, and the idea of historical progress around which Marx's argument is centred, have been largely rejected. Indeed, since the collapse of the Soviet bloc in 1989, many commentators have flatly reported the death of Marx's, and more broadly Marxist, concepts and ideas.

The legacy of Durkheim's work for modern social theory has taken various forms. These partly depend on how his arguments are interpreted and which aspects of his work are emphasized. For example, while some sociologists regard Durkheim's theory of modern society as the foundation of functionalism within the discipline, others suggest that Durkheim avoids precisely those theoretical difficulties which arise in the work of later functionalists such as Talcott Parsons. But the most significant feature of Durkheim's legacy for social theory arguably concerns his understanding of the relationship between society and the individual. His argument that we should 'treat social facts as if they are things' is still taken as a core methodological problem in sociological analysis. But Durkheim's work, like that of Marx, is also important for substantive reasons. For example, his argument that individualism – or utilitarian action – has a strong moral dimension cannot be lightly dismissed in the context of postmodern arguments about the triumph of consumer society and the decline of collectivism. Moreover, Durkheim's concept of the modern *conscience collective*, combining a cult of the individual with a core notion of citizenship, raises questions which loom large in more recent attempts to outline a politically inclusive social theory which is sensitive to cultural pluralism.

While taking these substantive concerns into account, I want to pursue a slightly different interpretation in this discussion. The main theoretical problem posed by the work of Marx and Durkheim – and it emerges in both modern and postmodern theories later on – arises from their treatment of modern society as a totality, or whole. They raise fundamental questions about how the relationship between society, or structure, and the individual, or agency, can be conceptualized in sociology without placing unwarranted causal emphasis on either. But as I argue towards the end of the chapter, this question is not only theoretically important but has far-reaching normative significance in so far as it tends to be closely allied to an idealized model of society: a general model of how society ought to be.

In the first section of this chapter, I shall focus on the theoretical arguments. In their analysis of social differentiation in modern society, Marx and Durkheim explore the tension between the integration of society as a totality on the one hand, and the specialization of functions brought on by economic development on the other. Marx regards this relation as contradictory, and incorporates his analysis within a dialectical theory of history. By contrast, Durkheim argues that the relationship between society and its functions is organic. This analysis depends on a distinction between forms of social solidarity in traditional and modern society.

The holistic approach of Marx and Durkheim plays an integral role in their normative arguments, and these are discussed in the second section of this chapter. According to Marx, the structural contradictions in modern society can only be resolved through a series of economic and political changes leading to a society, communism, which is based on collective ownership of the means of production. Only at this stage, he argues, will the potential of society to operate as an integrated whole without internal contradiction be fully realized. Durkheim argues that the potential of society to function as a coherent totality can be realized in modern society through internal adjustment, not wholesale structural change.

In the third section of the chapter, the critical discussion will begin to address questions which arise not only in relation to the work of Marx and Durkheim, but in the debate between modern and postmodern social theory. Three themes are especially important. First, both theorists advance a critique of classical economic reasoning which has hardly been surpassed, whether in modern or postmodern theory. This is not to suggest that the arguments of Marx, in particular, could be applied wholesale to late capitalism, for they rest on a production paradigm which is no longer, if indeed it ever was, tenable. But the point I want to draw out is not really about consumerism. It concerns the connection between culture and instrumental (or economic) reasoning, and remains a central source of dispute between modernists and postmodernists today. Second, modern and postmodern social theories divide across the fault line created by two visions of society: as a totality which is more or less integrated in the way that Marx and Durkheim suggest and of which modernists broadly approve; or as something much more fragmented, as the postmodernists maintain. Third, Marx and Durkheim take sharply different approaches to the relationship between theoretical and normative arguments in social theory. These differences have important connotations for our understanding of the role of social theory in society.

The Nature of Modern Society

In their accounts of the emergence of modern society, Marx and Durkheim engage in a critique of classical economics. For different reasons, they reject the idea that the division of labour alone can provide a sufficient basis for integrating the wider society. But while Marx identifies what he sees as structural contradictions in the organization of capitalist society, Durkheim argues for a general theory of society that provides a sociological, not economic, explanation for its systemic stability. These contrasting views of modern society are derived from a series of basic statements about the relationship between the individual and society. They are contained in Marx's philosophical anthropology, and in Durkheim's concept of the *homo duplex*.

Marx's philosophical anthropology

Marx's philosophical anthropology is derived from a critique of idealism and materialism in philosophy.[2] On one side, he argues against

Hegel that there must always be a material substratum to human consciousness. On the other, against materialist philosophers such as Feuerbach, he rejects the view that human consciousness is determined by the material world. In this way, Marx seeks to move beyond the dichotomy between subject and object. Crucially, however, modern capitalism prevents such a philosophy from being put into practice.[3]

Two basic propositions about the individual and society provide the foundation for Marx's philosophical anthropology. First, he argues that human beings must labour, or dominate nature, in order to survive. Second, he maintains that they must do so through interaction, in other words cooperatively, for this is just as important to their survival. These two propositions constitute the idea of *homo faber*,[4] and it is on this basis that Marx sets out his critical analysis of modern capitalism.

Durkheim's homo duplex

Like Marx, Durkheim argues that individuals are shaped in significant ways by the social conditions they inhabit. Society constrains the individual through a series of moral obligations. These obligations are objective, although we experience them subjectively: we have 'received them through . . . education' (1972: 64). This proposition is vital both for Durkheim's approach to methodology, particularly the concept of the social fact, and for his normative conception of the integration of modern society.

Durkheim argues that society cannot be seen as the sum of individuals within it because it has a reality of its own, or what he calls a reality *sui generis*. Society is made up of emergent properties, or social facts.[5] Social facts derive from the combined actions of a number of people. But it is the combination or synthesis of actions, not the actions in themselves, which gives social life and society a reality of their own. That combination occurs outside of us as individuals. As a consequence, particular patterns of social action and forms of judgement are instituted beyond the individual level: they do not depend on any one individual for their reproduction.

Against this background, Durkheim proposes a particular interpretation of the concept of constraint. This term can be defined literally as 'the exercise of force to determine or confine action' (*OED*). In connection with Durkheim's argument on moral obligation, the concept of constraint could be taken to imply that individuals follow normative principles through fear of sanction or punishment. For Durkheim, however, such a negative definition applies only to a minority of cases. For the most part, and increasingly in a modern society which operates according to organic principles, moral obligation derives from the recognition by individuals themselves that particular norms and values are legitimate, that is, that it is reasonable to follow them. In so far as society is a moral force, it is a benign one. Far from constraining us in a negative way, society provides the conditions through which the individuals who depend on it can make moral choices freely. We have, he argues, a 'liberating dependence' on modern society, whereby the 'individual submits to society and this submission is the condition of his liberation' (1972: 115).

This argument rests on the idea of the individual as the *homo duplex*, the human being of two parts or aspects. According to Durkheim, we are made up of sensations and sensory tendencies on the one hand, and conceptual thought and moral activity on the other.[6] Our sensory tendencies are egoistic. They do not derive from society and may even set themselves against it. Indeed, it is in preventing our enslavement to these impulses that our moral and conceptual activity, which derives from our dependence on society, can be said to liberate us.

Marx's political economy of capitalism

For Marx, modern capitalism is shaped by its own specific property relations. Economic processes such as the relationship between supply and demand, the price of goods and the production of profit do not arise from forces of the market but depend on these property relations, and can therefore be understood only in such terms. Whereas classical economic theory focuses on the idea of market equilibrium, that is, how supply meets demand through the price mechanism, Marx emphasizes structural contradictions within the capitalist economy that can be understood only by referring to the social and political relations on which economic production depends.

According to Adam Smith, economic equilibrium is made possible by virtue of the functional interdependence of specialized producers, that is, their dependence on the market to sell goods they have produced but which are surplus to their needs in exchange for goods they need. Crucially, the market depends on the 'propensity to truck, barter, and exchange one thing for another' (Smith, 1986: 117).[7] But whereas Smith focuses on the social and moral consequences of economic production, Marx emphasizes the social and moral nature of economic production itself.

The key to Marx's argument is contained in the idea that the creation of wealth is not merely socially consequential but actually consists of social, not just economic, relations. This is expressed in the labour theory of value, which suggests that profit does not derive from market relations but from an exploitative relationship between owners of capital and workers. Workers are forced to sell an abstract quantity of their labour-power in order to produce something which they will neither own nor control. The expansion of capital would not be possible without the systematic exploitation of workers. This argument has an important bearing on Marx's theory of ideology and alienation. The concept of reification, for example, refers to the way individuals treat economic processes as natural or given, rather than as consisting of social – and therefore politically *malleable* – relations.[8]

The labour theory of value plays a vital role in Marx's argument that the capitalist economic system is inherently unstable. This idea is expressed by the falling rate of profit (FRP) thesis. In essence, the thesis suggests that the growth of capitalism – its markets, institutions and profit levels – will mitigate against the prospects of its very survival as an economic system, and therefore the future of capitalist society as a whole. The FRP thesis provides the economic core of Marx's sociological argument that capitalist society cannot expand without damaging its own prospects of survival; and therefore that by its expansion, the conditions are set in place for a socialist, and later communist, society.

The FRP thesis hinges around the idea of the rising organic composition of capital. This idea is based on the proposition that there are two kinds of capital: fixed or constant capital, that is, investment that cannot really be withdrawn, such as in rent and machinery; and variable capital, or investment which can be adjusted or withdrawn, such as in labour. The notion of the rising organic composition of capital refers to the increase of one kind of capital, fixed, in proportion to the other. According to Marx, this increase occurs because, in their relentless search for profit and a competitive edge, capitalists tend to opt for technological progress. They therefore invest more in fixed capital, such as new machinery, than in variable capital, in this case, labour. Now in Marx's view, profit can only be derived from labour, that is, through the surplus value that remains once workers have been paid. Therefore the less capital is invested in labour, the lower becomes the capacity for profit. By this reckoning, because the ratio of fixed to variable capital increases, the rate at which profit is produced must decrease.[9] In narrow economic terms, this is what is meant by the claim, in *The Communist Manifesto*, that the bourgeosie are their own grave-diggers.[10]

Although the premises of the FRP thesis have been widely debated, especially the labour theory of value on which it logically depends,[11] the thesis is most significant for the way that Marx tries to combine economic and sociological analyses of modern society. To express this in another way, he argues that economic processes cannot be examined without reference to the social and political relations on which they depend.

Durkheim on the moral dimension of economic change

Durkheim's critique of classical economics does not deal with technical features of economic theory in the same way as Marx, but focuses on the social and moral consequences of a complex division of labour in society. He argues that the increasingly complex division of labour raises fundamental questions about the moral framework in which economic activity takes place.[12] He addresses these questions by distinguishing between individuation and moral individualism, and argues that economic integration by virtue of the division of labour is not a sufficient basis for the integration of society as a whole.

Whereas Marx views the interdependence of social functions in capitalist society as contradictory, Durkheim argues that modern society operates according to organic principles, rather like a living organism: 'Each organ, in effect, has its special character and autonomy; and yet the unity of this organism is as great as the individuation of the parts is more marked' (1972: 140). Unlike Marx, Durkheim does not challenge classical economic theory directly.[13] He accepts that the expansion of interdependent markets goes hand in hand with an increasingly complex division of labour, and argues that one important sociological consequence of this is the trend towards urbanization as the population moves in search of work.

Durkheim disagrees with the classical economists over the implications of the complex division of labour for society as a whole. In particular, he investigates difficulties of integration which arise from the fact that, in modern society, individuals have become isolated from wider structures of family and authority which had been present in traditional, or premodern, society. Economists are bound to overlook these difficulties because their notion of society is reductive, consisting of an aggregate of individuals in which 'everyone receives exactly as much as he gives, and in which one remains only as long as one profits from it' (1972: 67–8). In short, it is the increasing density of the population that arises from the complex division of labour, not that economic transformation by itself, which generates the pressure for change in modern society.

The Critical Analysis of Modern Society

I have argued that Marx and Durkheim focus primarily on structural or systemic problems of integration in modern society. Both undertake a form of functional explanation in order to investigate these problems. That explanation depends on a theoretical model of society as a totality which builds on the concepts of *homo faber* and *homo duplex*, respectively. Marx's analysis hinges on the notion of contradiction. Durkheim's approach rests on the idea of equilibrium. In the following discussion, I want to highlight the way in which these two modes of theoretical explanation, and the general models of society on which they depend, stem from an idealization of society. In other words, a normative project is not only implied by but inherent in these social theories as forms of analysis.

Marx's critique of capitalism

Marx's critique of capitalism focuses on the unequal property relations on which the accumulation and expansion of capital depends. For example, the concept of alienation appears in his work not as a result of the routinized nature of industrial production, as one might initially suppose, but as a critique of the fact that workers have no rights over the product of their labour at all. The commodification of labour under capitalism – it is bought and sold like any other commodity – is profoundly dehumanizing, making it impossible to realize the synthesis of conscious thought and material activity that Marx regards as integral to the progress of human society. Such a synthesis is impossible, he argues, because the capitalist system distorts the consciousness of all, both capitalists and workers, who are subject to its demands.

The key to Marx's normative argument lies with the concept of social class, particularly the distinction between a class in itself and a class for itself. This distinction focuses on the question of class consciousness. Marx characterizes social class not as a static entity but as a dynamic system of relations between human society and the material world. While a class in itself can be defined in objective terms by its relationship to the means of production, a class for itself constitutes a class in a subjective sense, that is, it is increasingly aware of itself as a class. Marx's explanation of how this transition will occur is closely tied to the FRP thesis. The contradictions inherent in capitalism produce periodic slumps in productive activity. Weaker businesses go bust or are taken over, producing a concentration of capital with fewer, larger industries. At the same time, even strong businesses are forced to cut back their workforce, and this, in conjunction with automation, causes a process of pauperization within the existing workforce as the increasing number of the unemployed, or the reserve army of labour, enables employers to keep wage levels low.

The processes of concentration and pauperization will render the objective conflict of interest between capitalists and labourers more stark, bringing it to the forefront of the minds of individuals themselves. Combined with the increasing social concentration of workers in larger factories as capital centralizes, this will enable the proletariat to begin transforming itself into a class for itself, a collective political agent in its own right. In accordance with the philosophical anthropology, all of this proceeds from the combination of material conditions – the economic contradictions that are inherent in capitalism – and the social relations which those conditions brought into being and on which they depend for their survival.[14]

In this way, Marx draws together a theoretical argument regarding the political economy of capitalism, and a normative argument regarding the position and political potential of the working class. He is therefore able to suggest that the transition from capitalism to socialism is inevitable: not, however, because the system will automatically be superseded, but because of a conjunction between structural contradictions and the conscious activity, or praxis, of the working class. Although Marx's reference to the law of the falling rate of profit might be taken to suggest that the transition to socialism and communism is theoretically preordained, this is not equivalent to saying that the collapse of capitalism is actually inevitable. Collective political action is a prerequisite for the overthrow of capitalism, in order to exploit the structural weaknesses described in the FRP thesis. The relationship between these two strands in Marx's argument, between the theory of capitalist instability and the praxis which ensures the transition to socialism, has been a central focus of debate ever since. But the question is not confined to Marxism. It arises in modern and postmodern social theory as a tension between theoretical and normative arguments. I shall discuss Marx's approach to this question in the critical discussion at the end of this chapter.

Durkheim on individuation and moral individualism

Durkheim's analysis of the risks posed by modernization is based on an analysis of the moral framework which is engendered by a society with a complex division of labour, in which mechanical solidarity no longer provides an appropriate basis for social integration. His argument is formulated through a critique of two contrasting accounts of the implications of the modernization of society. In effect, this analysis disagrees both with conservatives such as Comte and Tönnies on the one hand, and modernizers such as Spencer on the other.

Comte and Tönnies argue that institutions such as the family and the church must be maintained and even fortified in order to prevent the fragmentation of modern society. By contrast, Spencer contends that the economic interdependence of individuals in modern society will be a sufficient basis for social integration. Indeed, society will be more stable the more individuals pursue their self-interest in contractual relations with others. Durkheim rejects the basic dichotomy between these views. He concedes that functional interdependence within a complex division of labour can contribute to rather than detract from social integration, but only if it is accompanied by a specifically modern moral framework, namely individualism. In short, while Comte and Tönnies overestimate the dangers for social integration posed by an increasingly complex division of labour, Spencer tends to underestimate them. Durkheim's analysis of this question focuses on the distinction between individuation and moral individualism.

As I have already noted, the distinction between individuation and moral individualism stems from Durkheim's rejection of the idea that egoism is a sufficient basis for establishing social bonds. He argues that individualism is not reducible to the pursuit of self-interest, for 'the religion of the individual is a social institution like all known religions' (1972: 149).[15] Individuation entails the free expression of egoistic sentiments, without reference to society.[16] But this would amount to a condition of moral anarchy. For Durkheim, the growth of individualism in modern society therefore cannot be regarded as a process of individuation. Whereas individuation implies the absence of society, individualism contains ideals which depend on society for their very expression.

In distinguishing between moral individualism and individuation, Durkheim establishes a connection between the growth of modern society and a fundamental reshaping of the concept of the individual as citizen. Moral individualism consists of a cult of the individual, or a cult of personal dignity. The moral duty of the individual is important to this idea. The cult of the individual stresses our individual characteristics, and demands that we live and work as specialists.[17] At the same time, that demand is underwritten by a more abstract concept of the responsible citizen. In the context of society as a whole, the cult of the individual provides a more rational basis for social integration than can be found in traditional society, but is in no sense less dependent on society for its origins. This is why Durkheim refers to this form of social integration as organic, rather than mechanical, solidarity.

Individualism is a moral phenomenon because it is a product of society, not something which mitigates against the existence of society itself. Individuation, by contrast, must entail the atomization of society into a sum of individuals who act in their own interests without reference to collective concerns: a process which necessarily undermines society. In other words, only through moral individualism can society form a totality which is greater than the sum of individuals within it, and therefore provide a match for the *idea* of society as conceptualized by Durkheim in his social theory. In this way, Durkheim's normative argument is logically consistent with his theoretical concept of society and its relationship to the individual. It remains open to question whether either side of this argument has a disproportionate influence over Durkheim's work as a whole.

Critical Discussion

The following discussion focuses on three major themes. The first concerns the critique of classical economic reasoning advanced by Marx and Durkheim. I shall suggest that their sociological characterization of economic activity and institutions has a significant bearing on the conceptualization of instrumental reason. Their arguments remain important for the debate between modern and postmodern social theory because they highlight the interconnection between reason and culture. Second, the discussion moves on to the conceptualization of modern society, by both theorists, as a totality. I shall focus particularly on the use of functional explanation, and the problems that arise from it, in this context. Finally, I shall turn to the contribution by Marx and Durkheim to the theme which is central to the organization and argument in this book, that is, the relationship between theoretical and normative arguments in social theory.

Reason and economic life

One of the most significant debates regarding Marx's theory concerns whether his approach places undue causal emphasis on the economy: in other words, whether it is fair to characterize him as an economic determinist. Couched in this way, the debate tends to focus on the relationship between the infrastructure and superstructure in capitalist society. This does not, however, take sufficient account of the specific way in which Marx defines the economy. Both Marx and Durkheim advance a strong case for using a sociological characterization of economic life which, particularly in the case of Marx, makes it difficult to understand exactly what economic determinism might mean.

The question as to what constitutes economic life from a sociological point of view has been largely neglected in modern social theory, and is a specific area of weakness in the debate between modernists and postmodernists: not least because of a rather narrow association, which continues to be drawn, between economic action and instrumental reason. Whereas later theorists tend to regard economic processes and activities as sociologically significant without themselves *being* social in character, Marx and Durkheim suggest that there is an inherent social or cultural dimension to economic activity. For Durkheim, this is illustrated by the idea of economic progress: 'one would form an entirely false idea of economic development if one neglected the moral causes which play a part in it' (1972: 94).

This argument is important for two main reasons. First, Durkheim is in no doubt that reference to economic causes must play a vital part in the sociological analysis of modern society. But second, he also argues that these causes, and economic phenomena in general, must not be studied in isolation from their moral, and therefore societal, dimension. Few subsequent theorists, however, have acted on Durkheim's recommendation. On the contrary, they tend to treat economic life rather like a black box which affects or is affected by, but does not consist of, social action. Having said this, Durkheim's argument is weakened in as much as he seems to agree that economic and moral, or social, life are effectively two worlds. This might be taken to imply that they should be conceptualized in distinctive ways and only then bolted together in order to reach a fuller understanding of each world in its own terms. In short, Durkheim's argument may not go far enough towards incorporating a sociological understanding of economic action, economic reasoning and economic institutions into the framework of social theory.

Marx does try to open the economic black box. For example, his concept of reification is premised on the idea that economic processes and institutions such as the market or the price mechanism appear to us as natural, spontaneous or given, whereas in fact they consist of social and political relations. Marx's theory of modern capitalism, particularly of its contradictions, is arguably most significant in the context of the present day for the way that he tries to combine the analysis of seemingly objective economic processes with an interpretation of their interaction with the social and political relations on which they depend.

Critics of Marx increasingly argue that he places a disproportionate emphasis on production, as opposed to exchange, in his analysis of the economic conditions of capitalist development. This criticism applies in systemic terms when examining capitalist society as a whole, by underestimating the importance of the financial system; and to the question of human agency when investigating the role of individuals as workers rather than as consumers. The criticism gains particular importance in the context of theories of post-industrialism, the information society, and consumerism, which are discussed in chapter 6. Common to all three theories is the idea that the superstructure has become more important since Marx's time. This view is held even by those working quite closely within the Marxist tradition, such as the Frankfurt theorists, whose work is discussed in chapter 3.

The argument that the production paradigm in which Marx works no longer provides a tenable basis for examining economic life in contemporary society can be illustrated by considering the expansion of the international financial system during the past thirty years. In the third volume of *Capital*, Marx characterizes the financial system as an intermediary which shortens 'the technical operations that go with buying and selling' (1959: 321–2). In a marginal note added by Marx to his own copy of the first volume of *Capital*, he writes of the 'backwash' of monetary crisis having a disturbing effect on industry and commerce.[18]

Marx argues that the financial system does not, of itself, play a significant causal role in capitalism but merely facilitates the operations of industry. This may well be an accurate description of the actions and decisions of particular industrialists during Marx's time.[19] However, in view of the fact that money crossing geopolitical borders for purposes of commercial finance now far outweighs the quantity of money changing hands across borders for purposes of trade, Marx's approach is in need of radical revision. Monetary and financial networks are increasingly global, and play a significant role in creating conditions and constraints under which manufacturers must operate. The causal relationship between production and finance has, if anything, been reversed relative to Marx's theory.

While it may seem plausible to revise Marx's theory in the light of subsequent developments in the capitalist system, as neo-Marxists have sought to do, there is a more important theoretical difficulty in this approach which no amount of revision could resolve. The difficulty arises because the integrity of Marx's theory logically depends on the production paradigm. The analysis of central concepts within his theory

– such as alienation and social class, and indeed the very notion of the contradictions of capitalism, all of which are pivotal to the argument about the transition to socialism – derive from a philosophical anthropology which is underpinned by the idea of production, not exchange. For this reason, it remains open to doubt whether his theory could be revised to take account of major structural developments in the capitalist system without undermining the foundational principles on which that theory depends. But as I have already suggested, the analysis is most significant for the insight which has been frequently overlooked – to a large extent, this insight is shared with Durkheim: namely, that culture and ideological phenomena have an integral role to play in the reproduction of economic institutions, economic action and economic reasoning. It is an insight which we will not find, at least appearing with such clarity, in the work of the modernists and postmodernists as it is discussed later on in this book.

Society as totality

Marx and Durkheim have both been criticized for conveying the individual as overdependent on society. As to Marx's work, the criticism suggests that his arguments rely on unwarranted assumptions about the political consciousness of the individual, and potential differences of outlook between individuals. This stems partly from his preoccupation with the collective agent of social class, rather than with the individual as an agent or actor. As to Durkheim's theory, the criticism focuses on his analysis of the moral consciousness of the individual, and suggests that his theory overstates the level of coherence among the beliefs of individuals even when he writes of the cult of the individual. Both criticisms share a broader theme, however, which concerns the lack of flexibility in their characterization of modern society as a totality. This is the theme that I want to develop here, because it features strongly in the postmodern critique of modern social theory.

Marx and Durkheim employ functional explanation in their work. According to Cohen, functional explanation is employed where 'the character of what is explained is determined by its effect on what explains it' (1978: 278). In other words, the existence and operation of a social institution is explained by referring to its effects on other institutions, and ultimately on society as a whole. As Cohen points out, this form of explanation dominates Marx's theory of capitalist society: 'relations of production *correspond* to productive forces; the legal and political superstructure *rises on* the real foundation; the social, political and intellectual life *is conditioned by* the mode of production of material life; consciousness *is determined by* social being' (p. 278, Cohen's emphasis).

On the face of it, Durkheim uses a similar form of functional explanation. His theory of modern society examines the interconnection between parts of society, that is, their effect on each other and their contribution to the development of society as a whole. But there is also a fundamental distinction between the two approaches, because each theorist builds quite different assumptions into his argument. Marx's theory of modern capitalism, indeed his theory of history, begins with the proposition that successive societies contain a contradiction between the forces and the relations of production; or in the language of the philosophical anthropology, between those parts of society which correspond to labour and interaction. It is the unravelling of this contradiction that explains social change. By contrast, Durkheim bases his theory on the idea that elements of society exist *because* they make some contribution to its overall development. While he does not go so far as to say that this proposition is inevitably true – as references to the forced division of labour make clear – he does at least suggest that this proposition forms the basis of his general approach to understanding society and explaining its operation. This has immediate consequences for the interpretation of problems of integration in modern society. For example, as Giddens notes, 'division of interest between groups is treated only as a phenomenon of transitional phases in social development, in which the alignment of functions is temporarily out of equilibrium' (1978: 105–6).

Durkheim's theory of modern society can therefore be associated not only with functional explanation but with functional*ism*. And as Cohen explains, functionalism almost inevitably implies political conservatism: 'we may note how natural it is to conclude that if everything serves a useful purpose or is, indeed, indispensable, then there is no scope for desirable social change' (1978: 284). This notion of desirable social change suggests that there may be no room for normative argument in Durkheim's theory, nor indeed for human praxis. However, the blatant contrast between the accounts set out by Marx and Durkheim of the degree of long-term cohesion within modern society is perhaps less important than a fundamental similarity in their theoretical strategies. This is because both theorists seek to explain specific features of modern society on the basis of assumptions which are drawn from a general model of society, and which address its principles of integration and development. This is a familiar strategy in modern social theory, but has been called into serious question by postmodern theorists. It is important for our purposes in this book to understand the difficulties which arise from this approach.

One significant problem which has arisen with social theories that adopt a holistic concept of society concerns the extent to which theory either facilitates or conditions the interpretation and explanation of modern society. To express the same point from a narrower perspective, the problem concerns the extent to which a theory is capable of selective or wholesale falsification on the basis of empirical research. In the case of Marx and Durkheim, both theorists seem bound to draw specific conclusions about the nature and significance of what Durkheim calls the forced division of labour and what Marx calls class conflict. In short, their general theories arguably lead them towards drawing particular – and perhaps unwarranted – implications from events and processes as they are observed in society. Because, in either case, any other interpretation would come into conflict with the assumptions that lie behind the theory itself.

Durkheim suggests that moral individualism, and moral individualism alone, is functionally compatible with a society restructured by the complex division of labour. While there is no need for him actually to deny that problems of fragmentation exist, he must assume, by virtue of his general theory, that modern society has the capacity to correct them. For example, he argues that 'the functions that have been dissociated in the course of the upheaval have not had the time to adjust to one another.' In other words, and more explicitly, 'normally, the division of labour produces social solidarity.'[20] The problem, however, is that while Durkheim's distinction between normal and pathological states of adaptation to the development of modern society is certainly consistent with his general theory of society, his approach prevents him from characterizing such pathological states as anything *other* than transient difficulties. There is, in short, a problem of empirical closure with Durkheim's theory: genuine research questions are excluded, not illuminated, by theory.

According to Marx, class conflict defines modern society and therefore cannot be regarded as a symptom of maladaption. Only fundamental change in the organization of capitalist society, that is, in those property relations on which it depends, can lead to the resolution of class conflict. But this conclusion is not only circular but unavoidable once it is assumed that no society which is organized on the basis of asymmetrical property relations *can* survive. Indeed, it is the whole point of the dialectical method to identify and interpret the structural contradictions in society which stem from those relations.

For some critics, this particular instance of empirical closure is due to

Marx's normative commitments, that is, to a belief in the historical necessity of revolution. They suggest that he fails to recognize that history (and therefore revolution) are contingent, that is, they are not inevitable, they do not have to occur. This argument usually focuses on the allegedly deterministic content of Marx's theory, namely, its economic arguments. But I want to suggest a slightly different interpretation of the problem. It lies not with the alleged economic determinism of Marx's approach but with a form of *functional* determinism which is largely shared with Durkheim. In short, the problem begins with the deployment of a general model of society as the basis for making specific, empirical statements – some of which are explanatory and predictive – about a particular society or societal type. This raises the following basic question: how can the specific conclusions drawn from general social theories that employ functional explanation be evaluated, other than within the terms of reference dictated by the theories themselves? This question will recur a number of times in the following chapters.

Theoretical and normative projects of modernity

The relationship between theoretical and normative arguments in the work of Marx and Durkheim can be understood in two ways: first, in terms of the relationship between theory and praxis; and second, as the unintentional consequence of a theoretical conception of society itself. While the first of these interpretations presents difficulties which are addressed directly by each theorist, the second arises as a result of the general theory of society that, each in his own way, Marx and Durkheim propose.

Durkheim's analogy between society and a biological organism leads him to suggest that, just as the organism may be in various states of health, so society can be in a normal or pathological condition. The latter occurs because of some loss of equilibrium, or balance, in the way that constituent parts of society relate to and affect each other. That equilibrium is defined according to what Durkheim calls an average type of societal condition: 'If we call the "average type" that hypothetical being that is constructed by assembling in the same category the most frequent forms . . . one may say that the normal type merges with the average type, and that every deviation from this standard of health is a morbid phenomenon' (1972: 103). He suggests that it is the primary test of a scientific sociology that an average, or normal, type can be identified, for only this will give a solid grounding to the discipline. Otherwise, the mind of the sociologist would be 'no longer restrained by the matter which it is analysing, since it is the mind, in some manner or other, that determines the matter'. Indeed, Durkheim suggests that, with the help of sociology, 'the duty of the statesman is no longer violently to push society toward an ideal that seems attractive to him' but to prevent 'the outbreak of illnesses by good hygiene' and seek 'to cure them when they have appeared' (1972: 105).

In basic terms, Durkheim is proposing that, in order to proceed scientifically, sociology must derive its theories and explanations from the 'generality of phenomena'. But there is considerable scope for difficulty in this approach. At best, the analogy between a healthy body and a normal society appears to be naive and simplistic. At worst, Durkheim's argument threatens to achieve exactly the opposite of establishing sociology as a credible science. The problem arises because of the primacy of the notion of generality in Durkheim's theoretical strategy. In so far as he seeks a description of an *average* set of social conditions, this description must be in danger of becoming an ideal towards which other societies – or social groups, institutions, and so on – ought to aspire.

The broader, theoretical, difficulty here is whether it is possible to have a general theory of society which provides an objective or value-free measure against which to draw judgements about health and illness, diagnosis and cure. The problems posed for a scientific social theory by Durkheim's organic analogy suggest that the relationship between theoretical and normative arguments in his work may be unintentionally conflated, not clearly separated. To some degree, this question arises because of the commitment to functional explanation in his work, particularly when this is combined with an underlying assumption that a general or average type of society not only exists but can be defined as normal. As Barnes notes, 'it is part of our moral discourse to refer to what is normal and natural as opposed to what is abnormal and unnatural' (1995: 45). That we should then aspire to a condition resembling that society – just as we might aspire to our own physical well-being – suggests that Durkheim builds into his theory a set of normative arguments which he does not identify as such.

Whereas Durkheim tries to draw a sharp distinction between the theoretical and practical, or normative, aims of sociology, Marx explicitly seeks to combine them. He does so through the concept of praxis, which can be defined as 'the free, universal, creative and self-creative activity through which man creates (makes, produces) and changes (shapes) his historical, human world and himself'.[21] Marx maintains that theory is inseparable from praxis. As Cohen notes, 'common to theory and practice is an aspiration to establish congruity between thought and reality' (1978: 339–40). Thus although Marx's FRP thesis is set out as an objective analysis of the workings of the capitalist economy, as a theory it is closely allied to the normative argument that the transition to socialism, although historically necessary, can only be achieved through human praxis. This underlines the conviction put forward in the eleventh of the *Theses on Feuerbach*, namely, that 'philosophers have only interpreted the world, in various ways; the point is to change it' (Marx, 1977: 158).

In what sense, then, can Marx's theory be categorized as science? For Marx himself, the scientific test of theory appears to consist not of an average or general societal type which can be observed – this is Durkheim's solution – but rather an abstract, unobserved and unobservable notion of a society in which, consistent with his own philosophical anthropology, there are no contradictions between the forces and relations of production, that is, socialism. In other words, it is the extent to which a theory uncovers ways in which the present, capitalist, society masks its own contradictions that dictates whether it can be regarded as scientific. Theory must therefore be tied to praxis: and for praxis in this context, read the practical goal of socialism.

One important difficulty with this approach is that Marx can provide only a cloudy definition of the concept of socialism which underpins his theory. And for good reason. As he himself argues, to advance a utopian or idealistic depiction of a socialist society would compromise the notion of human praxis which is at the heart of his approach. It would be merely a theoretical exercise, an exercise whose practical value is therefore undermined. For this reason, the abstract ideas contained within the philosophical anthropology which underpins Marx's general theory of history are vital. According to him, a fundamental tendency towards the realization of these ideals is immanent in the progress of history, and it is the role of the theorist not only to articulate this but to further that progress. The problem, however, is that the theory which Marx builds on this basis is caught in a vicious circle: it can be verified only within its own terms.

It is therefore open to question whether Marx successfully manages the tension between theory and praxis. It should be emphasized that this is not a question about the extent to which revolution, the transition to socialism, can be regarded as necessary or inevitable. Marx's own reasoning renders this question meaningless in the sense that, as Avineri notes, the 'end-results of the revolution are ... historically formed and determined during and by its occurrence' (1968: 143). By that same reasoning, however, a more important question arises. This concerns whether Marx's theoretical map outlining the course of the transition to socialism should be regarded as arbitrary, or to express this another way, whether his theory has any outstanding claim to our credulity when compared with any other. Even if, as Avineri notes, Marx does not 'guarantee the success of the revolution in advance or take it for granted [but] only indicates the possibilities historically' (1968: 144), this hardly provides a sound basis on which to evaluate the status of the theory against which those possibilities are measured. The tension between theoretical and normative arguments in Marx's work has to some degree been reproduced by neo-Marxists: from the humanism of Gramsci which emphasizes the political engagement of Marxism, to the structuralism of Althusser which defines the science of political economy as undertaken separately from political thought and activity.

The questions raised by the work of Marx and Durkheim will be important as the discussion in this book proceeds. In different ways, both are seeking to grapple with the practical significance of social theory: for Durkheim, in a way which does not compromise its scientific status; and for Marx, in a way which redefines that status so as to avoid reducing theory to the passive and therefore misleading contemplation of a world which is independent of *homo faber*. Both strategies have been of undoubted significance for modern social theory, not least because they derive from a wide-ranging explanatory ambition, that is, from the advancement of general theoretical models of society. But the tension between theoretical and normative arguments to which these strategies give rise cannot, arguably, be avoided. And as I shall discuss in the following chapter, the search for a general model of modern society represents an enterprise which some theorists have rejected: not only for its difficulty, but because the aim itself is inherently normative. In short, there is an alternative approach to the aims and practical significance of social theory.

2
Modernity and Reason: Simmel and Weber

The work of Simmel and Weber is significant for the debate between modern and postmodern social theory because both theorists explore the impact of instrumental reason on modern culture.[1] This resonates with modernists and postmodernists alike: modernists, in so far as they allege that reason is a major source of authority and constraint over the individual; and postmodernists, because they argue that contemporary culture is marked by incredulity towards the claim that reason provides a universal framework that transcends belief systems. But there is another, equally important reason for continuing to read the work of Simmel and Weber in the present day. Neither theorist formulates a general theory of modern society: an enterprise which, by the reckoning of some postmodernists, represents the worst excesses not only of modern social theory but of the modern project. Postmodernists are drawn to Simmel's work, in particular, because of what they see as his anti-holistic understanding of society and, relatedly, the subjectivism of his approach.

The theoretical arguments of Simmel and Weber are quite closely related. As I shall explain in the first section of this chapter, both theorists characterize the development of modern society in terms of the concept of rationalization. Like Marx, they emphasize economic changes underlying the growth of modern society. But their approach is closer to Durkheim in so far as they tend to be preoccupied with the cultural significance of these changes. This theme is expressed in Simmel's arguments on money, and in Weber's analysis of the relationship between religious belief and the ethics of economic organization and activity.

In the second section of the chapter, the discussion moves on to the normative arguments advanced by Simmel and Weber. For both theorists, the critical analysis of modern society must focus on the ambiguous consequences of the growth of reason. Simmel argues that modern society is marked by the alienation of subjective culture in the face of an all-pervasive objective culture where nothing escapes the rational logic of commodification. He suggests that the pursuit of money for its own sake crystallizes a culture in which means have become ends. While more circumspect in his interpretation of the impact of reason on modern culture, Weber expresses doubts about the growth of bureaucracy, and envisages an individual who, as a consequence of that growth, becomes trapped inside a metaphorical iron cage. According to this view, reason must be allied to coherent objectives and ultimate values, otherwise technological advancement and economic growth will become meaningless and dispiriting.

In the third section of the chapter, two core themes will be raised for critical discussion. First, I shall examine the formalism which is integral to the theoretical strategy of Simmel and Weber. This is a distinctive strategy, and has since been taken up only rarely in modern social theory, while in many ways being incompatible with the arguments of postmodernists. In later chapters of this book, I shall try to explain why this might be so. In the second part of the critical discussion, I shall turn to the interpretation of the concept of reason in the work of Simmel and Weber. Simmel's conceptualization of reason is marked by an ambivalence which continues to resound in modern and postmodern social theory. Similarly, Weber's argument raises the question of the two dimensions of reason – as a means of instrumental calculation on the one hand, and as a basis for belief on the other – which have remained in some kind of conflict ever since. But there is another feature of their approach that I want to focus on. They are seeking to formulate concepts which address not only the relationship between instrumental reason and modern culture, but between reason and social theory itself. Weber, particularly, seems to acknowledge the tension which arises when reason is used as a framework for social theory while also being one of its principal topics of investigation. That tension will remain pivotal to the discussion throughout this book.

Reason, Economy and Society

In contrast to Marx, Weber and Simmel question the notion that the modern economic system is distinguished primarily by the private ownership of property, and by exploitative relations between owners and non-owners of capital. For Simmel, the modern economic system is defined by its own specific exchange relations, that is, the mature money economy. Weber undertakes a multifaceted analysis of relations between economy, state and culture, and argues that the impetus for the development of these relations lies less with changes in property ownership than with the rationalization of accounting procedures and the expansion of markets.

Reason and the mature money economy

Simmel characterizes reason in psychological terms. He argues that, as humans, we are distinguished by our ability to pursue goals in a conscious, strategic way. The emergence of money in society is a consequence of this. In so far as money is the most advanced expression of rational purposive action, it is a pure instrument which is open to a potentially limitless range of uses. The mature money economy, not capitalism, characterizes modern society. It consists of an extensive and interconnected network of monetary relations which span right across society. Its development is a consequence of the growth of reasoned thought and activity. In relation to money, social action is expressed in the form of calculating relationships. On a subjective level, this means that emotional reactions and decisions are progressively eliminated from social life.

Simmel does not, however, investigate the mature money economy because of an intrinsic interest in the operation of money itself. Rather, he argues that money is analogous with the most distinctive features of modern society and culture. Taking up the idea of the money economy as an extensive and interconnected series of contractual relationships, he argues that, from a subjective viewpoint, modern society is like a web whose 'delicate, invisible threads . . . are woven together between one person and another'.[2] But at the same time, the objective unity of this network empties social relations of their subjective content, effectively excluding those relations of their personal and specific character.

Monetary exchange provides a further analogy for what Simmel describes as the increasing tempo of modern life. He suggests that individuals use money not simply because it facilitates the exchange of goods but because it is desirable for itself. The abstract quality of money – the fact that it can be adapted to whatever purpose we choose – motivates people to acquire it. As a consequence, both the rate at which goods are bought and sold, and the range of assets that are turned into money, will tend to increase, and with them the tempo of social life more generally: 'every increase in the quantity of money has . . . a disturbing effect upon the pace of social life' (1990: 503).

Simmel's characterization of the mature money economy, and of its impact on modern culture, rests on a specific interpretation of the nature of social life itself. Like Durkheim and Marx, he emphasizes the interconnectedness of all social relations in modern society. He argues that all the individual elements of social life depend on one another.[3] Simmel does not, however, characterize the individual as a social entity. This theoretical stance is vitally important for his normative argument on the objectification of culture. But it is an approach which is embedded in a theoretical understanding of the nature and significance of society itself.

Simmel characterizes society as 'a structure which consists of beings who stand inside and outside of it at the same time' (1971: 14–15). There is a reciprocal relationship between society and the individual whereby the individual is both incorporated into society while simultaneously confronting it as something external. Thus, according to Simmel, the individual is both a product and member of society. As product, the individual is confronted with social forms that derive from the past. As member, the individual is woven into society as it exists now.

Simmel argues that society consists of a higher union which individuals are motivated to join by their own interests. These interests may be economic, idealistic, warlike, erotic, religious or charitable.[4] Whereas Durkheim, in his characterization of the *homo duplex*, suggests that only the most egoistic interests stand outside and therefore might work against society, Simmel suggests that all human motivations derive from the individual. Such motivations interact with, but do not stem from, the wider society. According to this view, even our sociability has psychological roots.[5] The impulse to sociability gives rise to various forms of association, or what Simmel calls social forms. In basic terms, social forms are forms of social interaction such as conflict, domination or exchange. Of these, exchange is by far the most important for Simmel because most social relationships among individuals can be considered under this category. Thus, in direct contrast to Marx, Simmel regards exchange, not production, as the basis of all social life. This has important consequences for his critical analysis of modern society, as I shall discuss later on in this chapter.

Weber's concept of reason

Weber characterizes the spread of reason as the intellectualization of modern culture. Whereas Simmel draws a distinction between the functions of reason, which are intellectual, and those of the passions, which are emotional, Weber suggests that reason can be applied both to matters of calculation and to questions of value. This corresponds to the two forms of reason which feature in Weber's analysis. First, there is the abstract and instrumental mode of calculation which, in neoclassical economics, best characterizes the reasoning of the economic actor.[6] Weber refers to social action in this context as goal-rational, or *zweckrationalität*. Goal-rational action can be defined as calculative action which is designed to attain a specific goal by the most effective or efficient means. As I shall discuss later on, the connection between instrumental reason and economic action in Weber's argument is a source of debate. The second form of reason consists of the concrete and applied judgement of values and political commitments. Weber characterizes this form of social action as value-rational, or *wertrationalität*. Value-rational action can be defined as action which is informed by an overriding ideal.

The distinction between goal-rational and value-rational action is heuristic. This means that neither definition is intended exhaustively to describe particular instances of reasoning and social action, but rather to provide a conceptual framework in which such instances can be interpreted and, above all, compared. For example, the types of rational action are formulated in order for irrational variations to be measured against them. Ideal-types are ideal not in the sense of being desirable but because they are abstract. They contain elements which are found in reality but not necessarily in the specific form suggested by the ideal-type. Crucially, the types are not literally descriptive.[7] Ideal-types are therefore not models in the sense implied by the theories of modern society which are advanced by Marx and Durkheim. They are tools that are intended to assist explanation. Weber's categories of rational action should also, in principle at least, be easily distinguishable from normative categories. This is not to say that ideal-types cannot be used in the context of a normative argument, but simply that they are not intended to have normative connotations in their own right.

Like Simmel, Weber emphasizes the importance of market, or exchange, relations in his account of the economic developments which underpin the modernization of society. But Weber's analysis also ranges more widely than this.[8] He argues that the application of instrumental reason to administration and accountancy was an important factor in the growth of market capitalism because it facilitated not only the activities of capitalists but the economic functions of the modern state. Although bureaucratic organizations existed in a fairly developed form in ancient Egypt and China, only in modern society does bureaucratic organization take on a fully fledged, that is, rational, form where officials are trained, appointed on the basis of their qualifications, and paid a salary. According to Weber, this is a vital precondition for the emergence of modern capitalism.

Weber argues that the modern bureaucratic state played a vital role in establishing standards of capital accounting on which capitalism depends in order to flourish. In particular, he emphasizes the importance of calculating profits and losses via double-entry bookkeeping.[9] But the modern state is also significant for establishing a rational fiscal system by collecting and administering taxes on a universal, state-wide basis, without the myriad exemptions and inefficiencies which characterized the absolutist system. Weber's argument is significant for present-day sociology, in which it is increasingly argued that contemporary society must be examined in its global context. Theories of advanced capitalism often suggest that the capacity of national governments to implement economic policy has been undermined by the process of globalization, while theorists of global culture ask whether the notion of a national culture is still valid.[10] Weber's work on the modern state has an important bearing on such questions because his approach to the state emphasizes both its internal organization and external relations.[11]

Despite focusing on the significance of the modern state for the growth of capitalism, Weber suggests that the functions of the modern state cannot be reduced to their economic context alone. He emphasizes that this is a complex question, because structures of power and political organizations vary in the extent to which they are conscious of external forces and constraints (1978a: 910). As a general principle, however, he suggests that most political communities would prefer weak rather than strong neighbours, and to be regarded by those neighbours as prestigious and as a potential threat. But the state also has a broader role in modern society, because it expresses and seeks to preserve qualities of nationhood which are both physical and spiritual.[12]

This is just one context, however, in which Weber discusses the interconnection between economics, politics and culture in modern society. In broad terms, his work consists of a multicausal analysis of the development of modern society. The analysis is more detailed than that of Marx because it is informed not by a general theory but by a series of concepts, or ideal-types, which enable different cases to be compared and contrasted. The approach is exemplified by his study of eastern Prussia, published during the 1890s,[13] and by his better-known work on the Protestant ethic. In the former, Weber examines the consequences of the development of commercial relations for the social structure of rural workers in the East Elbian region.[14] There are important connections between Weber's argument here and his reading of both *The Communist Manifesto* and the first two volumes of *Capital*, although socialist writers such as Lassalle and Rodbertus are also significant.[15] Crucially, however, it is the work of two economists of the German Historical School, Karl Knies and Gustav Schmoller – both of whom represent a narrative and evolutionary, rather than structural, approach to history – which informs Weber's thesis.

The argument is counterintuitive. Weber suggests that non-economic factors were key in the commercialization of the East Elbian region. Rural workers were attracted to the money economy by the freedom made possible by the monetization of exchange relations. In short, the money wage liberated serfs from landowners. They were even prepared to forego economic advantage in order to achieve this. Thus, in theoretical terms, the actions of serfs were rational in a substantive, not instrumental, sense: their gain was the psychological magic of freedom, not economic prosperity.

A similarly counterintuitive note is struck by Weber's account of the role of Calvinist belief in the development of capitalism. The most significant part of Weber's thesis is that it was the fear and inner loneliness engendered by the Calvinist doctrine of predestination which motivated intense economic activity. He therefore disputes any notion that the growth of capitalism was, psychologically at least, bound up with the pursuit of wealth as an end in itself. Indeed, he goes so far as to suggest that the unscrupulous pursuit of money for its own sake tends to be a characteristic of countries whose degree of capitalistic development remains quite backward (1930: 57). Weber maintains that the unprecedentedly rational pursuit of profit in which the Calvinists engaged sprang from an emotional or psychological response to religious teaching: the pursuit of economic prosperity to glorify God and sustain an inner belief that one has been chosen. It was only later on that the production of profit became an end in itself. That idea will provide the focus for discussion in the next section of this chapter, because it underpins Weber's normative argument.

Disenchantment and the Commodification of Culture

The normative arguments of Simmel and Weber focus on the cultural consequences of the growth of reason in modern society. Both are critical of what they regard as the increasing narrowness of modern culture, in which rational means such as monetary exchange and bureaucratic organization cease to be viewed as the most efficient basis for pursuing certain ends and are turned inwards to become goals in their own right. Simmel takes up this theme in his examination of the objectification of culture, and relatedly, of the weakening of subjectivity in modern society. For Weber, the development of modern culture is characterized by a process of disenchantment, that is, by our increasing detachment from spiritual values and a scepticism towards cosmic accounts of our relationship with nature.

Simmel on the objectification of modern culture

Simmel does not advocate clear normative principles in his work. Nor is he concerned, at least in a practical way, with the management of change in modern society. One important reason for this lies with the fact that Simmel does not formulate a general theory of modern society in terms of which a normative project would be framed. Nevertheless, his account of the character and development of the mature money economy, particularly its implications for modern culture, is implicitly critical and, according to some postmodernists, even contains the seeds of a new conception of society altogether.[16]

Simmel suggests that the development of modern society is associated in some way with increasing freedom for the individual: for example, our freedom to enter into exchange relations with others. But like the other classical theorists, Simmel argues that such freedom is double-edged. Its negative connotations are expressed in our pursuit of money. The freedom which money gives us is empty, a 'freedom *from* something' as opposed to a 'liberty *to do* something' (1990: 402, Simmel's emphasis). In other words, money frees us from economic and social constraints without, in and of itself, offering any guidance as to how we might exploit its range of possible applications.[17] Partly as a consequence of this, modern culture is spiritually vacuous. Our only attachment is to possessions, or even worse, to that shallow and fleeting satisfaction that is gained at the moment of their acquisition.

Simmel characterizes the prevalence of monetary relations in modern society in terms of the increasing solidity and autonomy of objective culture. He refers to this, and the fragmentation of subjective culture which it brings about, as the tragedy of modern culture.[18] Simmel suggests that, paradoxically, it is the fact that money empowers us that accounts for the fragmentation of subjective life. Monetary freedom is abstract, empty of substance. It becomes alive and valuable only through being incorporated into the substance of real social relations. But as soon as money is valued for its own sake there is no framework in which those relations can develop.

The diminution of subjective culture does not only arise from the development of the mature money economy. It is also expressed in the radical reorganization of social space in modern society, particularly within the city. Like Durkheim, Simmel argues that increasing social density – the movement of people into cities in search of economic survival, and the process of urbanization more generally – is one of the most important sociological consequences of modernization. But whereas Durkheim argues that this process enables a new form of individualism to flourish, Simmel suggests that it may threaten the integrity of individualism itself, not least because that integrity depends on the coherence of subjective culture. The city provides a spatial focus for the mature money economy, and its organization crystallizes the specifically modern, complex division of labour. It is therefore hardly surprising that Simmel's analysis of urban life is characterized by the same ambivalence that is expressed by his conceptualization of monetary freedom.

For Simmel, the city is a social space in its own right: 'not a spatial entity with sociological consequences, but a sociological entity that is formed spatially'.[19] The city embraces the full diversity of social life, just as money unifies people who – because of differences in their interests – could not possibly be integrated in any other way. Yet in so far as the city serves as a focus for monetary exchange and the division of labour, it expresses precisely those characteristics that, in the analysis of money, Simmel associates with the objectification of culture. These include intellectual rationality, mathematical calculability, abstraction, objectivity, anonymity and levelling. Thus, like money, the city provides a social space in which individuals depend on one another while simultaneously being dissociated from one other.[20]

Simmel's characterization of the fragmentation of subjective culture is developed further in his analysis of fashion. Focusing on the increasing turnover of successive fashions in modern society, he notes that the pursuit of fashion has broken into areas of society which were hitherto untouched by it. At the same time, those who were already interested in fashion are now becoming obsessed by it. Once again, however, fashion expresses the ambivalence of modern culture from the subjective point of view. On the one hand, fashion lends substance to our social identity, yet on the other, this substance is necessarily fleeting and ever changeable.[21] As with other forms of entertainment on offer to us in modern society, it is our exhaustion by the demands of economic life which renders us peculiarly open to trivial forms of amusement which serve merely to fill in what is otherwise vacant space and time: 'the nerves, exhausted by the bustle and anxiety of the day, no longer react any more to stimulations, except those which are, as it were, directly physiological, to which the organism itself still responds if all of its sensitivities have been blunted.'[22]

Prostitution represents the social relationship where all of these elements are combined: monetary exchange, insubstantiality, transitoriness and the satisfaction of shallow needs. According to Simmel, the transaction of money enables the relationship between prostitute and client to contain, however fleetingly, both the universal and the particular at the same time. The relationship is universal because it consists of an action which any and all of us can perform and experience. Yet it is also particular, because the mere presence of money is debasing. In prostitution, 'the most personal possession of a woman, her area of greatest reserve, is considered equivalent to the most neutral value of all' (1971: 122). The real danger, for Simmel, is that this debasement captures all that is essential in modern culture.

The disenchantment of the world

Weber's critical analysis of modern culture also focuses on the theme of subjectivity. He argues that instrumental reason places too high a value on subjective and ephemeral desires as opposed to morally informed needs.[23] There are further echoes of Simmel in Weber's description of the spirit of capitalism, where he berates the fact that, in modern society, to acquire more and more money is increasingly being thought of as an end in itself – to the extent that it begins to seem quite irrational. Like Simmel, Weber argues that exchange relations play a significant role in stratifying modern society, and that they therefore have a more powerful impact on the outlook and aspirations of individuals than Marx envisaged. These points are combined in Weber's reworking of the concept of class. While he largely agrees with Marx that property relations are a major determinant of class relations, Weber contends that our market situation, that is, our ability to marshall various resources, cannot be reduced to our class position. Moreover, a shared class position does not, logically or historically, go hand in hand with a shared political outlook, but is contingent upon a range of other factors. Of these, social status is the most significant. It is worth discussing this idea in more detail because it has a direct bearing on Weber's normative argument.

According to Weber, our status is likely to shape our conscious political affiliations because status consists of our social position as viewed by others. Social status cannot be conferred by virtue of wealth or property ownership alone, but depends on factors such as education and family background. There is no hard and fast rule governing this. The relative significance of status as opposed to class depends partly on the level of economic stability in society.[24] Weber therefore rejects Marx's contention that class struggle provides the only means of achieving social change, just as he rejects the holistic, revolutionary idea of societal transformation itself. For Weber, a constellation of interests and aspirations that is of sufficient coherence to generate significant social change is likely to have political, not economic, roots. Moreover, broader questions of power – of association and conflict between states, for example – are at least as significant as conflict and association between class or status groups within society for the phenomenon of social change.

Weber's most immediate practical concern is with the 'national question' confronting Germany at the turn of the century.[25] His normative arguments derive primarily from this, as do many of the themes in his economic writings. For example, he contends that national wealth is the goal not only of economic activity but of economic science. It is for this reason that a national economic policy should never be evaluated in narrowly economic terms alone.[26] Weber thereby reiterates the view that instrumental reason provides too narrow a basis on which to make judgements even on economic affairs.

An example of this normative orientation can be found in the typology of social action. Weber not only theorizes social action but directly addresses the difficulties posed within a society which is dominated by rational-legal administration. He seeks to convey and explore the implications of the fact that, within modern society, individuals find themselves increasingly unable to make clear, morally informed choices about important questions in their lives. The rational criterion of efficiency offers no guidance on the substance of political decisions. This normative argument is supported by Weber's theoretical distinction between *zweckrationalität* and *wertrationalität*.

The immediate practical questions preoccupying Weber must, however, be seen in the context of his broader critique of modern culture. This critique focuses on the narrowness of instrumental reason, and is crystallized by a distinction between the idea of calling or vocation as it arises, first, in Calvinist belief and, second, when we normally refer to paid employment in modern society. Two German terms, both of which can be translated as vocation, express this distinction. The first is *Berufung*, which literally means mission, while the second is *Beruf*, which can be translated as occupation or profession.[27] Weber employs this distinction when comparing the vocation or calling of the Calvinists with the sense of vocation as employment which we are expected to pursue in modern capitalism: 'The puritan wanted to work in a calling; we are forced to do so' (1930: 180–2).

Weber's account of the Protestant ethic can therefore be read metaphorically: less as a historical analysis of the emergence of capitalism than as an expression of a much wider transformation in modern society. This consists of the growth of an instrumental worldview in which ultimate values are debased. This theme is important to Weber's work on the world religions, for example, in which he investigates the connection between religious belief and the ethics that govern economic relations in different societies. More specifically, he suggests that the expansion of modern industrial capitalism necessarily goes hand in hand with the disenchantment of the world. He characterizes this process as the increasing intellectualization and rationalization of life. But this process does not provide us with a more rounded understanding of the conditions under which we live. Rather, it mistakenly suggests that we can master everything by rational calculation.[28]

The process of disenchantment can be defined as the gradual disappearance of magical thought and practice from the world. This process signifies not only a decline of religious belief but the rationalization of religious practice itself. The disenchantment of the world entails breaking up traditional worldviews into distinctive specialist areas of expertise: specifically, those of science, morality and art. The questions and values which are associated with these areas are no longer contained within an overarching belief system. Although he does not regard this development as irreversible, Weber offers a downbeat assessment of its implications: 'For of the last stage of this cultural development, it might well be truly said: "Specialists without spirit, sensualists without heart; this nullity imagines that it has attained a level of civilization never before achieved"' (1930: 182).

In institutional terms, the disenchantment of the world is expressed by the rationalization of economic life, particularly the process of bureaucratization which, according to Weber, too readily resembles a form of dehumanization. A bureaucratic organization grows in efficiency to the extent to which it is able to eliminate the emotions from its affairs. It is therefore paradoxical that the disenchantment of the world entails the disappearance of precisely those values and ideals which, as exemplified by the Calvinists, facilitated the emergence of modern society in the first place. The process of disenchantment, sucked into a self-perpetuating materialism, takes on a life of its own and thereby severs all links with its own history. A society and culture that is dominated by the criterion of instrumental efficiency and the logic of cognitive specialization is in danger of creating an iron cage into which the human spirit is propelled without any realistic prospect of escape. But while remarking on the fact that religious values have been banished from modern society and culture, Weber adds a significant question: 'whether finally, who knows?' (1930: 182). At the very least, this suggests that the iron cage he refers to should not be regarded as inevitable or irresistible, even if the process of bureaucratization and disenchantment rests on what he calls the mechanical foundations of capitalism. I shall return to this point later on, because it is arguably at odds with his analysis of the connection between instrumental reason and economic development.

Critical Discussion

In the following discussion, two areas of debate surrounding the work of Simmel and Weber will be discussed. Both raise important questions for modern and postmodern social theory. First, I shall examine the theoretical strategy of formalism and its implications for the normative arguments of Simmel and Weber. I shall ask whether this strategy presents a viable alternative to the general theories of society formulated by Marx and Durkheim. Second, the conceptualization of reason by Simmel and Weber will be examined. This concept provides an important, but problematic, focus for the arguments of both theorists, while being significant for the ongoing debate regarding the developmental trajectory of modern society.

Theoretical formalism

Neither Weber nor Simmel proposes a general theory of modern society. Paradoxically, however, this enables them to advance what are, if anything, more ambitious claims on behalf of their arguments and ideas than are to be found in the work of Marx and Durkheim. Simmel seeks to combine the disciplines of philosophy, history and sociology on the basis of a central juxtaposition between form and content. To some extent, this accounts for the liberal use of analogy in his work. By his own reckoning, Simmel adopts this strategy, which some commentators describe as impressionistic, in order to grasp the totality of relations in the world. By contrast, Weber's strategy is securely grounded in recognizably modern scientific principles. He argues against a general theory of history such as that proposed by Marx because it would gloss over important details in the analysis of specific cases. Instead, he formulates a series of heuristic devices, or ideal-types, as the methodological basis for comparative research which is arguably of greater scope than anything attempted by Marx.

It is open to question to what extent Simmel's work adds up to a genuine theoretical analysis of modern society. For some commentators, his work directly anticipates the postmodern thesis that society will move beyond industrialism and the realm of production into a world which consists of the circulation of symbols and signs: a world in which it is increasingly difficult to talk of reality as opposed to the representation of reality. For others, Simmel's analysis lacks critical edge precisely because of this confusion: unlike Marx, he fails to search for essential relations which lie beneath the surface of reality and which ensure that the appearance is sustained.[29] This would suggest that Simmel's analysis is of a reified world, but merely confirms rather than uncovers that reification.

In the light of these comments, it is worth reiterating that the core substantive theme in Simmel's work concerns the increasing asymmetry between objective and subjective culture. As expressed by the circulation of money and commodities, indeed the commodification of all aspects of culture, objective culture has acquired an 'ominous independence' from subjective culture. This argument can therefore be read in parallel with, not opposition to, Marx's analysis of reification and commodity fetishism. Where Simmel does depart from Marx in significant ways is in failing – or refusing – to situate his analysis within a general theory of society and history. To this extent, his approach is closer to Weber than to Marx. In other words, the distinctiveness of Simmel's approach when set against that of Marx may have more to do with his theoretical strategy than with the substance of his arguments. This strategy can be characterized as formalism.

Despite the range of analogies in Simmel's writings, there is what Levine refers to as a unity of method in his work: 'His method is to select some bounded, finite phenomenon from the world of flux; to examine the multiplicity of elements which compose it; and to ascertain the cause of their coherence by disclosing its form. Secondarily, he investigates the origins of this form and its structural implications' (introduction to Simmel, 1971: xxxi). This approach certainly generates rich empirical detail. Gadamer, for example, refers to the 'seismographic accuracy' of Simmel's depiction of Berlin (introduction to Simmel, 1978: 28). At the same time, it is a strategy which renders untenable any attempt to draw the threads of analysis together within a general theoretical system, that is, a set of interrelated concepts that provide a framework for understanding the operation and development of society as a whole. The advantages and disadvantages of this approach can be illustrated by considering Simmel's analysis of money.[30]

By defining money as the pure instrument of exchange, Simmel refers more to the *idea* of money in modern society – particularly of the range of potential uses to which it can be put – than to specific forms of money. As sociologists such as Viviana Zelizer later point out, no real form of money corresponds empirically to Simmel's abstract definition because all forms of money have a range of social, political, economic and even contextual restrictions on how, and to what purpose, they are used.[31] According to Simmel's basic methodology, however, he is concerned with money, in abstract terms, as a social form, that is, the purest form of exchange.

The reason for employing such an abstract definition of money becomes clear as soon as we consider the aims which lie behind his analysis. Simmel states that his two main objectives 'lie on either side of the economic science of money': first, to examine 'the conditions and connections of life in general'; and second, to uncover 'the preconditions that, situated in mental states, in social relations and in the logical structure of reality and values, give money its meaning and its practical position' (1990: 54). Simmel's theoretical strategy therefore mirrors core normative themes in his analysis, namely, the relationship between objective and subjective culture.

This unity of method and substance – or of form and content – is replicated by his characterization of money itself, both as a topic of study in its own right and as a means for exploring more general features of modern society and culture. In short, his treatment of money as an object of analysis is derived from his definition of money as a pure instrument of exchange. Just as he argues that, in modern society, money 'is nothing but the vehicle for a movement in which everything else that is not in motion is completely extinguished' (1990: 511), so he points out that his own philosophical treatment takes money as 'simply a means, a material or an example for the presentation of relations that exist between the most superficial, "realistic" and fortuitous phenomena and the most idealized powers of existence, the most profound currents of individual life and history' (p. 55).

Simmel's approach possesses a formal unity that one is most likely to find in an aesthetic context. Indeed, his approach is often described in aesthetic rather than philosophical or theoretical terms.[32] It is nevertheless doubtful whether this amounts to a coherent social theory. As Levine notes, Simmel's work has been widely criticized for its lack of theoretical coherence: 'The *results* of Simmelian inquiry are . . . a series of discrete analyses . . . This is what produces the appearance (and in the sense here specified, the reality) of disunity in Simmel's work. It suffers from the "type atomism" for which Talcott Parsons has criticized the work of Max Weber even more than does Weber's work' (introduction to Simmel, 1971: xxxi–xxxii). It is important to note, however, that Simmel's major achievement is to avoid the kind of theoretical inflexibility which apparently arises in the work of Marx. As Levine argues, Simmel's approach 'does not force all phenomena together into a general scheme nor does it molest them with arbitrary or rigid categories; at the same time it avoids mindless empiricism by providing a context of meanings for sets of observations. It enhances discovery' (ibid.: xxxii).

There are important similarities between the theoretical strategies employed by Simmel and Weber.[33] Like Simmel, Weber rejects the kind of theoretical system favoured by Marx. But whereas Simmel introduces concepts which tend to be specific, or useful to the particular study he is undertaking, Weber seeks to formulate a series of concepts and categories which are applicable to a wide range of empirical studies. In short, Weber suggests what might be seen as a middle way between the generalism of Marx and Durkheim on the one hand, and the particularism of Simmel on the other. For example, he defines capitalism in a more abstract way than Marx, that is, as a set of market, not property, relations. There are important theoretical reasons for this. Principal among these is the argument that a general theory of development such as historical materialism is untenable. Giddens summarizes the argument as follows: 'If "theories of history" as a whole are impossible, it follows on the more specific level that any theory which attempts to tie historical development to the universal causal predominance of economic or class relationships is doomed to failure' (1971: 163).

As I have already noted, Weber's references to economics are less concerned with classical political economy than with the historical school represented by Rosher and Knies. This approach rests on detailed empirical research, and can therefore be contrasted not only to Marx but to Simmel.[34] Commentators such as Tenbruck and Habermas have suggested that Weber's understanding of economic development is based on an evolutionary interpretation of history, although others disagree.[35] I shall return to this question later on, because it arises in connection with Weber's conceptualization of instrumental reason in terms of economic calculation. Of greater importance in the context of this discussion is Weber's argument against historical generalization.

For this, more than anything else, underpins his approach to historical and comparative social theory.[36]

While Marx seeks to discern laws underlying the development of capitalist society, Weber's approach is both more sweeping and more narrow. Where Marx formulates developmental laws, Weber outlines what he calls developmental tendencies. These are frameworks which outline, but do not theorize in detail, patterns of development in society. Developmental tendencies are conceptualized in an abstract, not general, way. That is to say, they are intended to provide an abstract framework against which particular cases can be compared, not an explanatory model for generalizing across such cases. Weber's strategy is therefore less ambitious than that of Marx in so far as he offers no general explanatory schema for understanding the development of society. Weber's focus is also narrower. He suggests that a society develops in ways which may be specific to that society alone. These patterns must be compared, not merely subsumed within a more general theoretical framework.

Weber's approach to social theory is closely informed by the argument for a crisp distinction between facts and values in the social sciences. This distinction should not, however, preclude the possibility that the social sciences might have practical and even normative significance. According to Weber, value-freedom is not equivalent or reducible to impartiality. To express this in another way, objectivity in social science cannot be achieved merely by remaining aloof from political or moral questions: '*Scientifically the "middle course" is not truer by a hair's breadth* than the most extreme party ideals of the left or right . . . An *attitude of moral indifference* has no connection with *scientific "objectivity"*' (1969: 57–60, Weber's emphasis). Weber does not suggest that such objectivity is easy to achieve. In his discussion of the tension between science and politics, for example, he concedes that scientific work cannot proceed in a moral and political vacuum: 'Scientific work is chained to the course of progress; whereas in the realm of art there is no progress in the same sense' (1991: 138).

Weber argues that a scientific approach to social theory must be based on the formulation of specific analytical techniques. To this end, he recommends that we construct concepts and categories – ideal-types – which enable detailed empirical research into specific historical cases. This approach suggests a direct analogy between the social and natural sciences, because it is as close to the experimental model as we are likely to get. The formalism of Weber's approach is exemplified by his argument on the non-economic motives lying behind key economic developments such as the commercialization of agriculture in the East Elbian region, and the role of Calvinism in the development of capitalism. In both studies, he treats the role of economic motives in the transformation of societies as a matter for empirical investigation, not theoretical assumption. He is able to proceed in this way because, as with the ideal-type more generally, Weber's typology of social action is formulated for heuristic purposes, as a tool for research rather than a general theoretical model which may in some cases prejudge the outcome of that research.

In chapter 1 above, it was noted that Durkheim's general theory of society – and especially his interpretation of its normal and pathological states – is derived from observations that are intended to lead to the formulation of a general or average type. Weber's strategy presents an instructive contrast to this.[37] According to Weber, the most important problems in the social sciences tend to concern specificity, not generality or commonality. In other words, he suggests that it is the differences *between* social and cultural phenomena, much more than the characteristics they share, which are most likely to generate significant insights into the social world. Ideal-types are formulated in order to investigate, not gloss over, such differences. Moreover, they are designed to discover *degrees* of difference between various cases: a discovery which, as I suggested in the preceding chapter, general theoretical models of society such as those formulated by Marx and Durkheim seem likely to mitigate against. Crucially, it is only by formulating concepts which are abstract[38] – and which therefore enable differences between cases to be highlighted or even accentuated within the ideal-type – that Weber's strategy can be implemented. But more important than this, it is a strategy which is not intended to preclude the discovery of those characteristics that various social and cultural phenomena do have in common.[39] In other words, Weber's strategy is designed to overcome the disadvantages of a general theoretical model of society, that is, its lack of specificity, without losing sight of its advantages, that is, the identification of commonality. He appears to be convinced that this is only possible because the ideal-types do not literally describe society or aspects of society as if from the outside, but facilitate the empirical investigation of society from within.

There are therefore clear advantages to Weber's strategy when compared to that of Marx or Durkheim. The use of ideal-types enables a more flexible approach to historical and comparative research, minimizing the possibility of theory prejudicing either the focus or the outcome of investigation. Furthermore, this enables a closer association between theory and research: after all, Weber's main criterion for evaluating ideal-types is that they are useful in the context of research. But the potential disadvantages of Weber's strategy must not be ignored. There is always a risk of lapsing into what Levine calls mindless empiricism, where theory passes merely for a set of concepts and categories for processing information without providing a basis on which to interpret that information. In this case, the interpretation of social phenomena might appear to be merely arbitrary or wilful. Moreover, as Marxists might argue, the criterion of usefulness – as applied to ideal-type concepts – is unlikely to be especially robust in the face of the interests, however unwitting, of the researcher. There is also a potential problem of coherence, although this can be understood only in the light of some notion of the objective of social theory: for example, whether it is to advance a general model for sociological explanation which cannot be directly incorporated into social research; or whether theories should consist of concepts, categories and modes of explanation which are open to modification in the light of research. I shall be returning to these questions, and the answers suggested by modern and postmodern social theorists, in later chapters.

Instrumental reason and economic calculation

As I have already discussed, both Simmel and Weber define instrumental reason as a form of economic calculation. Furthermore, both theorists provide a critique of economic calculation which focuses on its narrow or apparently 'asocial' character. The social relationship which most sharply expresses this form of reasoning consists of exchange, and both Simmel and Weber devote considerable attention to this in their analyses of economic life in modern society. There are significant differences between their approaches, however, which will be important as our discussion proceeds.

Simmel is at pains to conceptualize economic exchange in a broad way: 'exchange is a sociological phenomenon *sui generis*, an original form and function of social life. It is in no way a logical consequence of those qualitative and quantitative aspects of things that are called utility and scarcity, which acquire their significance for the process of valuation only when exchange is presupposed' (1990: 100). Indeed, one might say that one of the major arguments of *The Philosophy of Money* consists of the insight that monetary exchange, and monetary relations in general, cannot be understood within the limited terms suggested by neoclassical economics. Even if, as Frisby suggests, Simmel's analysis starts out with a theory of value derived from the marginalist school of neoclassical economics, his subsequent insistence that exchange is a sociological phenomenon suggests that his work 'contains a sociological and philosophical critique of its own economic presuppositions' (1992a: 97). Nowhere is this clearer than in Simmel's rejection of the idea that all relationships involving money have a rational and calculating character. His analysis of modern society and culture therefore contains what is, in effect, a double-edged critique: on the one hand, of a culture increasingly characterized by narrow forms of economic calculation; but on the other, of the notion that this development could ever be understood or explained in terms of an equally narrow economic theory.

On the face of it, Weber's treatment of economic action and exchange, and particularly its relationship with instrumental reason, is more straightforward than that of Simmel. He argues that the spread of instrumental reason into more and more areas of social life is problematic for modern culture. As Brubacker notes, this is because a belief system 'cannot in itself be guided by reason, for . . . there is no rational way of deciding among the plurality of conflicting possible value commitments' (1984: 9). In this context, the significance of reason appears to be twofold. Intellectually, reason guides rigorous analysis and thought. But at the same time, reason provides a framework for principles which have normative significance for the way we organize our political system or societal space. In basic terms, Weber warns that the intellectual side of reason will be reduced to a demand for technical efficiency; and that this will become valued for its own sake. This appears to run parallel to Simmel's argument that monetary exchange will turn into a craving for money for it's own sake.[40]

Another way of addressing these questions, however, would be to ask what *drives* the process of rationalization as characterized by Weber. In the economic sphere, he lists three institutional 'preconditions' which must be met if economic calculation is to thrive in society (1978a: 108). First, economic units, or actors, must be sufficiently autonomous from each other to facilitate the struggle of interests which is necessary for the price mechanism to work. Second, market freedom, defined as the absence of monopoly, is necessary for that struggle of interests to prevail. Third, calculation must concern effective demand, not demand *per se*, because this enables the adequate distribution of goods for supply and demand to be in equilibrium: 'What is produced is thus determined, given the distribution of wealth, by the structure of marginal utilities in the income group which has both the inclination and resources to purchase a given utility' (1978a: 108).

While Weber associates the spread of formal rationality with increasing economic freedom, he argues that this process may compromise *human* freedom on a more general level.[41] But as Turner notes, this might well be taken to suggest that 'rationalization in Weber's sociology has a variety of meanings' (1992: 177). For example, it is possible to distinguish between two forms of intellectualization that he associates with the spread of reason in modern society, corresponding to formal and substantive rationality, respectively. In formal terms, intellectualization would entail 'the subordination of all areas of life to systematic scientific inquiry and management'. In substantive terms, intellectualization would refer to 'the dominance of expert cultures over traditional authorities in the sphere of morality, social relations and interpersonal behaviour' (Turner, 1992: 177).

Unlike Simmel, of course, Weber does seek to develop a dualistic understanding of reason: as applied, basically, to both means and ends. He characterizes this distinction in terms of the difference between formal and substantive rationality. Formal rationality refers to the calculation of the most efficient or effective path for achieving a predefined goal. Substantive rationality entails measuring 'the results of economic action, however formally "rational" in the sense of correct calculation they may be, against those scales of "value rationality" or "*substantive* goal rationality"' (1978a: 85–6, Weber's emphasis). Weber is less clear, however, when it comes to the relationship between formal rationality and modern culture. He tends to treat instrumental calculation as an abstract system of logic: not, as later theorists such as those associated with the Frankfurt School and Foucault have suggested, as a system of thought which is embedded in historically and culturally specific systems of power. In other words, Weber's analysis begs the question as to the epistemological status of formal rationality as he defines it. Is formal rationality a culturally and historically grounded worldview? Or is it a purely abstract framework which has no cultural underpinnings?

This question raises two serious problems. The first concerns the relationship between formal rationality and economic calculation. If these are equivalent to one another, as Weber might well be suggesting, his argument regarding the predominance of formal rationality in modern culture implies that economic values will take precedence in modern society. This would help to explain why later theorists such as Habermas have argued that Weber's characterization of modern society is untenably skewed towards a narrow conceptualization of economic life and institutions: not, however, as a result of the analysis – which is explicitly multicausal – but *of the way in which reason itself is defined*.

The second difficulty which arises from Weber's argument concerns the relationship between reason and culture, or more precisely, tradition. In so far as he associates the spread of formal rationality in modern society with the erosion of values, the process of disenchantment as

Weber defines it can be interpreted as the decline of tradition. As Benhabib observes, this would mean that overarching value systems from the past which grounded specific beliefs in the 'normative regulation of the social order' have been superseded (1991a: 41). In turn, this implies that all normative judgements must now come under the scrutiny of reason, and would therefore explain why the process of rationalization is meant to have such an unsettling or alienating effect on modern culture.

The contrast between Weber's argument and that of Durkheim is especially instructive in this context. Both theorists address what Sayer calls the 'violence of abstraction' which is brought about by the spread of reason in modern society (1990: 54–5).[42] For Weber, abstraction occurs when we lose touch with ultimate values and become preoccupied with instrumental efficiency. For Durkheim, by contrast, abstraction entails the internalization of moral values, or something akin to the incorporation of society within the individual. To some extent, this contrast can be explained by the distinctive way in which each theorist approaches the notion of society. While Durkheim's definition of society presupposes that it has an in-built capacity to maintain its own integrity as an organism, Weber advances no such general proposition.

The contrast is also due, however, to the abstract way in which Weber defines reason itself. As I have already suggested, it is unclear whether he associates the spread of reason with the transcendence of tradition, or whether he regards instrumental reason as a culturally and historically situated framework of thought. It is equally unclear just how 'irresistible' the advance of reason will be, according to Weber. Take, for example, this question, posed right at the beginning of *The Protestant Ethic and the Spirit of Capitalism*: 'A product of modern European civilization, studying any problem of universal history, is bound to ask himself to what combination of circumstances the fact should be attributed that in Western civilization, and in Western civilization only, cultural phenomena have appeared which (as we like to think) lie in a line of development having *universal* significance and value' (1930: 13, Weber's emphasis).

Two somewhat different interpretations of this question are possible. To suggest that these developments might have universal *significance* is an empirical statement which is, in principle, capable of verification, that is, it poses the question as to whether *all* cultures will eventually be defined by a rational worldview. To suggest that reason has universal *value*, on the other hand, is to suggest a rather different claim. It implies that formal rationality has cognitive superiority over, not simply more powerful support than, any other mode of thought.

According to this view, reason would be independent of culture, consisting of an objective, neutral and free-standing methodology governing the pursuit of knowledge. In this form, reason would be of vital importance to the epistemological principles which underwrite modern social theory. The contrast between these interpretations of Weber's question is stark: while the first might imply a relativist account of the significance of reason, the second manifestly would not. Weber's qualification to his own question – he suggests that 'we like to think' that our notion of reason has universal significance and value – implies a relativist position. As Benhabib points out, to say that 'we like to think' that reason has universal validity seems to be an implicit acknowledgement that 'it is only our "cultural interest" that motivates us to pose this question.' According to Benhabib, at the very least his question expresses the 'tension between the universalist and perspectivalist positions . . . [which] runs through the corpus of Weber's writings on modernity and rationalization' (1991a: 83 n2).

Taken together, the two problems which have been raised here regarding Weber's interpretation of reason suggest that this might be an account of rationalization which is rather different from the one that is often attributed to him. That is to say, we might infer from his argument that the dominance of rational thought in the modern world derives not from its inherent cognitive superiority but from its alliance with an economically powerful culture, namely, the West. Despite Weber's explicit advocacy of a multicausal approach to sociological explanation, this would amount to a somewhat narrow economic explanation for the growth of reason in modern society.

This nagging ambiguity in Weber's work has been taken up by subsequent theorists of both modern and postmodern society. For modernists such as Habermas, the characterization of reason must be widened to incorporate political ideals in a way that Weber implicitly intends but ultimately fails to do. Only then, Habermas suggests, can the full potential of reason to realize the good society – rather than the iron cage which Weber predicts – be appreciated. For postmodernists, by contrast, Weber suggests an interpretation of reason which has come to fruition only towards the end of the twentieth century, namely, that it represents a form of thought which does not have universal validity but merely a global significance by virtue of its advocacy by an economically powerful culture.[43] The contrast between these readings of Weber's analysis presents a problem for social theory which has become more significant the more we have become conscious of the need to verify or justify our own, specifically Western, worldview. Postmodern theorists have argued that social theories of modernity have advanced an implicitly Westernized perspective on the world: in other words, that the form of reasoning which underpins contemporary social theory cannot accurately be cast as independent or neutral in relation to culture.

In this context, it is important to reiterate the distinction between generality and abstraction in social theory. As I shall argue in part II of this book, modern social theory is closely associated with constructing a theoretical system, that is, a set of interrelated concepts that provide a general model for understanding and explaining how society works. Of the theorists discussed so far in this book, the work of Marx and Durkheim comes closest to this definition. The theorists discussed in this chapter reject such an approach as too generalized. Weber argues that social and economic change depends on causal variables which may be specific to individual societies. Any general approach to historical development across several societies is bound to gloss over what are often the most significant causal variables in any particular instance. Weber's argument that the Protestant ethic was an important catalyst that helps to explain the uneven development of capitalism in Europe illustrates this point. Here, he advances not an alternative general theory of the development of capitalism but rather a more detailed analysis which, by his reckoning, helps to explain variations which cannot be accounted for within the more general framework of historical materialism. For Weber, a social theory does not in itself seek to explain the development of society but serves as a tool of explanation through the construction of abstract ideal-types. He suggests that to conceive of social theory as a theoretical system makes it impossible to distinguish between the dispassionate observation of facts on the one hand, and normative commitment towards beliefs and values on the other. For Marx, by contrast, such a clear-cut distinction between fact and value is not only impossible to sustain in practice but, in the context of modern capitalism, serves unwittingly to sustain inequality and injustice in society under the smokescreen of objectivity. According to this view, a truly objective approach to theorizing modernity must be critical.

Weber comes closer than Simmel to formulating an abstract rather than general social theory. His rigorous approach to theoretical analysis derives from his commitment to the scientific application of reason in sociology. Yet it is on this very question that his approach causes confusion in so far as the growth of reason and its relationship with modern culture is also a topic of investigation in his work. In this second respect, he shares common ground with Marx, Simmel and Durkheim. In their treatment of the relationship between modern society and reason, all of the classical theorists suggest that reason, the form of knowledge discovered during the Enlightenment, is universal in its potential reach and significance. This view has been more recently manifest in some of the more celebratory accounts of globalization. As I shall move on to argue in subsequent chapters, however, the uncertainties associated with ecological decay, economic instability and the ongoing possibility of thermonuclear war must mean that such claims are at least brought into question. In turn, this suggests that the roots, nature and significance of modernity as a project must be subjected to reappraisal: and also, perhaps, the claims which are made on behalf of our social theories. It is the purpose of the remaining chapters of this book to trace out what seems, from the perspective of present-day social theory, to have been a significant reversal of fortune in the development of modern society and social theory. In particular, I want to ask what the origins are of the overwhelming loss of confidence in modern society and culture which contemporary social theorists seem not only to have diagnosed but which they themselves, in all but a few cases, have increasingly come to share – not least towards their own normative projects.

Part II
Modern Social Theory

3

A Critique of Reason: Horkheimer, Adorno and Marcuse

In the following three chapters, I shall explore a dilemma that originates in the dual application of reason in modern social theory. As I argued in chapter 2, this is a dual application because, on the one hand, reason provides an analytical framework in which theories are constructed and against which they stake their claim to validity, while on the other, reason provides a topic of investigation for social theory due to its importance for the development of modern society. How, then, can we engage in a critical analysis of the consequences of the spread of reason in modern society without falling back on that self-same form of reason to validate our critique? As conceived by the Frankfurt theorists, critical theory takes this dilemma to its farthest extent. It sets itself up as a critique of the consequences of the growth of reason for modern society, but refuses to rely on reason to provide the foundation for that critique. My task in this chapter is to examine the implications of this approach as taken up in the work of Horkheimer, Adorno and Marcuse.[1]

The basic aims of critical theory are clarified by Horkheimer's distinction between traditional and critical theory.[2] Traditional theory merely affirms society as it appears to us, and therefore suggests that the appearance does not disguise any deeper or hidden reality. From the perspective of critical theory, the outcome of this process is quite similar to what Marx calls reification. By contrast, critical theory addresses the rift between appearance and reality directly. It is also premised on an inherent interest in the emancipation of social classes. And it is totalistic, claiming to express the interest of all members of society in overcoming exploitation. Like Marxism, critical theory is based on a conflation of theoretical and normative aims, whereas, according to

Horkheimer, traditional theory will always seek to keep these apart. But critical theorists take a more open-ended stance than Marx towards the future trajectory of modern society. Although they agree that it is impossible to predict the outcome of radical social change in a concrete way until it actually occurs, they go further than this to question whether the developmental trajectory of modern society has any underlying logic at all. That questioning derives, in large part, from a rejection of the universal concept of reason which they associate with Enlightenment thought.

From the outset of our discussion, it is important to understand that there is no singular, coherent view among the Frankfurt theorists about the theoretical and normative aims of critical theory.[3] This is partly because critical theory seeks always to position itself relative to changing social conditions. It sees itself as an integral part of the social reality under investigation, and must therefore change its terms of reference as society itself changes. Critical theory cannot be formulated on the basis of general principles because such principles must be derived from and engage with the ongoing reproduction of society itself. By definition, critical theory is in a constant state of flux. It is because of the subsequent difficulty entailed in treating the work of these theorists in a general way that I shall focus mainly on the arguments of Horkheimer, Adorno and Marcuse, although comparisons sometimes will be drawn with the work of other theorists associated with the School.

Although there are serious difficulties entailed in portraying the work even of these three Frankfurt theorists as intellectually coherent, it is possible to identify a number of core theoretical features of their work, and I shall seek to do this in the first section of this chapter. Two areas are particularly important. First, there are some very basic differences between their conceptualization of modern capitalism as against that of Marx. The impact of the authoritarian state is one important aspect of this. In simple terms, critical theory relies on a synthesis of ideas drawn from Marx, Weber and Freud. Second, and relatedly, critical theory tends to focus primarily on the role of culture and ideology – or more specifically, the culture industry – in sustaining the capitalist system. In the work of Horkheimer, Adorno and Marcuse, this theme is closely interwoven with a broader critique of positivism as a foundation for social thought and science.

In the second section of the chapter, I shall discuss critical theory as a normative project. Two major components of this project will be identified. First, these theorists argue that the capitalist system reduces the individual to an infantile dependence on superficial distractions and gratifications which merely affirm that they have been subjugated by that system itself. This argument will be discussed initially by explaining some general features of the culture industry, and then by considering specific examples of Adorno and Horkheimer's critique of its role in modern society. Second, the concept of the culture industry can be understood fully only against the background of their broader-based critique of reason that deals with the consequences of Enlightenment thought for the development of modern society. I shall examine this theme by comparing the work of Adorno and Horkheimer on what they call the dialectic of enlightenment, with Marcuse's argument which draws together the concepts of reason, Eros and liberation. Both approaches focus on what I shall call a dialectical critique of reason, and provide a much clearer sense of the way in which we can characterize critical theory as a normative project.

In the critical discussion, differences and disagreements among the three theorists will be considered only in so far as they have some bearing on questions raised by critical theory on a more general level. I shall identify two themes in particular. The first concerns the concepts of culture and the culture industry that they develop. In theoretical terms, these might be seen as an extension of the holistic concept of society employed by Marx. But they raise similar questions and potential difficulties. The second theme concerns the dialectical critique of reason which is put forward in critical theory. When taken to its farthest extremes, this critique leaves critical theory itself, and above all the normative project associated with it, in a somewhat precarious position.

Modern Capitalism and the Authoritarian State

The historical context in which the Frankfurt theorists were writing provides an important background to their distinctive approach to capitalism. Confronted by successive failures of radical movements across Europe during the 1920s, and by the development of National Socialism in Germany under Hitler, these theorists shared two fundamental concerns. The first was common to other scholars working within the Marxist tradition such as Lukács and Gramsci, and addressed the problem of understanding superstructural or subjective reasons for the survival of the capitalist economic system despite severe structural problems following the First World War. The second issue was peculiar to the German situation, and concerned the specific features of a capitalist system which is managed by an authoritarian state.[4] The key question for the Frankfurt theorists was whether principles of Marxist analysis could be applied to authoritarian capitalism, or whether an altogether distinctive theoretical approach was required.

Weber: Marx: Freud

The analysis of modern society that is advanced by the Frankfurt theorists relies on a combination of two theoretical syntheses. The first draws together Marx's dialectical critique of capitalism and Weber's analysis of rationalization. It is easier to describe this in negative terms. Critical theory places greater emphasis than Marx on subjective and cultural features of modern capitalism, while rejecting Weber's suggestion that the process of rationalization will necessarily follow a predefined path. The second theoretical synthesis seeks to combine psychoanalysis and Marxist thought in a critique of capitalist culture and ideology. In what follows, I shall provide a very basic account of the principles and significance of each synthesis.

The Frankfurt theorists argue that Weber's analysis of the spread of instrumental reason is too narrow, although they largely accept his argument that rationalization in modern society is characterized primarily by the prioritization of means over ends. They argue that the concept of the iron cage wrongly implies that the social, political and economic developments associated with the spread of reason are inescapable. Weber's approach is seen by Marcuse, for example, as fatalistic, because it appears merely to surrender to the inevitability of the iron cage, rather than to develop a social theory which is set against it. He argues that this approach rests on the mistaken supposition that the institutional manifestation of reason in modern society stems from inherent features of reason itself. On the contrary, the way that reason has been translated into organizational form in capitalist society depends on other significant factors.[5] In short, there are different possible modes of rationalization. Weber envisages only one.

Although the Frankfurt theorists emphasize the importance of the relationship between the process of rationalization and the growth of capitalism, they reject Marx's argument that the spread of instrumental reason in modern society is primarily a function of capitalist political economy. The problem, in fact, is that neither Weber nor Marx adequately explains the causes or implications of the growth of reason: Marx, because he relies too heavily on the concept of the forces of production; Weber, because he fails to account for alternative directions that the process of rationalization might take. In order to explore these alternatives, critical theory places much greater emphasis on the relationship between reason and subjectivity, and on the consequences of capitalist production for subjective identity.

Like neo-Marxists such as Lukács and Gramsci, the Frankfurt theorists – Grossman is the notable exception[6] – suggest that Marx's theory of capitalist society underestimates the importance of the superstructure in maintaining capitalism. The relationship between economy and culture is just too complex to theorize in terms of the base/superstructure model. Culture does not merely interact with other dimensions of society such as the system of production. It can play a significant role in shaping them. Likewise, the state is a much greater determinant of capitalist relations than Marx estimated, particularly in its authoritarian form.

The Frankfurt theorists divide into two broad camps when addressing the significance of the authoritarian state for the capitalist system.[7] Neumann, Marcuse, Gurland and Kirchheimer maintain that authoritarian capitalism is merely a monopolistic form of the capitalist system as characterized by Marx. Indeed, it confirms Marx's argument that capital would become more concentrated, or centralized, over time. By contrast, Horkheimer, Adorno and Pollock argue that authoritarian capitalism is an altogether distinctive economic system, in which the state begins to supersede the function of markets (although it is still a far cry from state socialism). According to Pollock, authoritarian capitalism presents an increasingly risk-free environment to the capitalist: the state invariably supports capitalist enterprise through crisis, 'since its collapse would bring about the most severe consequences – both for the body economic and political situation'.[8]

Critical theory nonetheless retains important features of Marx's basic approach.[9] The Frankfurt theorists agree with Marx that productive forces play a key role in shaping institutions right across society. They accept that the abstract character of commodity exchange debases human relationships, and that economic relations are reified by capitalist ideology. They retain the assumption that the capitalist economic system is contradictory, prone to crisis, and that capital will tend to be concentrated in the hands of fewer and fewer capitalists. Finally, they accept Marx's argument that the pursuit of profit, being inherently unstable, will expand into new territories and that this expansion may rely on state and even military support.

If there is one theoretical question around which the debate among the Frankfurt theorists on the relevance of Marxist theory crystallizes, however, it concerns the extent to which structural crises within the capitalist system can be regarded as inevitable or necessary. While Grossman seeks to clarify this question by focusing on the role of collective struggle in the deliberate and planned overthrow of capitalism, Adorno and Horkheimer make much more of the difficulties posed for the individual personality by the strictures of commodity production and exchange, and emphasize cultural and psychological questions that, in their view, Marx underestimates. In order to explore these questions, the analysis turns to Freud, and to the function of the family.

Freud's account of the family is centred around the concept of the Oedipus complex. He argues that a child's sexual desire for the opposite-sex parent is invariably repressed through fear of punishment from the other parent. As a result, the child will tend to identify with the same-sex parent as a disciplinary figure, internalizing their commands and sanctions. This is crucial to the formation of the ego. According to Adorno and Horkheimer, however, the capitalist system compromises the capacity of either parent to serve as the figure of authority which is demanded by the Oedipus complex. The father's status is undermined by the insecurity engendered by the instability of the capitalist economy, while the mother's role is undermined by her economic dependence on the father. Under such conditions, the ego-identity of the child is bound to be weakened.

Adorno and Horkheimer argue that the family has a dual function in capitalist society which makes it inherently unstable. On the one side, it provides the crucial link between the economic and ideological functions of the capitalist system, and therefore has a vital role to play in maintaining that system. On the other, the family provides a private arena in which individuals can be valued in their own right – rather than as mere wage-labourers – and in which they can find a degree of emotional security.[10] The first of these functions fatally undermines the second, however, thereby compromising the psychological stability of family members. The expressive vacuum which this creates can only be filled from outside. It is this role which is taken up by the culture industry.

Critical theory and culture

The concept of the culture industry is conceived by the Frankfurt theorists so as to avoid the populist connotations of the concept of mass culture. The idea of mass culture implies 'a culture that arises spontaneously from the masses themselves' (Adorno and Horkheimer, 1979: 12). By contrast, the culture industry imposes culture from above. It is an industry not because it is a singular entity, but because its products are produced and sold as commodities rather than for their inherent aesthetic value. But the Frankfurt theorists do not put forward a theory of the culture industry so much as explore specific aspects of it, such as popular and classical music, advertising, cinema and television. They regard these cultural forms as an expression of the relationship between culture and the capitalist system on a more general level. Nevertheless, their account of the development of the culture industry does tie in with the theme of social differentiation which, as I have already explained, is central to sociological accounts of the origins of modern society. I shall discuss this here, before moving on to contextualize the Frankfurt theorists' concept of culture against the background of their broader critique of positivism.

Adorno and Horkheimer argue that the arts, that is, intellectual and artistic culture, have become increasingly differentiated from other dimensions of society as capitalism has developed. The reason for this lies primarily with the commodification of art works. In traditional society, the arts were tied to a system of religious and private patronage. This ensured that, although artists depended on patrons for a living, art works were not themselves regarded straightforwardly as commodities. They were not bought and sold as goods in the marketplace, but commissioned in the context of a long-term relationship between artist and patron.[11] This system broke down with the development of capitalism, not least because the wealth and power of traditional sources of artistic patronage were being rapidly eroded. Increasingly, individual artists had to rely on independent buyers in one-off transactions for economic survival. But this was merely a transitory phase on the way towards the development of a fully fledged culture industry. As long as artists could work independently, they were able to produce works that were still governed by aesthetic, not market, principles. This ceased to be possible with the development of the culture industry.

The centralization of capital is predicted by Marx, of course. But for the Frankfurt theorists, it has consequences not only for finance and industry. Culture too is monopolized as its production becomes increasingly dependent on centralized sources of capital.[12] In institutional terms, there is an interlocking of industry, finance and culture as modern capitalism develops. This process hinges not only on the ownership of capital but on the control and development of technology. Nevertheless, the logic which governs the process cannot be reduced to technological factors, as some critics would allege. Technology has indeed enabled greater standardization of cultural products, and thereby their production in vastly increased numbers. But this is the result 'not of a law of movement in technology as such but of its function in today's economy' (Adorno and Horkheimer, 1979: 121).

The Frankfurt theorists do not always agree about whether to reject accounts of the development of the culture industry which rely on technological determinism, or materialism. For example, Walter Benjamin seems more inclined to regard technology as autonomous, relative to economic forces, than Adorno.[13] Where the Frankfurt theorists do tend to concur is in arguing that a vulgar Marxist account of the function of ideology in capitalist society is inadequate and simplistic.[14] In basic terms, this account suggests that capitalist ideology is a straightforward expression of the interests and worldview of the ruling class, that is, the owners of the forces of production. The approach of the Frankfurt theorists places much more emphasis than Marx on the power and significance of reification in capitalist society, particularly its role in underpinning the reproduction of capitalism as an economic system. This is vitally important both to their concept of culture and to their critique of positivism.

The key to the Frankfurt concept of culture can be found in their interpretation of the process of commodification. This process can be defined as the objectification of social relationships: they are turned into abstract and objective things that are bought and sold as commodities. For Marx, the process of commodification occurs most clearly in the definition of work as labour-power. The pricing of labour severs the social relationship between the labourer and the product of labour. Similarly in the context of the culture industry, the process of commodification undermines the connection between the artist and the work of art, and disrupts the relationship between the work of art and any aesthetic values that might have informed its creation. In basic terms, an aesthetic logic is replaced by an economic logic which has been dictated by the market, and by the structure of the ownership and control of finance and technology in capitalist society. But the link between the artist and the work of art is disrupted not only by the fact that the work is bought and sold. The real point is that the work of art is *conceived* for that purpose. In the context of the culture industry, the logic of commodification affects the work of art from the outset, not simply once it has been completed.

For Adorno and Horkheimer, the products of the culture industry are therefore shaped not by the substance of a ruling class ideology, but by the formal logic of production which the capitalist system dictates. Culture is inexorably tied to the cash nexus of capitalism. To subject the production of art works or cultural products to the needs of consumers is necessarily and irreparably to alter the function and character of culture itself: 'Culture as a common denominator already contains in embryo that schematization and process of cataloguing and classification which bring culture within the sphere of administration' (Adorno and Horkheimer, 1979: 131). Thus the culture industry uniquely expresses the alliance between the development of capitalism and the growth of reason which underpins the Frankfurt theorists' approach to modern society.

As I explained in chapter 1, the concept of reification plays an important role in Marx's work because it is the objectification of social relationships as natural, spontaneous or given which, by his reckoning, enables economic processes in capitalist society to be unquestioningly reproduced by those on whom those processes depend. For Marx, this explains why theory must seek to unveil the hidden realities of capitalist society; and why to do so has an inherent practical function. This argument also underwrites his rejection of positivism as bourgeois science, that is, a form of thought which, by conveying the world as it appears, fails to uncover its deeper reality and merely affirms its false appearance. The Frankfurt theorists seek to build on this rejection, and to follow it through with their conception of the aims and function of critical theory. From the preceding discussion of the culture industry, it is clear that there is a close connection between the Frankfurt theorists' understanding of the commodification of culture and the process of reification as characterized by Marx: the more cultural products are conceived and consumed as commodities, the greater will be the hold that the logic of commodification has over our perception of the world. The central point, however, is that the culture industry does not so much advocate that logic in ideological terms, as express it in its mode of organization.

The Frankfurt theorists' concepts of culture and the culture industry are closely allied to their rejection of positivism in social thought and in science.[15] The key to that rejection, as spelled out by Horkheimer when he distinguishes between traditional and critical theory, lies with the notion that science is not external to but part of the reality it seeks to address. By extension, knowledge in whatever form does not exist outside of its subject-matter but is inherently tied to the nature and reproduction of that subject-matter. Thus for Horkheimer, critical theory 'has for its object men as producers of their historical way of life in its totality' (1972: 244). In the context of the critique of modern society and the culture industry, this approach has two obvious ramifications. First, it underpins the significance of culture not as ephemeral or coincidental in relation to the capitalist system, nor as determined by it, but as something which is *both* distinctive from *and* integral to the reality of that system. According to this view, ideology is much more than merely an illusion.[16] Second, the approach of the Frankfurt theorists places critical theory at the very heart of its subject-matter, underlining that this is a critique of society which has been mounted from within.

In this second respect, the Frankfurt theorists arguably go much further than Marx. He writes of the laws and inner logic of capitalist development, and therefore implicitly conceives of his own theoretical enterprise as privileged science in *some* form. By contrast, the Frankfurt theorists appear to eschew any claim to be offering a privileged account of social reality. Now, if it comes from anything at all, that privilege must be derived from an association between knowledge and reason; and in Weber's terms, from a strict separation of fact and value. The Frankfurt theorists reject both the association and, in particular, the separation. As Adorno argues, a value-free science 'fails to apprehend reality just as much as one which appeals to more or less preordained and arbitrary established values' (Adorno et al., 1976: 118). In the context of modern society, such a science would be merely an expression of alienation. This argument suggests that the Frankfurt theorists must search for a grounding for their critique of modern society – and, moreover, their critique of the trajectory and consequences of the spread of reason – in something other than reason itself. Alternatively, they might suspend that search altogether. As I explain in the next section of this chapter, this is exactly what they seem inclined to do.

Modern Society and the Dialectic of Reason

In the following discussion, I shall begin by exploring specific examples of the Frankfurt theorists' critique of modern society, and of the culture industry in particular. Their analysis ranges widely: across patterns of work and consumption, politics and the state, and forms of media such as television, cinema, music and even cartoons. But these surveys need to be placed in proper perspective if critical theory is to be understood as a broader-based normative project. For the purposes of this discussion, that perspective will be provided by the work of Adorno and Horkheimer on the dialectic of enlightenment, and by Marcuse's analysis of the relationship between reason, Eros and liberation.

Administration and stupefaction

According to Adorno and Horkheimer, our cultural tastes are both a contrivance of the culture industry and a result of the infantilization of our needs by modern capitalism. On the one side, as I have already discussed, the production of cultural commodities according to the logic of capitalism radically alters their intrinsic meaning and value. Works of art, once bought and sold as commodities, lose their uniqueness. The logic of mass production standardizes cultural objects and erodes innovation and originality. Moreover, the logic of capitalism dictates that, in order to sell as many commodities as possible, any variety in what we consume will become increasingly superficial. As a consequence, cultural commodities are pseudo-individualized by features which prioritize marketability over intrinsic value. On the other side, the organization of society and its institutions according to the stifling rationality of administrative bureaucracy diminishes our capacity to engage with cultural practices in a sustained or critical way. The system effectively atomizes our sense of social identity, and renders us peculiarly vulnerable to stupefaction. The Frankfurt approach therefore depicts modern culture as an alliance of capitalist accumulation and instrumental reason. I shall focus initially on that connection here, because it is vital to understanding the role of the culture industry in modern society.

As I have already discussed, the Frankfurt theorists criticize Weber for suggesting that the growth of instrumental reason has its own independent dynamic, whereas in fact it is interdependent with capitalist political economy. Marcuse defines the outcome of this relationship as technological reason. In work and consumption, in education and training, in transportation and public policy and in the development of communications media, technological reason underpins a process of unrelenting fragmentation and specialization. In the tasks they fulfil, individuals are increasingly atomized. They are deprived of any holistic conception of the organization in which they work. As a consequence, institutions throughout society appear to operate according to their own irresistible and impersonal logic, remote from the real experiences of those individuals whose actions, after all, are vital to their being able to function at all. In this context, instrumental reason gains an unwarranted dignity and universality, as an objective principle which must be followed, rather than a form of thought and organization which is embedded in the cultural and economic constraints imposed by capitalism.[17]

The Frankfurt theorists argue that the monotonous regularity imposed on social life by the workings of administrative reason creates a rather different class system when compared to earlier stages of liberal capitalism. In advanced capitalism, and to a much greater extent under the auspices of the authoritarian state, social classes have no positive basis for collective identity. They can be defined only in negative terms, that is, in relation to the conglomeration of interests that opposes them. Whereas the interests of capital and state can be regarded as a totality, the interests and outlook of social classes cannot. Those political struggles that do manifest themselves are marginal, disconnected from society as a whole and its foundations, and therefore tend merely to further rather than undermine the process of atomization. Objectively speaking, workers represent a shapeless and incoherent mass, dominated by mechanistic procedures which are formulated according to the so-called law of instrumental reason. But in subjective terms, they experience no association with others, and therefore no sense of common identity and interest. A considerable part of the responsibility for this must lie with the culture industry. In an absolute sense, the culture industry negates the classical notion that the development of modern society goes hand in hand with a process of cultural specialization. The culture industry 'impresses the same stamp on everything' (Adorno and Horkheimer, 1979: 120). The appearance of specialization, the association of taste with individualism, is exactly that: an appearance.

The marketing of culture, or leisure, in modern society feeds off and affirms the experience of fragmentation and alienation in the workplace. The culture industry takes full advantage of the fact that we have been infantilized by an economic system which reduces us to components of a great machine and subjects of an objectifying reason. As a result, our activities as consumers mirror our lives as workers: as Adorno and Horkheimer describe it in *Dialectic of Enlightenment*, 'mechanization has such power over a man's leisure and happiness, and so profoundly determines the manufacture of amusement goods, that his experiences are inevitably after-images of the work process itself' (1979: 137). Both in their content, and in the way they are produced, the commodities of the culture industry affirm the appearance of a society that operates according to a universal logic which is out of our control and beyond our comprehension. But the culture industry does not merely bolster the process of reification. Although the Frankfurt theorists' work on the culture industry ranges across a variety of art forms and media, the argument is fundamentally the same. The most basic function of the culture industry is stupefaction. It disables us psychologically and emotionally. It acts as psychoanalysis in reverse. I shall illustrate this point very briefly with three examples: music, the cinema, and cartoons.[18]

Adorno's analysis of the culture industry is frequently concerned with music. In broad terms, he argues that our ability to listen to music has regressed in modern society.[19] Because the organization of the music industry has taken priority over the substance of the music itself, we have lost the ability to engage with and listen critically to what we hear. Increasingly, we content ourselves with the familiar. For example, well-known passages from classical works are played and replayed, often in isolation from their original context, that is, the work as a whole. This process has been assisted by the use of musical fragments in advertising. We may even associate musical passages less with composers than with the products their music has been used to advertise. Moreover, what ought to be somewhat marginal aspects of the music industry – relative to the music itself, at least – have increasingly taken centre-stage. Star performers – conductors, singers, and instrumentalists – tend to receive our real interest and acclaim. We applaud the performers much more than the performance – and the music itself considerably less than either. This holds true irrespective of whether classical or popular music is played. Even with jazz, according to Adorno, the illusion of spontaneity and improvisation masks what is merely the monotonous repetition of familiar and standardized formulae.

The cinema provides a further target for this critique. Films are valued for their technical gimmickry – which is itself merely an index of the size of the budget used to produce them – much more than for their content. In both its production values and its products, cinematography is centred around opulence and conspicuous consumption, not intrinsic value or artistic merit. Like music, the movies themselves are uniform and formulaic. Indeed, it is on exactly this basis that they are sold to us. With predictable plots and one-dimensional characters, there is nothing to surprise or unsettle the audience, which in any case wants merely some minor variation on an old and recognized formula. But the cinema is not just a place where we can escape from reality. On the contrary, reality itself is increasingly filtered by it. So-called realism in cinematography merely provides a means of sustaining the illusion that 'the outside world is the straightforward continuation of that presented on the screen' (1979: 126). And in that cinematic world there is no room for imagination, for critical engagement or disharmony. Technical effects require 'quickness of observation'. But they rule out sustained thought. Our reactions, however fast, are automatic because they are repeated so often. We think in a mechanistic way: 'The might of industrial society is lodged in men's minds' (p. 127).

When the critique turns to the cartoon, a degree of romanticism – a yearning for some ideal, now past – becomes implicit in this approach. There is, further, a more explicit reference to content in this context, to some ideological message. Cartoons once provided a fantastical counterpart to technological reason. They now embrace it. No longer is justice invariably done. No longer do the maimed characters have countless further lives. No longer does the cartoon provide pure fantasy. Cartoons are now focused on motive, violence and retribution. They are an expression of 'organized cruelty'. Characters such as Donald Duck, who are subjected to unrelenting punishment, affirm to us that to break down individual resistance is 'the condition of life in this society' (p. 138). Cartoons no longer function for amusement and slapstick. They are about the wielding of absolute power. They convey to us that resistance is useless.

Supporting the culture industry is a parallel industry of critics and connoisseurs, whose comments and distinctions merely 'perpetuate the semblance of competition and range of choice' (p. 123). What they seek to disguise is a relentless generality. Individualism is contrived by the culture industry, and thereby – in essence – destroyed: 'only because individuals have ceased to be themselves and are now merely centres where the general tendencies meet, is it possible to receive them again, whole and entire, into the generality' (p. 155). The process of individuation was never fulfilled. Instead, each individual is just a manifestation of a generalized species-being: not in any idealized sense, but as a lowest common denominator. The products of the culture industry have even begun to appeal to us precisely because they are cheap, generally available, average. Art is ready to admit that it is merely a commodity, rendered faceless by the anonymity of the market. Whereas patrons had objectives and demands, the market has a series of intermediaries: so many, in fact, that the artist is 'exempt from any definite requirements' (p. 157). This process has become so extensive, so predominant, that cultural 'commodities' are hardly worthy of the name: there is no 'exchange', no 'use', only blind consumption. Even advertising has ceased to engage us other than as a negative filter: we do not trust anything that is not advertised. Advertising does not appeal to us in any positive sense because its message is transparent: 'The triumph of advertising in the culture industry is that consumers feel compelled to buy and use its products even though they see through them' (p. 167). The core argument of this critique is not that the culture industry deceives us. We are not simply the unwitting victims of an illusion. The culture industry operates a universal swindle. But we are its willing accomplices.

The dialectical critique of reason

The concept of reason which the Frankfurt theorists take up in their critique of modern society is dialectical, that is, they suggest that reason contains its other, non-reason. In particular, they reject the notion – which stems from Enlightenment philosophy – that reason possesses a stable, universal and objective logic: in effect, that reason exists outside of society. Drawing on Freud, they define non-reason in psychoanalytical terms, as consisting of impulses and drives. These impulses and drives have been repressed by the growth of instrumental, or technological, reason in modern society: first, because reason in this form sets itself up as absolute; and second, because in doing so it represses its other, non-reason. If critical theory has a primary normative goal, it is to reconcile these two sides of reason, and thereby to liberate the human subject. As the following discussion will clarify, however, individual critical theorists have somewhat different views on the extent to which that goal is feasible.

According to Adorno and Horkheimer, the growth of instrumental reason in modern society derives from a fear of uncertainty. This fear has its roots in our relationship with the natural world. Instrumental reason takes the specific form that it does in modern society because of our desire to dominate nature. Given the calculating character of instrumental reason, the Enlightenment signals not so much the disenchantment of the world as the disenchantment of nature. The consequence of this, however, is to sever the relationship between humans and nature, or subject and object: a relationship which, in traditional societies dominated by mythology, tends to be unitary, not dualistic. And although the drive underpinning this process is oriented towards the domination of nature, its outcome is exactly the reverse: instrumental reason appears to us as external, as an abstract law that we must obey, not a tool of human consciousness and activity. Our relationship with nature does not liberate us from fear but oppresses us. Our use of instrumental reason does not empower us but renders us helpless. The predominance of instrumental reason in modern society raises calculability to the level of an absolute standard. It is the only legitimate measure of the true worth of all processes and ideas. Anything which cannot be enumerated is regarded as hopelessly metaphysical. Indeed, metaphysics is banished from a world in which mathematics is the 'ritual of thinking' (Adorno and Horkheimer, 1979: 25). Thought is mechanized, confined to factuality and repetition. This condition does not signal the realization of the potential of reason for society but its subversion, a denunciation of 'the rationality of the rational society as obsolete' (pp. 38–9).

In their own individual writings, Adorno and Horkheimer tend to agree that the only means of resisting this state of affairs is through critical negation. In short, critical theory can only pave the way for a reconciliation of the human and natural worlds – a reconciliation which they define as a genuinely rational society – by positioning itself squarely against society as it exists. As I mentioned earlier on, this strategy must proceed from a position within, not outside, society: as a form of immanent critique. But what of reason in this context? Adorno and Horkheimer do not seek to ground the critical analysis of modern society in a universal concept of reason. But nor do they abandon the notion of reason altogether.[20] For Horkheimer, reason is grounded in ongoing social practices.[21] The key to this is human labour, which contains both the idea of, and the interest in, a condition in which society and nature, or subject and object, are reconciled. This argument is broadly in agreement with Marx's philosophical anthropology, which I discussed in chapter 1. Marx argues that humans need not only to interact with nature in order to survive but, no less important, to interact and cooperate with each other as they do so. Likewise for Horkheimer, only collective social action offers the promise of genuinely fulfilling human potential. But there is no requirement to ground this idea in anything other than human experience as it already is, because inherent to that experience is 'man's striving for happiness'. Quite simply, that striving is a 'natural fact' which is in no need of philosophical justification (Horkheimer, 1972: 44-5).[22]

Like Horkheimer, Adorno also conceives of critical theory primarily as the negation of modern society from within. However, Adorno seems to have somewhat less faith than Horkheimer in the idea that the striving for happiness is inherent in human praxis, and that an idea of the rational society is already implicit in the labour process. Adorno's conceptualization of the nature and aims of critical theory as a normative project is expressed by the idea of negative dialectics. This approach rests on a distinction between a concept, that is, an idea, and an object, that is, the thing to which that idea refers. Adorno proposes that, in modern society, the relationship between concepts and objects is not identical. That is to say, our concepts invariably contain features and ideas, or some sense of potential, which their corresponding objects have failed to realize. The point of negative dialectics, or what Adorno calls non-identity thinking, is partly to exploit this gap and thereby to understand something more of what objects in the world might potentially become. But first and foremost, its purpose is to underline the fact that such a loss of potential exists, that objects in the world are not as their concepts suggest them to be. For Adorno, unceasing negation is the real key. But if critical theory does have an overall normative goal, it is to achieve a rational identity between concepts and objects, that is, to realize the inherent potential of society in its relationship with nature. However, in so far as negative dialectics can only proceed from a position within society – that is, society cannot be grasped from the outside as a totality in the way Durkheim suggests – it must apply to itself. In short, this means that Adorno cannot actually define his own concepts, for to do so would be to suggest a sense of identity, or harmony, in theory which has yet to be achieved in the relationship between society and nature. According to this view, critical theory must always be in a somewhat shaky position.[23]

Like Adorno and Horkheimer, Marcuse also seeks to unearth the potential which is already present in modern society. Moreover, he too regards reason not as abstract and universal but as concrete, as grounded in specific social contexts and practices. But Marcuse draws on Marx's earlier writings – on alienation and labour – to a much greater extent than either Horkheimer or Adorno, and engages more consistently with political debates which were ongoing at the time he was writing. More importantly, Marcuse holds the ideal of revolution at the centre of his conception of critical theory. In short, he outlines a rather more optimistic vision of the future.[24]

In a similar way to Horkheimer – who characterizes labour as the basis of human experience, of reason, and of our striving for happiness – Marcuse defines labour not in terms of human goals, but as driven by needs and impulses. For Marcuse, labour derives from the need to fulfil our potential as creative beings. He agrees with Marx that in capitalist society workers are alienated from the products of their labour; and with Freud, that this has its roots in the repression of sexual drives and their translation into purposeful economic activity.[25] According to Marcuse, there is an inextricable relationship between Eros – the erotic impulse – and human labour: 'the impulse to preserve and enrich life by mastering nature in accordance with the developing vital needs is originally an erotic impulse' (1966: 113–14). This position, in this particular respect, is not so very different from that outlined by Horkheimer. But whereas Horkheimer seems ultimately to lose faith in the notion that these basic drives might ever be liberated, Marcuse does not. Although negation plays an important role in Marcuse's approach, it is never allowed to suffocate the positive function of critical theory as he conceives it. For Marcuse, critical theory is as much about the liberation of drives as it is about the critique of capitalist political economy.

The key difference between Marcuse's idea of negation and that of Horkheimer and Adorno hinges on this positive function. For Marcuse, although truth is indeterminate and theory provides no guarantees, it is nevertheless the task of the critical theorist to outline concrete courses of action. In contrast to Adorno's idea of negative dialectics, Marcuse's approach to negation entails grasping society as a totality and discovering the essence of a particular historical epoch. The aim of this should be to falsify and thereby transcend that totality: a goal which Adorno could never countenance because it assumes what he would call rational identity in the context of theory itself. Grasp the totality, Marcuse appears to be saying, and you can reach a higher form of reason, not least because you can uncover those social relationships that 'condition the appearance of society from its core structures' (1968: 70–1). Theory in its critical form is still a transcendent normative project.

It is worth noting that none of the three theorists discussed here denies that there is at least some connection between reason and liberation. Adorno and Horkheimer argue that the 'critique of enlightenment is intended to prepare the way for a positive notion of enlightenment which will release it from its entanglement in blind domination' (1979: xvi). As Gebhardt notes, this is to regard reason as 'a kind of historically evolving capacity for self-transcendence, inseparable from the notion that humans make their own history'.[26] As I discussed at the beginning of this chapter, Adorno and Horkheimer argue for a reflexive notion of reason, where the criteria according to which a theory can claim validity are, at the same time, part of its topic of investigation. It is for this reason that – especially in Adorno's case – their vision of critical theory consists of unremitting negation: theory, of and for itself, can provide no basis for its own validity. Similarly, while Marcuse notes that reason has been 'instrumental in sustaining injustice, toil and suffering', he moves on to argue that 'Reason, and Reason alone, contains its own corrective' (1968: 450). This might be taken to suggest a concept of meta-reason.[27] But this is certainly not something which features in the arguments of the Frankfurt theorists. If anything, their position is closer to Romanticism, which emphasizes the ideal of a personality, a spirit, which is in harmony with nature.

This takes us to the heart of the notion of immanent critique. By this, these theorists appear to mean a form of practical criticism which cannot rely on reason as a framework for justifying its claims. Critical theory must be conscious of its own role in society, and above all, watchful over the inherent tendency of theory to become hypostatized and lose its practical relevance. The form of critique advanced by these theorists must never allow itself to become stabilized as anything approximating a unified theory of the historical development of society. This approach does not reject Enlightenment thought but suggests that it has been misappropriated in modern society: distorted, especially, by the narrow tenets of positivism. This error must be redeemed through a critical theory which is conscious of the fact that reason does not provide us with a series of timeless, abstract guidelines for thought. Finally, and most importantly, all three theorists discussed here emphasize one core point: that reason is historically situated. Reason is grounded in, not the ground of, human praxis. According to this view, reason should not predetermine our needs, but enable us to realize them. I shall focus on this point in the critical discussion, because it suggests what is potentially most significant, but immediately most problematic, in the Frankfurt contribution to modern social theory.

Critical Discussion

The core interests of the Frankfurt theorists, with which critical theory should be identified most readily, are the concept of culture and the dialectical critique of reason. These two themes will form the basis of this discussion. The concepts of culture and the culture industry that are employed in critical theory are characterized above all by their generality. In the first part of this discussion, I shall ask whether, for an incisive analysis of the role of culture and ideology in helping to sustain the capitalist system, a more refined conceptual framework might be needed. Their dialectical critique of reason, which is scrutinized in the second part of this discussion, shares that characteristic of generality. But it also contains a significant insight: namely, that we need to develop a concept of reason which, first, recognizes its interconnection with, not domination of, human praxis, and second, acknowledges that the growth and spread of reason in modern society can take a number of different forms.

Culture as a totality

It must be said that the Frankfurt theorists seek as far as possible to avoid simplistic notions of culture and the culture industry. Such notions might see culture as a straightforward expression of ruling class interests. But critical theory refutes the idea that the collective interests of *any* class can be represented explicitly through cultural media. As Adorno writes with reference to music, the class position of a composer cannot be 'translated into tone language' (1973a: 56–7). The Frankfurt theorists do, however, suggest that the twin pillars of modern society as they conceptualize it, instrumental reason and the logic of capitalist accumulation, are directly implicated in its culture. While their explanation of this is not as rudimentary as it first appears, and certainly not elitist in the way that some critics allege,[28] it does have serious deficiencies as an account of culture.

The Frankfurt theorists rebut the argument, which they associate with Weber, that the development of modern society brings about a process of cultural differentiation or disenchantment. As I discussed in chapter 2, Weber suggests that questions of science, morality and art – which in traditional societies were embraced by one overarching belief system – have sheered off from each other to become areas of specialist expertise, each with its own language and terms of reference. The Frankfurt theorists disagree. For them, all areas of knowledge in modern society fall under the jurisdiction of the culture industry and are subjected to the same fundamental logic of commodification. Where specialism appears to exist, as in the case of so-called art movies, they denounce it as contrived and superficial. Where distinctions seem to arise, they are ironed out as part of the same basic logic: 'Something is provided for all so that none may escape; the distinctions are emphasized and extended' (Adorno and Horkheimer, 1979: 123).

There is more than a hint of circularity in this approach. As a characterization of the role of culture in modern society, it is so general that it becomes difficult to imagine any art form or cultural medium which cannot, with a little imagination, be redescribed in such a way that it fits the rationale of commodification, whatever its specific features might be. If one musical style engages the intellect more than most, it is merely in order to ensure that the whole market is monopolized. If a cultural form revolves around political satire, as in the films of Chaplin, it must be berated for its bourgeois sadism: because, when all is said and done, it merely affirms the system it pretends to undermine.[29]

The problem here is twofold. First, the Frankfurt theorists define the culture industry as monolithic and all-embracing from the outset. They then seek to use examples – and refute counterexamples – in order to verify this definition. If the culture industry is a totality, it *must follow* that it contains all instances of cultural production: even those that do not immediately appear to conform to the definition. Second, the concepts of affirmative culture – and its opposite, autonomous art – which the Frankfurt theorists formulate are highly non-specific. They are difficult to apply to particular cases without passing judgements which overextend the concepts themselves. Thus whenever the Frankfurt theorists highlight art forms or works which they consider genuinely critical, that conclusion all too easily appears to have been arbitrary, almost to the extent of being just a question of taste.

The first of these difficulties arises as an inevitable consequence of the Frankfurt theorists' characterization of culture as a totality. This applies particularly to the work of Adorno, whose disagreement with Benjamin's argument on the mechanical reproduction of art works illustrates just how readily he slips back into a rather crude Marxist orthodoxy. Benjamin focuses on technical features of cinematography, and suggests that the intense experience of cinema may enable the 'critical and receptive attitudes of the public [to] coincide'.[30] But Adorno is dismissive of cinema on the grounds that it is an industry whose organization is dictated by the logic of capital accumulation. It is inconceivable, according to Adorno, that such an industry could undermine, even in a partial or unintended way, the economic and political system on which it depends. In any case, as he writes to Benjamin, the real point is that 'in a communist society work will be organized in such a way that people will no longer be so tired and so stultified that they need distraction' (Adorno et al., 1980: 123). Does he really mean to suggest that there will be no need for cinema in a communist society? One way or the other, as a critical analysis of so complex and varied a medium as cinema, this borders on the facile.

The second difficulty which I referred to above concerns the generality of the Frankfurt theorists' approach to the concepts of affirmative culture on the one hand, and autonomous art on the other. According to them, affirmative culture literally validates and confirms the reified appearance of modern society as filtered through the culture industry. Autonomous art, as defined by Adorno, contradicts that appearance. It is not autonomous in the sense of having no attachment to reality, but because it expresses within its formal structure the contradictions – or what Adorno would call non-identity – which that reality inherently contains. But just as critical theory must always position itself in relation to changing social circumstances in order to negate them, so must autonomous art. For this reason, Adorno is unable to provide a definition of autonomous art other than in relative terms.[31]

This, it must be said, is a theoretically consistent position. Yet it is also unhelpful from the point of view of critical analysis. We are left with no clear sense of the aesthetic criteria which must be met for a work of art to be autonomous. It seems that to a large extent we must rely on our own judgement. Even the concept of negative dialectics provides no real guidelines as to how we might proceed. How exactly should one set about deciding to what extent a work of art, a film or a piece of music expresses non-identity within modern society? In *Aesthetic Theory*, Adorno insists that autonomous art must combine elements of mimesis, constructiveness, sensuality and rationalism.[32] He writes that the autonomous work of art will outlive the moment of its reception: not in the sense of being especially memorable, but of demanding lasting critical reflection. One might as well add that the work of art should be accompanied by a critical philosophy in order to be appreciated to its fullest extent. But these are hardly rigorous theoretical guidelines on which to develop a critical analysis of radical aesthetics.

One important feature of Adorno's argument is that autonomous art must be contextual, that is, historically and culturally relevant.[33] For example, while he applauds Arnold Schönberg's development of the serial technique of musical composition during the 1920s, he is critical of later composers such as Pierre Boulez and Elliot Carter who, during the 1950s, sought to replicate and in some ways extend this technique.[34] But according to Adorno, in their hands serialism ceases to be a musical form that expresses the contradictions inherent in modern society, and becomes instead the 'bad heir of tonality' (1967a: 167). One is tempted to ask exactly why. Serialism was no easier to listen to during the 1950s than the 1920s. And presumably, modern society was no less contradictory by then. On what criteria, then, does Adorno base his judgement? He argues that Schönberg's serial music served to 'bind together centrifugal, recalcitrant and more or less explosive musical forces' (1956: 22).[35] His objection to its resurrection by Boulez and Carter seems to be, quite simply, that it has become old hat. Are we to conclude that one of the central features of autonomous art must be that it is original? Adorno does not say. Nor, it should be added, does he define exactly what originality might mean in this context. We are left only with his own specific judgement. And this may just as well concern what is good or bad music. Certainly, when Adorno writes on jazz, perhaps the most that can be learned is that it is just not to his liking.

One important aspect of the Frankfurt theorists' analysis of the culture industry concerns the relationship between a cultural form and its audience. They make clear that no art form contains features which can determine or guarantee how it is interpreted. Whatever the aims of a film-maker, composer, painter or cartoonist, it is possible that their efforts may go unheeded if an audience responds in a way that is unintended and unforeseen. Benjamin, for example, makes much of the fact that printed art works lose the aura that the original paintings possess when they are hung in a specific space. The aura derives partly from uniqueness, partly from an association with place. Even Adorno, in articles written during the late 1960s, agrees that the radical potential of culture rests with its capacity to provoke an audience and 'wrest the collectivity from the mechanisms of unconscious and irrational influence'.[36]

Despite these admissions of the unpredictability of public taste and mood, however, the critical theorists rarely venture beyond quite basic content analysis in their studies of the culture industry. In their work on film, music, horoscopes, television and theatre, they focus on the medium in question and what it contains: rarely on how it is used. Without clear guidelines as to what constitutes autonomous or radical art and culture, this amounts to little more than second-guessing how an audience, reader or listener might respond. They imply, moreover, that although the audience might be unpredictable, its response is nevertheless likely to be uniform. This ignores the indisputable fact that cultural forms are experienced in a variety of contexts, and that these contexts might well affect not only how they are interpreted, but the way in which they are assimilated and discussed.[37] In short, these are questions for research, not elementary content analysis informed by vague notions of radicalism, critical engagement and formal contradiction.

When it comes to the analysis of culture, the deficiencies of critical theory are all too clear. As a theory of culture and the culture industry, the arguments put forward by the Frankfurt theorists are too vague to enable even the most basic distinctions and conclusions to be drawn about what does and does not fall into the category of autonomous or radical art. Their characterization of the culture industry itself is so generalized that virtually anything can be described as coming under its auspices. If culture is a totality in the way they suggest, it would seem that – *by definition* – nothing can escape the logic of commodification. When translated into an empirical context and addressed to specific instances, there seems to be little in this approach that can prevent the individual tastes of the interpreter from shaping the analysis. As a theory of culture, the problem is not so much that the approach of the Frankfurt theorists has no critical foundations. It is, first and foremost, that their concepts and definitions are almost entirely lacking in analytical precision.

Reason and Romanticism

The critique of reason is at the heart of critical theory as a normative project. This is the source of the greatest potential strength of critical theory, but also of its most serious difficulties. The strength stems from an inversion of what the Frankfurt theorists take to be the Enlightenment concept of reason and of its relationship to the natural and social world. According to them, Enlightenment philosophy conceives of reason in absolute and universal terms, and above all, as independent from the world. They argue, on the contrary, that reason is grounded in human praxis, and cannot therefore be regarded either as universal or as following a predetermined pattern of development. They characterize reason as ambivalent, as containing its opposite, non-reason. Yet in seeking to reconcile these two sides of reason, the commitment of the Frankfurt theorists to critical negation means that if their argument falls back on anything at all, it must fall back on Romanticism. Unfortunately, this rather undermines their work as a normative project.

The ambivalent concept of reason which informs critical theory relies on psychoanalysis. The key to this is the concept of non-identity. Although this concept is actually formulated by Adorno, it is relevant to the arguments of Marcuse and Horkheimer. They largely agree with Adorno's suggestion that the notion of a centred or unitary self that underwrites Enlightenment thought is untenable in the context of modern society. It is the work of Freud, and to some extent Nietzsche, that exposes this. For Adorno, Freud demonstrates just how deeply laid destructive impulses are in modern society,[38] while Marcuse praises psychoanalysis for exposing the idea of a self which is 'prior to' society as a myth.[39] It is when Adorno and Marcuse disagree, however, that serious problems with this approach begin to arise.

According to Adorno, psychoanalysis serves as a precise expression of the contradictory relationship between modern society and the individual.[40] That contradiction arises because, on the one hand, the individual is caught up in a form of narcissistic identification with authoritarian leaders which feeds off the pleasure principle, while on the other, the individual has to internalize the repressive demands of modern society. As a consequence, the ego becomes a conscious expression of the pleasure principle at the same time as being the very agency which represses it. This contradiction renders individuals peculiarly vulnerable to the culture industry and to fascism.[41] The normative goal of critical theory must be to release the individual from this basic contradiction. But for Adorno, liberation can only come from society, that is, from changes in its political economy and culture. And the role of critical theory in bringing about such change can consist only of negation. To seek to envisage change in any more constructive way would be to lose grip on the idea of non-identity which critical theory must express.

As with the concept of autonomous art, Adorno cannot be criticized for theoretical inconsistency. On the contrary, he follows through the implications of the concept of non-identity thinking to their farthest extremes. The outcome, however, is theoretical stalemate. Unremitting negation leaves the critical theorist with nothing to fall back on, no grounding for critique and no basis for seeking a way forward (for that would be to assume a sense of harmony in theory which does not exist in society). The price of theoretical consistency, it would seem, is critical paralysis.

Marcuse does not allow himself to be caught up in this way. But the price of his escape is an apparent theoretical contradiction. Having argued that human labour, not reason, is the basis of 'truth' in the world, Marcuse sets about investigating how the rational side of labour can be reconciled with the impulses and drives on which it depends. In crude terms, he seeks to rediscover and unleash labour as play. For this, Marcuse turns to Freud's argument on group psychology, and to the idea that impulses and drives must be channelled into labour, and thereby repressed, in order to ensure that civilization can survive. According to Marcuse, this process does not have to go on forever. Once a certain level of technological development is reached – as he alleges it has been in modern society – it should be possible to liberate surplus drives, that is, the energy associated with functions that technology can now perform.

There are two serious difficulties with this more positive conception of critical theory. First, Marcuse's position dictates that liberation must begin at the level of the individual. In the context of his broader critique of modern society – of its structural domination of the individual and its inherent contradictions – this not only appears to be naive but does not make a great deal of sense. In effect, Marcuse appears to be caught in a vicious circle. It is one thing to suggest that modern society contains space for the liberation of impulses and drives, that is, that there is surplus repression; it is quite another, however, to demonstrate just how that liberation might even begin to come about. Marcuse appears to conflate these questions, whereas they must be treated as distinctive. The second difficulty arising in this argument concerns a theme which might have provided an answer to the first. In fact, it compounds it. If there is a grounding for Marcuse's approach, it rests with labour, not with reason. Yet his concept of labour as play is controversial, at least in as much as it contradicts Marx's argument against the romanticized view of labour as genuinely free. Marcuse can provide no basis on which to defend this position, however, because in effect the concept of labour he employs serves as the basis for his entire conception of critical theory. In short, there is nothing against which this concept can be argued for.[42] In Marcuse's hands, not only the idea of liberation but the entire enterprise of critical theory as he sees it rests on a presupposition which must be accepted on faith.

That faith, if it exists at all, can only be derived from an attachment to the self-same Romantic values which are implicit in the work not only of Marcuse but of other critical theorists as well. For example, Marcuse argues that the real value of psychoanalysis to critical theory derives from its invocation 'not only of a past left behind but also a future to be recaptured' (1970: 60–1). In a similar vein, Adorno conceptualizes the element of sensuality in autonomous art in terms of 'man's prehistoric oneness with nature'.[43] Horkheimer, too, suggests that 'men are determined by "elementary reactions of pleasure and pain"'(1972: 45). For the Frankfurt theorists, the Romantic impulse is vital because it is constitutes the other of reason. It therefore provides the core of the potential of modern society which critical theory must unearth and unleash.

This brings us to what is perhaps the most profound difficulty raised by critical theory. The Frankfurt theorists argue, against Weber, that the development of reason in modern society can take several distinctive forms. They reject the Enlightenment concept of reason as a universal and external framework, and replace it with a notion of reason that is grounded in human praxis. Yet their commitment to negation renders them unable to demonstrate precisely what form this connection between reason and praxis might take in modern society. Instead, they fall back on an idealized notion of harmony between human beings and nature, a past which they urge us neither to forget nor abandon. The picture this conjures up, however, is incapable of verification. Moreover, it is just as totalizing as the modern society against which the Frankfurt theorists position themselves.

The Frankfurt approach to critical theory is defined by its extremes. Both are asserted as articles of faith, rather than by a core set of concepts which can in some sense be argued for. On the one side, these theorists invoke a totalizing vision of modern society in which all human thought and deed is but an expression of the unrelenting logic of commodification. This, they suggest, stems from the blind domination of instrumental reason. Indeed, on the strength of their critique, the ideological system in modern society appears so pervasive and far-reaching that it becomes doubtful whether liberation is feasible at all.[44] Against this, however, they portray a total state of harmony between humans and nature which, they allege, houses all the essential features of human freedom. These features are ever-present in society. They must be rediscovered. Critical theory is the driving force of that process of rediscovery. But it can assume such a role only in negative terms: continually setting itself against the world as it appears without actually defining the world as it is meant to be, other than in the vaguest of terms. It is suggestive that the critical theorist who holds to this position most rigorously and consistently, Adorno, is the theorist who seems to have been most paralysed by the commitment to negation above everything else. It is his work that stands out for its combination of theoretical ambition and political defeatism: a combination which is expressed by the idea of negation. Marcuse is the most positive and constructive of the Frankfurt theorists discussed here. But he is also the least consistent in theoretical terms, falling back on an ideal of liberation derived from a concept of labour which he is unable to verify or support.[45]

The source of these difficulties does not lie in the Frankfurt theorists' refusal to embrace the universal concept of reason, but in their apparent failure to follow through the idea that reason derives from the social and cultural activities of human beings, and in relation to the political economy of modern society. That failure stems largely from the fact that the critical theory rests on a conceptualization of modern society and culture as a totality. The conviction that universal reason overshadows modern society prevents them from asking, in a constructive way, what different forms reason might take; and whether, indeed, it has taken such forms already in specific areas of modern society. So profound and far-reaching is the abhorrence they express towards Enlightenment thought – so deeply held the conviction that it presents a structure which overwhelms human freedom from the outset – that they do not even begin to search for its weaknesses. For all of their commitment to negation, this suggests a curious tendency to take modern society at face value, and to buy into the concept of universal reason – if only to reject both out of hand. They do not mount a sustained critical challenge to modern society and culture. They mirror both in negative form. If there is a counterhistory to modern society and to the Enlightenment, the Frankfurt theorists do not provide it. For that, we must turn to Foucault.

4

Reason and Power: Foucault

Foucault and Habermas carry forward the critique of modern society which the Frankfurt theorists began. But each moves in a somewhat different direction. While Habermas identifies his work most explicitly with the Frankfurt tradition, it is Foucault who more closely captures the spirit of their approach to modern society as an authoritarian system, and to the growth of instrumental reason as an extension of administrative power. But whereas critical theory appears to maintain some notion of the latent potential of modern society – albeit as the neo-Romantic promise of a return to nature – Foucault seems to abandon all such notions, even if some interpreters regard his later work in a more positive light. Like the Frankfurt theorists, he repudiates the teleological, or goal-oriented, idea of history which the project of modernity implies. But he also rejects the connection between reason and human freedom which is retained even within critical theory. Unlike Horkheimer and Marcuse, he berates the ideal of collective political agency as derived from Marxism. Above all, he dismisses the idea that knowledge is anything other than an accomplice for the exercise of power. This latter argument, in particular, makes his work peculiarly difficult to evaluate as a social theory.[1]

Foucault develops an interpretation of history which does not need to rely on the notion of historical agency, that is, of reasoning actors pursuing interests through conscious strategies. He seeks 'to free the history of thought from its subjection to transcendence' (1972: 203). But the real point of this approach is difficult to discern, not least because Foucault continually reinterprets his arguments in the light of his later work, and in response to his critics. For this reason, a conclusive account of his writing is all but unattainable. In the discussion which follows, I shall seek to interpret Foucault's arguments in terms of the specific themes which are being developed in this book. Foremost among these will be his interpretation of the concept of reason, and his analysis of the consequences of its growth for modern society.

In the first section of this chapter, I shall discuss Foucault's theoretical arguments regarding the relationship between reason, discipline and the body in modern society. These arguments are premised, first, on his understanding of history as defined by the concepts of archaeology and genealogy, and second, on a conception of the interrelationship between knowledge and power.

In the second section, the focus moves to Foucault's historical writings on madness, discipline and sexuality. These hinge on the notion of a decentred subject, that is, a view of society and history which excludes the individual as an agent of knowledge and social change. This notion arises in Foucault's analysis of the body, in connection both to discipline and sexuality. But his later work, on ethics, arguably deviates from this approach to suggest a more humanist position, that is, one which is centred around the concept of human agency.

The critical discussion in the third section of the chapter will evaluate Foucault's approach in terms of its implications for modern social theory. I shall ask whether Foucault suggests a viable alternative to modern social theory as it has been conceived so far in this book. The discussion will focus on the concept of the self, and more broadly, on his interpretation of the relationship between knowledge, reason and power. I shall ask to what extent Foucault's theoretical concept of power lends itself to meaningful sociological analysis. I shall then explore its implications for his normative position.

History, Knowledge and Power

When considering theoretical ideas which feature in Foucault's historical writing, it is important not only to discuss the arguments themselves but to ask why he selected particular topics for investigation, such as madness, the body and discipline. The answer lies somewhere between two conventional descriptions of Foucault's role as a historian. The first, which tends to be applied to his earlier work, suggests that he is a *counter*historian who uses the archaeological method to provide a subversive account of the origins of modern society. To this end, a topic such as madness serves as an ideal focus for presenting the case against conventional interpretations of the Enlightenment, particularly of its association with humanitarian values. The second description of Foucault, which applies to later works outlining a genealogy of power and knowledge, is as an *anti*historian who rejects modern approaches to historiography altogether. Here, Foucault does not so much outline an alternative – and therefore implicitly more accurate – version of history, as reject the notion of historical truth altogether. In this context, he focuses on the interrelationship between power and knowledge through a study of the discursive practices surrounding discipline and sexuality. The aim here is to show how the modern subject is really the outcome of an alliance between discourse and power. Crucially, power in this context is conceived not as repressive, but as producing both knowledge and the individual.

The concept of archaeology

The discipline of archaeology is conventionally defined as 'the scientific study of the remains and monuments of the prehistoric period' (*OED*). Foucault uses the concept of archaeology in order to describe what he does as a process of unearthing or digging out the historical conditions for various forms of knowledge. These forms of knowledge are defined as 'epistemes' or 'epistemological fields', and he regards them as the 'conditions of possibility' of knowledge (1970: xxii).[2] To unearth them is to discover how forms of knowledge became established as knowledge at all. Foucault contrasts his approach to modern historiography, which merely describes the progress of knowledge towards a level of objectivity which we like to identify with modern science. In place of this, he brackets questions about the objectivity or truth of knowledge, to the extent that his approach is neither 'the history of knowledge, nor history itself' (1971: xiii).[3] The archaeological method characterizes Foucault's work on madness, the birth of the clinic, the human sciences and historiographical methodology.

Two theoretical themes are important to Foucault's archaeological approach. First, he rejects interpretations of history as progress, that is, interpretations that deal with incremental stages culminating in the achievement of a goal or a form of ultimate convergence. Foucault's own approach emphasizes discontinuity and historical rupture.[4] For example, in *The Order of Things* – which focuses on four epistemes, that is, the preclassical, the classical, the modern and the contemporary – he writes of the relationship between the classical and the modern age as 'a discontinuity' which is 'enigmatic in its principle, in its original rupture' (1970: 217). Second, Foucault stresses the importance of non-formal knowledge. This is partly a question of subject-matter, partly of historical sources. With regard to the former, Foucault focuses not on the so-called noble sciences but on disciplines that concern 'living beings, languages, or economic facts', and which are conventionally thought to have been tainted by empiricism, and to be too contingent for us to imagine that they are 'anything other than irregular' (1970: ix). With regard to historical sources, Foucault's archaeology is replete with references to apparently marginal texts. This approach underwrites his main aim at this stage, that is, to provide a counterhistory which emphasizes the unfamiliar.[5]

According to Foucault, the archaeological method decentres the subject in so far as it characterizes subjectivity and volition as socially constructed, not innate. He alleges that conventional historiography merely assumes that human consciousness is the foundation of all historical development, an approach he dismisses as 'anthropologism' (1972: 12). The idea of a decentred subject is closely associated with structuralism. In basic terms, this is the theory which holds that unobservable social structures generate observable social phenomena. According to Foucault, the archaeological method describes a field of historical research in which questions concerning the human subject, human consciousness and historical origins are raised, and in which their interconnections are explored, mingled, and separated off from each other.

The concept of genealogy

A basic understanding of Foucault's use of the concept of genealogy can also begin with a conventional definition. The *Oxford English Dictionary* defines genealogy as 'an account of one's descent from an ancestor or ancestors, by enumeration of the intermediate persons'. Perhaps the most important difference between Foucault's own interpretation and deployment of the archaeological and genealogical methods is that the latter brings to the forefront what was only implicit in the former, namely, the entanglement of knowledge with power. Foucault's understanding of the concept of genealogy is drawn partly from Nietzsche's argument that there are no fixed or essential properties in history, or even in human nature or the body.[6] For Nietzsche, history has no immanent logic but consists of a struggle between competing configurations of power. This struggle will never be resolved.

According to Foucault, genealogy must record events in their singularity, that is, they must not be subsumed beneath a teleological account of history as proceeding towards some kind of inevitable goal.

This approach deliberately focuses on unpromising areas, hitherto thought to be either without history or to lie outside of history. These include the sentiments, love, conscience and instincts.[7] Foucault argues that the world consists of a multitude of interconnected events. History has no underlying logic, no hidden structure, but relies on accidents and contingencies, and can be driven by apparently trivial human emotions. The concept of power/knowledge lies at the heart of Foucault's genealogical approach. One might see this as his alternative to the concept of ideology. The notion of ideology suggests that thought is distorted by oppressive power relations. By extension, non-ideological knowledge could be attained only in a society where such power relations do not exist. But according to Foucault, power is always a precondition for, not an obstacle to, the definition of truth.[8]

The concept of power/knowledge is consistent with Foucault's non-linear understanding of history, for this consists not of progress towards a humanitarian society but, rather, a series of systems of domination. Foucault dismisses the concept of progress as a 'language of liberation'. In short, whereas the archaeology suggested that history consists of a series of incommensurable epistemes, the genealogy interprets history as a series of incommensurable discursive systems that are and always will be inextricably tied to the struggle for power. The concept of power/knowledge is also consistent with Foucault's understanding of the decentred subject. To see power as oppressive would be to imply that there are fixed or essential properties in human nature which will be set loose when that oppression is lifted. But for Foucault, the struggle for power is intrinsic to the process by which we are able to become individuals at all.[9]

According to Foucault, discourse governs what counts as knowledge and as truth. The aim of genealogy is therefore to explore relations between three forms of social practice: human experiences such as madness, illness, deviance, sexuality and self-identity; knowledge such as psychiatry, medicine, criminology, sexology and psychology; and institutionalized power such as that contained in asylums and prisons. These interconnections form the basis of Foucault's critique of modern society, which I shall turn to in the next section of this chapter.

Reason, Unreason and Modern Civilization

Foucault does not have a normative theory. But his arguments have unmistakable normative connotations. These derive from a critique of the conventional characterization of Enlightenment reason as necessarily leading to a more civilized and humane treatment of the individual. In his historical analyses of madness, punishment and sexuality, Foucault suggests that the Enlightenment concept of reason has actually given rise to greater levels of discipline and surveillance over the individual: to the point, with sexuality, that those controls are almost completely internalized.

Archaeologies of madness and the clinic

Foucault first investigates the subject of madness in *Mental Illness and Psychology*, where he draws a connection between mental illness and the conflicts which are endemic to capitalist society.[10] But later on, in *Madness and Civilization*, he goes further and uses the concept of insanity as the basis for a critique of what he calls bourgeois reason. Foucault argues that there have been four kinds of discourse, or epistemes, surrounding madness since the Middle Ages. In the Middle Ages, madness, and more specifically leprosy, were linked to holiness in so far as they were viewed as a sign both of God's anger and God's grace. In the Renaissance, madness was associated with the wisdom of folly, and thereby with an ironic or comic access to truth and reason. This was symbolized by the ambivalence of the Ship of Fools, which expelled the insane while, at the same time, carrying them on what seemed to be a voyage of destiny.[11] In the classical age, madness became an illness that was attributed not to sickness but to idleness and bodily deterioration. The insane were confined, and subjected to sometimes bizarre, often inhumane physical and moral remedies. The classical treatment of madness is significant because it disrupted the link, or dialogue, between reason and insanity, or reason and unreason. It was during this age that any trace of dignity in madness was lost, or rather expelled.

Major changes were instituted in psychiatry during the late eighteenth and the nineteenth centuries under the guidance of the two great reformers, Tuke and Pinel. In broad terms, their works were responsible for converting the asylum into a 'medical space' (1971: 270). According to Foucault, however, medicine was introduced into the asylum not for its scientific objectivity but as a guarantor of judicial and moral imperatives. The asylum was organized around the concept of work as moral treatment. According to Tuke, a Quaker, it was only through hard physical work that we could conform to the order of God's commandments. But for Foucault, the real point of this approach was not philanthropy but the requirement for labour. In effect, the asylum became a mirror of bourgeois society, a microcosm of its structures and values. Far from signalling the emergence of a more humanitarian and civilized approach to insanity, the reform of psychiatry – and above all its drive towards medicine – merely established the asylum as an instrument of moral homogeneity and social condemnation.

In modern society, Freud's concept of neurosis has narrowed the gap between madness and reason. By focusing on the capacity of the doctor to treat madness, he has effectively liberated the insane from the asylum. But at the same time, the institutional powers of the asylum are merely transferred, concentrated directly into the hands of the therapist. According to Foucault, psychoanalysis is unable to liberate or explain the 'sovereign enterprise of unreason' because it rests on the ultimate authority of the analyst (1971: 278). The relationship between patient and physician is 'quasi-divine'. The disappearance of madness into this relationship merely compounds the alienation which the modern treatment of the insane has engendered. The so-called scientific definition of mental illness in modern medicine, and above all in psychoanalysis, is entirely post hoc, that is, a rationalization which kicks over the traces of the punitive moral practices from which that modern conception is derived: 'What we call psychiatric practice is a certain moral tactic contemporary with the end of the eighteenth century, preserved in the rites of asylum life, and overlaid by the myths of positivism' (1971: 276).

Foucault maintains the focus on medicine, but within a shorter timespan, in *The Birth of the Clinic*. As suggested by its subtitle, 'an archaeology of medical perception', this study focuses on three different manifestations of the medical gaze from around 1770 to 1830.[12] The first was a medicine which characterized diseases as species that are independent of the body. Its aim was to classify these species. During the last third of the eighteenth century, classification gave way to a second perceptual structure, namely, clinical medicine. This focused on symptoms, characterizing disease not as an essence but as a dynamic mixture of symptoms. Third, at the beginning of the nineteenth century, a medicine emerged which focused on body tissues. This characterized disease as originating in hidden causes, namely, lesions within specific body tissues. For this approach, study of the body after death was the key to advancing knowledge. According to Foucault, the most important consequence of the second and third structures was that, once medicine turned its gaze to symptoms, and even further towards body tissue, disease ceased to be its object at all. The sick body was now the focus of the medical gaze. In this way, clinical medicine replaced the concept of health with a repressive idea of normalcy, similar to the notions of sanity and reason which emerge as positivist myths in his study of madness.

The genealogy of discipline

Discipline and Punish is a study of penal institutions and discourses. Foucault identifies two penal styles, beginning with the era of public torture in late eighteenth- and early nineteenth-century France. During this era, torture as a spectacle was intended to exact retribution on behalf of the monarch because to commit a crime was to offend against his person. In other cases, torture was employed as a means of eliciting confession. Yet the use of public torture during this era was actually quite rare. Moreover, the public execution opened up a space for resistance. In the face of imminent death, 'the criminal could say everything and the crowd cheered' (1977b: 60). Thus although public torture and execution were designed to serve as gruesome affirmations of the terrorizing power of the prince, they also carried elements of carnival, in which rules were disobeyed, the authorities laughed at and criminals lauded as heroes.

From around the 1830s, rational reforms of this system were undertaken for two main reasons: first, because public torture and execution were seen as inhumane; and second, because they came to be regarded as ineffective deterrents. The focus shifted from revenge to punishment, with crime regarded less as an attack on the monarch than as an assault on society. The point of reform was to exact a punishment which corresponded to the crime while ensuring that the offender would be rehabilitated into society. In short, crime and punishment were subject to a system of classification which was based on the notion of social utility. The penal system therefore combined three strands of rationalist thought: 'social contract theory, utilitarianism, the semiotics of representation' (Merquior, 1991: 89). But in this apparently humane combination, Foucault sees the construction of a more general system for the exercise of power over individuals, and the subjection of the body to controlling ideas. In short, this was primarily a more effective, not more just, system of punishment, able to 'punish more deeply into the social body' (1977b: 82).

With echoes of the Frankfurt School, Foucault uses the themes of punishment and discipline to argue that the Enlightenment brought forward a 'military dream of society': a society based not on nature but on the 'meticulously subordinated cogs of a machine'; not on social contract but 'permanent coercions'; not rights but 'training'; not the general will but 'automatic docility' (1977b: 169). This was a society premised on the supervision of the smallest details of life and of the body. The idea of supervision was encapsulated by the surveillance techniques of the modern prison. The architectural model for these techniques was derived from Bentham's panopticon, with all of its cells visible from a central watchtower. But the key to prison surveillance was administrative. Inmates were continuously observed, dossiers kept, and the minutiae of their daily lives regulated.

According to Foucault in *Discipline and Punish*, the panopticon symbolized the disciplined society of the modern age. Whether in the asylum, the hospital, the prison or the approved school, the disciplined society exercises control, first, by branding individuals according to binary categories such as mad or sane, normal or abnormal, and second, by what he calls coercive assignment: 'who he is; where he must be; how he is to be characterized; how he is to be recognized; how a constant surveillance is to be exercised over him in an individual way, etc.' (1977b: 199). Individuals are segregated, their activities controlled, their bodies exercised, and their movements organized strategically. In short, they are transformed into docile bodies, not merely in order to be constrained but, in the context of the military for example, because discipline is seen as benefiting the individual. In this latter guise, discipline spreads outwards into factories and schools. Workers and pupils are subject to a whole series of penalties for lateness, behaviour, speech, even sexuality: each individual is caught within a 'punishable, punishing universality' (p. 178).

At the heart of this network of discipline and punishment lies the concept of normalcy, which is derived from a universal concept of reason and symbolized by an individual who is obedient, hard-working and useful. The modern individual has a rational conscience, and is therefore vulnerable to modern forms of discipline, surveillance and control. According to Foucault, every one of us has become subject to examination according to this central norm: in medicine, in education, and in work. The human sciences, also, owe their origins to this disciplinary mentality: 'knowable man . . . is the object-effect of this analytical investment, of this domination-observation' (p. 305). Turning Durkheim's concept of organic solidarity inside-out and revealing its darker side, Foucault argues that the main outcome of the discourse on normalcy and sanity in the disciplined society is not to eliminate but to produce notions of abnormality and delinquency, and thereby to assimilate them within a general system of subjection which is disguised by the dignity of reason. The prison does not lie at the margins of modern society. It is its purest form: 'Is it surprising that prisons resemble factories, schools, barracks, hospitals, which all resemble prisons?' (p. 228).

Sexuality, the body and an ethics of the self

Foucault's work on sexuality focuses on the internalization of power/ knowledge within the modern subject. Where his analysis of discipline suggests how power constitutes the subject from the outside, his study of sexuality examines the role of power in producing the self from within. Foucault explains this process by exploring what he calls techniques of the self. Once again, the concept of discourse is pivotal here. Modern sexual discourses produce modern sexual practices. And as with power, there is no natural substratum of drives which could, at some stage in the future, be liberated. Sexuality is not autonomous. It cannot be reduced to physiology or biology. It does not have features which are fixed or essential. In short, sexuality does not exist prior to its articulation through discourse. The history of sexuality therefore cannot be a history of repression.

Foucault's analysis of the emergence of modern sexuality focuses on the theme of confession. In the Renaissance, the confession served as a means of supervising sexuality. But given that this was required only on an annual basis, it hardly amounted to thoroughgoing supervision. Instead, 'the individual was vouched for by the reference to others and the demonstration of ties to the commonweal (family, allegiance, protection)' (1978: 58). This began to change under the Council of Trent, which reformed the church between 1545 and 1563. Among the reforms was a requirement for priests and monks to subject themselves not merely to more regular confession but to more rigorous techniques of self-inspection. This came to be reflected more widely in modern culture by an increasingly inward, confessional attitude towards sin and desire: a requirement to admit to oneself matters that should never be divulged to others. According to Foucault, the modern subject is a confessing animal. It is as if truth were lodged deep inside us, demanding to surface. But he disagrees with Marcuse that modern attitudes towards sexuality derive from the translation of sex drives into labour. Modern sexuality is not an instrument of repression but an expression of a bourgeois idealization of the self which is formed around the heterosexual, monogamous couple. The apparatuses of sexuality, that is, those strategies of power which both support and are supported by forms of knowledge, designate any other sexual practices as delinquent.[13]

Foucault's arguments on sexuality are set in a more straightforward historical framework than his earlier work on madness, the clinic and discipline. Whereas those earlier studies tend to use a three- or four-fold periodization of history, the first volume of his work on sexuality focuses on one central historical break, between the Renaissance and the modern age. This break hinges on the idea that after the Renaissance, the confessional was turned inwards to the core of the self. Towards the end of that volume, he draws a further historical contrast: between an ancient blood society and a modern 'sex society'.[14] But in later volumes, Foucault's historical focus shifts again. Here, in an approach he describes as archaeo-genealogical, he examines ancient texts which prescribed rules of sexual behaviour. He calls these texts operators which enabled individuals to examine their own behaviour and thereby construct an identity for themselves. His stated aim is to replace a history which focused on the prohibitions imposed by moral systems, with a history of ethics governing the self.

Foucault argues against the conventional view that, while pre-Christian attitudes towards sex tended to be positive, those which characterize Christianity are largely negative. In the ancient world, chastity and monogamy were praised, just as they are in the Christian world. The key difference, however, is that whereas Christianity outlines a moral code that applies to everyone, the ancients expected them to apply only to the ruling class, that is, free males. Moreover, the point of the moral code in the ancient world was to avoid physical danger, not sin. The notion that physical needs should be mastered derived from a belief that 'renunciation has a high spiritual value by itself' (1985: 245). To allow oneself to believe or behave in any other way was to be caught in a form of self-enslavement. Gender was an important aspect of this. Paradoxically, self-mastery was associated with virility: 'the man of pleasures and desires, the man of nonmastery or self-indulgence, was a man who could be called feminine' (1985: 84–5).

In the third volume of his work on sexuality, Foucault brings the historical focus forward. He argues that there was a conjugalization of sex in Greece and Rome during the first two centuries AD. This consisted of an increasing emphasis not only on monogamy but on emotional commitment within marriage. Bisexual practices were discouraged on more explicit moral grounds, because it was believed that sexual relations between younger and older men could not possibly be consensual. None the less, the emphasis remained on a largely aesthetic interpretation of human existence, that is, some notion of the art of living.[15] Only with Christianity are sexual needs in themselves, or the libido, looked on with moral suspicion, hence the requirement for inward confession: 'The more we discover the truth about ourselves, the more we have to renounce ourselves.'[16] In short, while classical Greek morality basically consisted of a search for a more personal ethics, Christian morality consists of a system of rules.

The central point of Foucault's analysis of sexuality is to argue that in modern society, control is achieved in less visible ways than we have conventionally understood. Because control is exercised through inward confession, which gains its purest form in psychoanalytic therapy, it is disguised as a liberating form of self-knowing which originates in Enlightenment reason. But psychoanalysis does not lead us towards greater self-knowledge. It merely enables disciplinary power relations to penetrate the self more deeply. Whereas penal institutions control the body from the outside, sexuality is now deployed as a form of biopower, that is, an internalized mechanism of control. In this sense, Foucault's work on sexuality restores the individual to the heart of the analysis: the subject is effectively recentred. However, this approach can be compared with Foucault's earlier argument on other, more contentious grounds. That is to say, the analysis of sexuality might be taken to suggest not a gradual softening of Foucault's stance towards the modern subject, but as carrying to fruition a deeper logic that was implicit in his work all along. According to this view, Foucault has not merely sought to provide a critique of modern society and its treatment of the subject: from the beginning, he has endeavoured to serve as an advocate for the subject against that treatment. This brings the discussion to Foucault's more explicitly political writings on power, ethics and resistance.

Foucault's concept of resistance is implied by his interpretation of power. He argues that power has no agent but is articulated in and through discourse. This implies that resistance to power is an inherent feature of power itself: 'there are no relations of power without resistances; the latter are all the more real and effective because they are formed right at the point where relations of power are exercised' (1980: 142). Resistance to injustice is therefore possible only at the exact points, or moments, where injustice manifests itself.[17] By referring to techniques of the self, Foucault outlines a new politics of resistance which is centred around a modern subject which may be vulnerable but is not as helpless as his earlier work might have implied. This approach focuses not on a collective struggle against power but on the goal of practical self-mastery itself. Liberty means 'not being a slave to one's self and to one's appetites' (1988a: 6). In an interview, Foucault remarks that an outline of the political future is most likely to be found in 'experiences with drugs, sex, communes, other forms of consciousness and other forms of individuality' (1977a: 231).

Foucault's political arguments suggest an anarchist position. But as Merquior notes, whereas the classical theory of anarchy – as laid out by Peter Kropotkin and Michael Bakunin, for example – tends to outline a future utopia, Foucault is as rigorously opposed to utopian thinking as he is to all forms of institution. Moreover, there is a strong anti-rationalist strand to Foucault's normative arguments – derived from a theoretical understanding of Enlightenment reason as a form of administered discipline – which is absent from the work of the classical anarchists. For Merquior, three basic features of Foucault's work on the ethics of the self – anti-utopianism, negativity towards all forms of institution, and anti-rationalism – suggest that he can most accurately be portrayed as a 'neo-anarchist' (1991: 156). But if this analysis is correct, it raises major questions about the coherence of Foucault's theoretical argument, and the viability of his normative project. These questions will form the basis of our critical discussion.

Critical Discussion

Foucault's critique of the project of modernity has two main strands. First, it is a critique of modern historiography and philosophy. Their preoccupation with evolution and progress reflects a belief, derived from the concept of reason, that modern society is a more efficient, humane and just society than anything that has gone before. To disrupt the modern view of historiography is therefore implicitly to undermine that belief.[18] Second, it is a critique of modern society itself. Foucault characterizes modern institutions as having the sole objective of discipline, subjugation and control. There are no agents of control, no ruling class with which the oppressed can engage in collective struggle. Disciplinary control in modern society is expressed through forms of discourse that are entangled with power, and disguised by a scientific reason whose objectivity is a myth. By developing the concept of power in conjunction with knowledge, Foucault seeks to question the modern idea of collective political identity, and to undermine the notion of society as a totality, a notion at the heart of modern social theory. But does any of this add up to what, in social theory, we might call a normative project? Could the different strands of Foucault's work be pulled together into a coherent framework, or would such an exercise contradict some of his most basic arguments?

One major question that must be addressed in relation to the coherence of Foucault's work concerns how to interpret his earlier analyses of madness and discipline in the light of his later writings on ethics.[19] The decentred, then apparently recentred, subject lies at the heart of this difficulty. Might this reveal a deeper unity in Foucault's work when taken as a whole? Or does it indicate a serious theoretical disjuncture? The argument for unity would suggest that Foucault gradually shifts towards a tighter focus on the subject in order to gain a better grasp of the development and experience of our sexuality. According to this view, Foucault's argument on ethics draws attention to an interrelationship between social forces and human agents which is not only centred around the concept of the self but is oriented towards the ultimate goal of emancipation. This might be plausible to the extent, first, that one develops a theory of the subject, and second, that one can account for the interrelationship between that subject and wider social forces and relations. Foucault, however, does neither. Some commentators have suggested that Foucault's approach consists of a progressive broadening of perspective. For example, Davidson argues that the three stages in his work – archaeology, genealogy, and ethics – represent different levels of analysis, each with a different aim. Archaeology is descriptive and offers a new interpretation of history. Genealogy is analytical, and argues against received notions of historical truth. The work on ethics is normative, and neither displaces nor undermines the earlier work but offers a reassessment of its methodological implications.[20] A similar view is taken by Dreyfus and Rabinow, who argue that Foucault develops a unique combination of genealogy and archaeology. This consists of identifying the problem of the modern age, analysing how it arose, and using his 'rhetorical skills' to increase our awareness of it (Dreyfus and Rabinow 1986: 115).[21] One might well ask whether rhetorical skill provides a sufficient basis for constructing a normative project from the theoretical strands of Foucault's writing. Compared to Marx, for example, this is a rather thin fabric on which to weave theoretical and normative threads together.

As I argued in chapter 1, Marx outlines a normative project which builds on his theoretical argument that the ideological framework of capitalist society rests on the process of reification. In this approach, theory has necessary practical implications because it seeks to reveal hidden structures and processes within capitalist society: and to reveal them is to render them politically malleable. The practical aim of theory in Marx's hands is therefore to establish a closer connection between thought and reality. By contrast, the Foucauldian strategy appears to involve the deployment of rhetoric to sensitize us to a different reading of history and of our present situation. But this generates a major difficulty for characterizing that strategy as a project.

Because he rejects any notion of objective historical truth, the relationship between theoretical and normative arguments in Foucault's work can be understood in one of two ways. On the one hand, his theoretical and normative arguments can be seen as independent of each other and therefore to be read separately. This would suggest that the different strands of Foucault's argument do not need to support each other because they have no basis in truth or historical necessity: whereas, for example, Marx claims that his arguments are bolstered by both. On the other hand, we might collapse the distinction between theoretical and normative arguments altogether. After all, Foucault denies the concept of objective truth on which theory should rest.[22] But in this latter case, Foucault would need all the rhetorical skill he can muster, because to all intents and purposes his approach would have no greater claim on our credulity than any other. Against this background, it is rather appropriate that in an interview he suggested that his books be regarded as 'Molotov cocktails' that 'self-destruct after use'.[23]

In normative terms, Foucault's argument might well be seen as presenting us with a fairly stark choice between an established ethical paradigm – humanitarian discourse centred around a reasoning and autonomous individual – and something much more vague and considerably less well known.[24] By his own reckoning, just about the most that can be said of the concept of an ethics of the self is that, rather like the approach developed by Marcuse, it seeks to liberate a bundle of self-enhancing experiences for the individual. But at the same time, Foucault's arguments on sexuality and the self reject the idea of a coherent self. The notion of the decentred subject merely dissolves the question of identity into a vacuum.[25] Indeed, the apparent victory of humanism in Foucault's later work might be regarded as a sign of failure for his strategy as a whole. In that case, however, we would be left with little more than an expression of Foucault's own personal repulsion towards the project of modernity.[26] But is there nothing whatsoever that we might regard as constructive in Foucault's work on the self? Some feminist theorists argue that there is.

Foucault's work on sexuality is significant for feminist theory because he presents a powerful historical case against biological accounts of sexual difference. Within feminism, such accounts are regarded as essentialist because they suggest that there is a natural basis, or essence, to sexuality.[27] They normalize differences in the status of men and women in society in so far as they suggest that they are natural. While most feminists agree that Foucault tends to gloss over questions of gender, some theorists argue that his analysis can be extended to analyse how techniques of the self might apply specifically to women.[28] For example, Foucault suggests that discursive practices surrounding sexuality effectively construct the body, acting as the source of its identity and material integrity in the world. According to one view, he avoids mistaking the collapse of one particular discursive system governing the body for a liberation from discipline altogether.[29]

Foucault's concept of the self appears to have no intrinsic connection with the social world. It is solitary and isolated. But for some feminists this can be a source of strength because it enables us to take account of real differences of outlook and experience among women. Thus while McNay concedes that there are 'lacunae' in Foucault's argument, she goes on to suggest that these are outweighed by the strong historical case that he makes against essentialism, and by his concept of ethics (1992: 38). So could this concept of ethics form the basis for a positive normative theory? Closer inspection of just two of the lacunae to which McNay refers reveal more serious difficulties.

First, while Foucault makes a strong negative case against reducing sexuality to biology, he provides little by way of a positive case for overcoming gender inequality in modern society; indeed he says little about gender inequality at all.[30] Theoretically, feminism is fundamentally concerned with the question of women's identity. It is from this question, after all, that the political aspirations of feminism derive.[31] But Foucault's arguments on the self suggest that no such identity actually exists. Moreover, his microphysics of power denies precisely the form of collective politics that this conception of feminism would imply.

A second significant difficulty in Foucault's work on sexuality arises with the concept of discourse. In general terms, it is difficult to discern exactly what Foucault means by this concept. He provides only a generalized characterization. This somewhat monolithic approach leaves little room for the study of inconsistencies and contradictions within discourses on sexuality, whereas it is precisely such inconsistencies which, historically, have tended to open up spaces of resistance for women. By ignoring these, Foucault not only undermines his own understanding of the microphysics of power – which focuses, after all, on local points of resistance – but he also ignores an important feature of the political history of women.[32] The genealogies of sexuality, discipline and psychiatry mostly take account of official sources of knowledge. Such an approach is bound to overemphasize that particular perspective, and accordingly, overstate the extent of its grip over individuals.[33]

Foucault's skill in arguing against what he regards as a received wisdom – about sexuality, power or insanity – tends not to be matched by a corresponding argument for a specific theoretical position. But this question not only concerns the relationship between his theoretical and normative arguments; it reaches into the heart of the theoretical arguments themselves. Foucault's historical writings introduce a highly complex, multifaceted array of variables. Even in his work on the birth of the clinic, which to many commentators is the closest he gets to structuralism,[34] Foucault seeks to explain complex patterns of causality which embrace not only medical discourse but broader-based economic, social and political transformations. For example, he suggests that, at least in part, the clinic emerged in France as a consequence of government attempts to alleviate pressure on hospitals during the Revolution. Because these clinics were less likely to be dominated by traditional medical practice, they opened up a space for new discourses. As Foucault describes it, such connections show how medical discourse, in the hands of politicians and lawmakers and having specific functions to exercise in society, 'is articulated on practices that are external to it, and which are not themselves of a discursive order' (1972: 164). In other words, this is not a straightforward, point-by-point interpretation of history – linking events and their causes – but an investigation of how discursive practices come to be articulated in conjunction with a wide range of institutions and social practices.

One might reasonably assume that such an approach would require a complex social theory in order to explore these connections or articulations. Foucault does not provide one. Nowhere is this clearer than with his arguments about discipline and power. The most serious problem here is that the notion of the decentred subject threatens to disable his concept of power altogether. Whereas the Frankfurt theorists' account of domination in modern society retains the idea of social class and some notion of the individual subject of domination, Foucault rejects both. But as a result, he outlines a concept of power which is so difficult to break down, or operationalize, that it tends to obstruct thoroughgoing sociological analysis. This might explain why, in the details of his writing, the subject keeps reappearing.

Foucault seeks to outline a productive, not merely oppressive, concept of power. In short, he suggests that power helps to constitute, rather than merely constrain, the individual. The primary reason for this is that, according to him, there are no features belonging to the subject – such as sexuality – that can be designated as natural or innate. And the existence of such features as natural would be implied by an approach which holds that, in some way, power reins us back. But there is one other important point. By Foucault's reckoning, the most appropriate way to proceed with the analysis of power is in ascending order, that is, from the individual to society. He therefore outlines a microphysics of power that begins with the specific, the body, and moves to an increasingly general level, dealing with such concepts as the 'general tactics of subjection' in modern society. At both ends of the spectrum, power is exercised neither by, nor over, an agent.

It is important to be clear about what is at stake here. In historical terms, it may well be difficult, if not impossible, to identify in precise terms who the agents of power might be in particular circumstances. Those circumstances might well be so complex, and the causal sequences so multifaceted, that a more abstract terminology is required to describe them.[35] In such cases, we have a research problem. For example, Foucault refers to instances where the historian has to deal with strategic necessities that are not reducible to interests, that is, where a whole range of factors and needs come into play in bringing about a sequence of events, and which therefore cannot be understood in terms of the interests of a particular group or class. But in broad terms, he outlines a theory of power which holds that, by definition, all instances of the exercise of power have a highly abstract, intangible quality. In effect, he does not simply state that agents or interests are difficult to identify, but that there are *no* agents or interests: power is simply 'a machine in which everyone is caught' (1980: 156). It is one thing to suggest that power permeates all social relations. It is quite another to argue that everything in society is *defined by* power.[36] If all social relations are shaped by the imprint of power, they must be reducible to power. It then becomes difficult to understand what is distinctive about power relations as opposed to any other social relations. In other words, this approach places such importance on power, and accords power such an omnipresent role in social life, that the concept itself loses all specificity.

This difficulty stems from Foucault's rigid, self-imposed theoretical requirement to eliminate the subject from historical analysis. He is constrained by this because he seeks to demonstrate that the growth of reason in modern society has shattered, not liberated, that subject. But in developing a counterhistory of reason and modern society, he must use a ubiquitous and generalized concept of power which services his understanding of the decentred subject. A finessed definition of power would allow that subject back in, because it would have to distinguish between forms of social relations: in simple terms, those social relations that are defined primarily by power and those that are not. And one important explanation of the differences between those forms would entail referring to the interests of those involved, be they individuals or groups. For a historian who is supposed to work unencumbered by a broader-based social theory, Foucault seems unusually caught in a self-imposed theoretical bind.

Foucault is sometimes associated with the earliest stages of postmodern thought. But he is not a postmodernist. Admittedly, his liking for dramatic historical schisms lends itself to the idea of a break with modern society. Moreover, important themes from his work have been taken up within postmodern social theory. But the real significance of Foucault's work lies elsewhere. If anything, he is an antimodernist, a philosopher and historian who seeks to implode the mythology of human progress that we inherited from the Enlightenment: not, however, in order to lead us in a new direction, but so as to dispute our beliefs regarding the origins of our present historical situation and thereby contribute to our understanding of that situation.

As I argued in chapter 3, the Frankfurt theorists adopt a critical stance towards modern society which leaves little room for the normative aims espoused by Marx. Nevertheless, they hold on to the idea that modern society *just might* enable greater levels of justice and egalitarianism. They merely refuse to imagine that the realization of such ideals might be inherent in the progress of history, or could be derived from a universal concept of reason. Foucault provides the counterhistory of modern society that the Frankfurt theorists so clearly lack. But in doing so, he constructs a concept of power which is just as totalizing as the idea of culture becomes in their work. As in their case, Foucault's unmistakable normative aversion to the project of modernity tends to overwhelm a rather weak theoretical account of its problems, and a discussion of alternatives that is weaker still.

Whereas Adorno and (increasingly) Horkheimer suggest that all resistance to modern society and the culture industry is useless, Foucault implies that resistance is everywhere: only, however, as a necessary counterpart to the relentless exercise of disciplinary power. And while Marcuse tends to fall back on a neo-Romantic depiction of harmony between society and nature, Foucault lurches forward into an idealization of sensory experience which is not only anarchic but rendered shapeless by his refusal to articulate a concept of identity. If the primary aim of the Frankfurt theorists is to negate modern society and culture, and thereby to undermine the incessant logic of instrumental reason, Foucault seeks to discredit its myths and subvert its certainties. Both enterprises nonetheless share key traits. They argue that Enlightenment reason is contradictory, that it contains and implies its other. This leads to a rejection of reason as a criterion for validating objective truth, and thereby to a refusal of its role as a framework for social theory and historiography.

If Enlightenment reason, and the administrative and disciplinary machinery it engenders, is as sovereign as Foucault and the Frankfurt theorists suggest, their exploration of its 'other' seems rather shallow by comparison. In seeking to oppose reason, they merely amplify the grip of instrumental reason over modern society, and therefore, by default, reinforce that grip. If their aim is to turn reason against itself by spotlighting its other, this requires a more sustained critical evaluation of Enlightenment thought than they provide. For that evaluation, we must turn to another theorist who shares a sense of scepticism towards the growth of instrumental reason in modern society, but moves against it from the opposite direction. According to Habermas, reason is not contradictory in the way that Foucault and the Frankfurt theorists suggest, but genuinely ambivalent: a duality not in the sense that reason contains its opposite, but in that it has two *complementary* dimensions. This enables Habermas to retain the concept of reason as the basis of his theoretical and normative project. His arguments are discussed in the next chapter.

5

The Potential of Reason:
Habermas

According to Habermas, critical theory has two core features. First, it seeks to explain the development of modern society up to the present day. Second, it sets out a normative project which aims to realize universal ethical principles. In both respects, this is a more positive and affirmative conception of critical theory than that which was advanced by the Frankfurt theorists. In theoretical terms, Habermas's account of the development of modern society, particularly his conceptualization of society as a social system, is formulated from an objective or external standpoint which the Frankfurt theorists would largely reject. Normatively, Habermas's project is unashamedly affirmative. He agrees that reason is grounded in human praxis. But while the earlier critical theorists seek to expose the contradictory nature of reason, Habermas characterizes reason as a duality. There are two dimensions to reason: instrumental and communicative. These correspond to parallel but distinctive patterns of development in modern society: technological progress and moral progress, respectively. This theoretical argument provides the foundation for Habermas's conception of critical theory as a normative project.[1]

In the first part of this chapter, I shall examine some of the main features of Habermas's theory of the development of modern society. His earlier work seeks to reconstruct historical materialism as conceived by Marx, and consists of a theoretical synthesis which combines the arguments of the classical social theorists with the developmental psychology of Piaget and Kohlberg. Habermas argues that there are two dimensions in modern society, the system and the lifeworld. These correspond to the two dimensions of reason on which the development of modern society depends.

In the second section of the chapter, I shall discuss Habermas's interpretation of modernity as a normative project. He argues that an asymmetry between the system and the lifeworld in modern society is the primary cause of its problems. These are chiefly problems of social integration, and they account for the failure of modern society successfully to constitute itself as a just and open political community. The argument rests on the idea that the operating logic of the system has invaded, or colonized, the lifeworld, distorting its capacity for integration. But according to Habermas, this problem can be resolved by drawing on a potential for political self-determination which already exists within the lifeworld. His major concern lies with how such potential can be released; and once released, what its impact will be on major institutions within society such as education and the law.

In the third section of the chapter, the critical discussion will focus on two themes. First, while critics have argued that the incorporation of systems theory into Habermas's work undermines its radicalism, I shall suggest that the most important questions raised by this are theoretical. These primarily concern the extent to which functionalist reasoning can be applied to actual institutions, and social and economic practices, within modern society. Second, I shall discuss the questions raised by Habermas's normative arguments, particularly whether his universalistic conception of the project of modernity is compatible with cultural pluralism.

The Development of Modern Society

In his analysis of the development of modern society, Habermas seeks to broaden both Marx's understanding of the forces of production and Weber's interpretation of the process of rationalization. These are regarded by Habermas as untenably narrow because they express a preoccupation with economic integration at the expense of a finer-grained approach to social and cultural integration. Marx's theory of capitalism implicitly abandons the most important insight contained in his philosophical anthropology, namely, that labour and interaction are equally important to human survival and to the development of society.[2] Although Habermas regards culture as a superstructural phenomenon, he argues that it plays a more prominent role in the development of society than Marx appears to suggest. It is the understanding of this which can lead to a 'renewed historical materialism' (1979: 98). Weber, too, fails to build on the basis of the most important distinction in his work, namely, between instrumental and value rationality. The concept of the iron cage overstates the importance of instrumental reason in modern society. Habermas seeks to reincorporate the weaker half of these two distinctions – the concept of interaction in the case of Marx, and of value rationality in Weber's work – into critical theory. They form the basis for his own division of modern society into two dimensions: the system, which corresponds to labour and instrumental reason; and the lifeworld, which corresponds to interaction and value rationality. He then seeks to explain their separate, although interrelated, patterns of development.

Reason and moral progress

We are all familiar with notions of economic and technological progress. They are an integral feature of the historical narrative of modern society, and accordingly, play a major role in classical social theory under the broad category of rationalization. Whereas Marx and Durkheim investigate the problems raised by this form of progress for the integration of society as a whole, Weber and Simmel focus on its unintended consequences for modern culture and the individual. Habermas pulls these two approaches closer together. He agrees that economic and technological progress generate problems of integration for modern society. But he disagrees with the way in which those problems are conceptualized by Marx and Durkheim. And whereas Weber and Simmel suggest that the growth of reason has overextended itself in modern society, Habermas argues that it has not been extended enough. His argument depends on a dualistic concept of reason which balances the idea of economic and technological advancement against the less familiar and more problematic notion of moral progress.

Habermas's understanding of the concept of moral progress stems partly from developmental psychology, particularly the work of Piaget and Kohlberg. In basic terms, he seeks to transpose their arguments regarding the development of the moral reasoning of individuals on to the level of society. Just as individuals are increasingly able to seek rational solutions to personal conflicts as they mature, so societies can become more mature and more rational in dealing with problems of integration. That, for Habermas, is moral progress.

Piaget argues that as a child learns, its cognition becomes less egocentric or self-centred, that is, the child is increasingly able to distinguish between self and other. Kohlberg translates this basic idea into an account not only of cognition but of moral reasoning. He suggests that at the highest stage of learning the individual is able to recognize rights and values which can be applied to everyone in an abstract way, rather than merely to oneself in a concrete, punishment-oriented fashion.[3] For Habermas, communication provides the key at this stage, which he calls postconventional morality. For only broad-based agreement through rational dialogue can establish such universally recognized and generally applicable rights. The process must be rational because it involves setting aside local conventions and parochial leanings.[4]

To this extent, morality can be characterized as a learning process. But whereas Kohlberg focuses only on the maturation of the individual, Habermas must establish that there is some connection between the individual and society in this regard. In order to do this, he draws on Mead's concept of the generalized other. Mead argues that our socialization depends on the internalization of norms, integrating us with a social group without the need for authoritarian sanctions. We are able to achieve this by adopting the role of the generalized other, that is, the outlook of the community as a whole.[5] But according to Habermas, Mead's analysis lacks a satisfactory account of the development of the generalized other itself. This can only be provided through a fuller understanding of cultural aspects of social evolution. That understanding is drawn partly from Durkheim. Although the concept of the *conscience collective* explains the moral integration of society in quasi-psychological terms, that is, it underemphasizes the significance of communication, it complements Mead's argument in so far as it focuses on the idea that society itself is a moral force. Thus while Mead underlines the importance of symbolic communication to moral integration, Durkheim helps to broaden the argument by focusing on the development of the society against which and through which this form of communication takes place. Habermas draws on this combination in his account of the uncoupling of system and lifeworld.

The uncoupling of system and lifeworld

Habermas agrees with Weber that the development of modern society is driven by an underlying logic of rationalization. Unlike Weber, however, he maintains that this logic has a dualistic quality, consisting of the two dimensions of reason I discussed earlier on in this chapter. Habermas therefore sustains the broad line of argument formulated by the Frankfurt theorists: namely, that Weber focuses only on a historically specific form of rationalization, whereas the growth of reason can take on a number of different forms. But in a much more systematic fashion than the earlier critical theorists, he argues that the process of rationalization follows two basic patterns, each with its own distinctive logic. In principle, these patterns should run in parallel. The first derives from the growth of instrumental reason, the second from the development of value rationality, or what Habermas calls communicative reason. Together, these patterns of rationalization underpin the process of social differentiation in modern society. The principal feature of this process is the uncoupling of the system and the lifeworld, which I shall explain now.

While the growth of instrumental reason underwrites economic and technological progress in modern society, the growth of communicative reason enables society to achieve a higher level of moral and political maturity, that is, to constitute itself as an open, just and egalitarian community. In the first instance, it is the gradual separation of these forms of reason which is responsible for the process of social differentiation. But whereas the classical theorists characterize social differentiation in terms of the specialization of key functions in society, Habermas points to a more basic division between two major dimensions of modern society, namely, the system and lifeworld. He defines the system and lifeworld in two ways, focusing on their operating logic on the one hand, and their empirical manifestation on the other. The operating logic of each dimension is determined by the form of reason which is inherent to its formation. In empirical terms, the system includes economic and administrative organizations: the latter are associated with the state's role in taxation, for example. The lifeworld consists of the education system, media and family life. Thus in simple terms, while the character of the system is broadly economic, that of the lifeworld is broadly cultural.

In traditional society, there was no such division between specialist functions and institutions. For example, the family was a unit of economic production, thereby straddling the system and lifeworld as Habermas would define them. According to Habermas, it is the task of modern social theory not only to understand how each dimension of society operates in its own terms, but also to explore the interrelationship between them. In order to do this, he draws on the theory of the social system which was devised by Talcott Parsons during the 1960s and 1970s.[6] It is worth briefly explaining Parsons's approach, because it provides a vital counterpart to Habermas's account of the relationship between the system and lifeworld.

According to Parsons, modern society – which he characterizes as a social system – consists of four interdependent subsystems. These subsystems emerge as a result of social differentiation. Each has its own specialist function which contributes to the operation of the social system in its entirety. The functions performed by each subsystem are characterized by Parsons in terms of the AGIL schema: the economy consists of processes whereby the social system adapts to its environment (A); the polity is concerned with setting and attaining particular goals (G); socialization through the family and education ensures that the social system is properly integrated (I); and the maintenance of tradition means that deep (or latent) patterns of values and beliefs are sustained (L).

The AGIL schema depicts a hierarchy. According to Parsons, the social system operates by balancing inputs of physical energy against forms of symbolic communication which conserve energy. Thus the more advanced our mechanisms of symbolic communication become, the more efficient the social system will be. This approach is based on the principle of cybernetics, that is, 'the theory or study of communication and control in living organisms or machines' (*OED*). At the bottom of the hierarchy (A), in economic life, relatively high levels of energy are consumed and the level of symbolic communication is fairly unsophisticated. But as we move up the hierarchy, less energy is consumed and the process of symbolic communication becomes more abstract. The relationship between one subsystem and each of the others is controlled by a particular steering medium which operates within each subsystem, while also conveying information to the others. It is the steering medium which is responsible for communication, encoding information in a symbolic form. Money is the steering medium for the economy; power for the polity; influence in the family and education; and value commitment in tradition and culture.

Habermas employs the idea of the steering medium to explain the relationship between the system and lifeworld in modern society. But in doing so, he questions Parsons's assumption that each subsystem operates according to an identical underlying logic. According to Habermas, this unjustifiably assumes that the social system will normally achieve a certain level of integration. It therefore cannot provide a satisfactory framework in which to examine any problems of integration that might arise in modern society. Parsons merely suggests that when such problems do arise, cybernetic adjustments elsewhere in the system will ensure that they are rectified. For Habermas, this is an unwarranted theoretical assumption.

Habermas's argument focuses on the principle that a steering medium encodes information in a symbolic form. The principle is exemplified with particular clarity by money. According to Parsons, money conveys information – such as the promise that it can be re-exchanged with other transactors later on – which bypasses the kind of energy-sapping procedures that are associated with barter. Before goods are bartered, much more specific information is required regarding the objects exchanged and the other transactor involved. Habermas broadly accepts this description of money. When it comes to the other steering media, however, he expresses serious doubts.

In a somewhat infamous article, Parsons seeks to draw a direct analogy between money and power: voting in elections is like depositing money at a bank; withdrawing money is like withholding political support; and a sliding poll-rating for a politician in office is broadly similar to price inflation.[7] The difficulties raised by this analogy are well documented, and Habermas agrees that the form of symbolic communication associated with the exercise and exchange of power is far more complex, and therefore more difficult to encode, than it is in the case of money.[8] But for an even better reason, Habermas entirely rejects Parsons's argument that the other two steering media – influence and value commitment, which are broadly cultural – operate in a similar way to money and power. This rejection is crucial, because it forms the basis of Habermas's argument that the system and lifeworld each have a distinctive operating logic, and in the context of modern society, may not be integrated successfully at all.

According to Habermas, the form of symbolic information which is involved in the maintenance of culture and tradition is of an entirely different order than the form that is involved in the exchange of money and the exercise of power. With money and power, the encoding of information genuinely can conserve energy. But our values and beliefs require more explicit forms of dialogue which, when encoded in the way envisaged by Parsons, will not be facilitated but distorted, with damaging consequences for society as a whole. The encoding of information in this context is inappropriate because it rules out precisely those features of communication which, according to Habermas, can lead to genuine consensus around core values and beliefs. Such a consensus is only possible by opening up the process of communication to rational discussion, not through narrowing it down and bypassing it with encoded symbols. In short, the 'success' of our values and belief system cannot be measured by the same criterion of efficiency that we use to evaluate our monetary system. Culture follows different patterns of development because it is reproduced according to another dimension of reason. Our values and belief system depend not on instrumental but on communicative reason, and in this way, constitute our lifeworld. Our monetary system and polity rely on instrumental reason and constitute the system. Socialization and education, and more broadly the maintenance of culture and tradition, entail a learning process which cannot be compared straightforwardly to the development of a successful economy and state.

In Habermas's view, Parsons is compelled by the logic of his theory of the social system to reduce the role of culture and tradition in society to the narrow criterion of instrumental reason. In doing so, he compounds, rather than identifies and explains, what may in fact be a major source of tension in modern society. The development of modern society depends on the uncoupling of the system and lifeworld, not the differentiation of society as a whole into subsystems which operate according to instrumental reason. The subsequent stability of society hinges on the maintenance of equilibrium between these two dimensions. In failing to understand this, Parsons is in no position to identify problems of cultural integration in modern society. He merely threatens to replicate those problems in his social theory.

The Project of Modernity: A Defence

Habermas's conception of the project of modernity builds on the dualistic interpretation of reason which he develops in his critique of the classical theorists and Parsons. Not only does this new understanding of reason enable him to explain problems of integration in modern society in a distinctive way. It also provides the foundation for a much more positive conception of the normative role of critical theory in exploring how those problems might be resolved. The problems derive from what Habermas calls the internal colonization of the lifeworld, and I shall describe this in the first part of this discussion. In the second part, I shall move on to examine Habermas's broader-based defence of the project of modernity.

The internal colonization of the lifeworld

In simple terms, the lifeworld consists of the stock of knowledge we need in order to enter into social relations. In traditional society, such knowledge was unquestioningly a matter of tradition. In modern society, the values and beliefs which constitute the lifeworld tend to be articulated and questioned. In principle, this is a rational process. That is to say, we increasingly accept particular values and beliefs only with good reason: not on the basis of faith, force, or the charisma of leaders. We do so, however, not because these values might be efficient, but because they have been agreed upon through open dialogue. Crucially, that dialogue enables us to ensure that those values and beliefs apply to everyone, not just a privileged or powerful minority. The problem, however, is that the development of the lifeworld has been compromised by the predominance of the system in modern society. We have mistakenly applied criteria derived from instrumental reason to lifeworld questions, and to institutions that properly reside in their own dimension of society. Habermas refers to this process as the internal colonization of the lifeworld.

During the early 1960s, Habermas explored the history of what he calls the public sphere in modern society. The concept is an important precursor of, although not exactly equivalent to, the idea of the lifeworld, and is therefore worth brief consideration before we discuss the process of internal colonization in more detail. Habermas defines the public sphere as the 'sphere of private people come together as a public' (1989a: 27). The public sphere was distinct from the state. From its earliest inception among the intelligentsia in Europe, this was primarily an arena for discussion and debate characterized by the 'people's public use of their reason' (ibid.). But during the eighteenth and nineteenth centuries, the public sphere underwent an important transformation, largely as a consequence of the expansion of market capitalism. The liberalization of market relations helped to make the public sphere less exclusive and to protect its affairs from state intrusion. This led to what Habermas calls the privatization of civil society. With greater inclusivity, however, came a tendency to bring more specialized interests into play. This undermined what, for Habermas, had hitherto been the key factor in the success of the public sphere, namely, that special interests were set aside in a rational dialogue which addressed only the common cause. In short, the wider the public sphere was opened out to participants from all areas of society, the narrower became the expression of interests that were brought into its compass by participants. Habermas argues that the primary goal of the public sphere – and of what he later calls the lifeworld – should be to reverse this trend. Greater inclusivity should not go hand in hand with the intrusion of special or marginal interests. The public sphere, or the lifeworld, must be an arena for dialogue and debate in which the only questions addressed are those that can, in principle, be applied to everyone.

Habermas's critique of modern society is premised on the argument that such a lifeworld has not been allowed to develop in modern society. It has been compromised not only by a tendency for political discussion to be anchored to private interests; there are deeper, structural, factors at work. Of these, by far the most significant derives from the expansion of the system, and more specifically its mode of reasoning, into areas of society that properly belong to the lifeworld. The system has increasingly invaded, or colonized, the lifeworld, stunting its development and distorting the operation of institutions – such as the family and education system – which reside there. He illustrates this point with two examples: the process of juridification and the phenomenon of cultural impoverishment.

The process of juridification is characterized as a growth in formal (or positive) law in modern society. According to Habermas, this has resulted primarily from the expansion of the welfare state. Social welfare issues that were once regulated and controlled beyond the law have been increasingly subject to detailed legislation, thereby increasing the density of the law and extending its penetration into people's lives. The key problem, however, is that this expansion has been driven by instrumental reason, that is, by the operating logic of the system. This is why Habermas refers to the internal colonization of the lifeworld: priorities and imperatives that properly belong to economy and state begin to operate within areas of society – above all in the family – where they are not only inappropriate but deforming. As a consequence, the family has become merely an extension of the labour market; the education system has devoted itself to the assignment of employment and life prospects; and leisure has come increasingly under the grip of commodification.[9]

The process of juridification is distorting not so much because it detracts from the functions that these lifeworld institutions should fulfil, but because it fundamentally alters the manner in which they are perceived and performed. If socialization is the primary role of the family and education system, it cannot be reduced to the narrow requirements of the labour market without seriously undermining the capacity of those institutions to impart values in an open, just and rational way. Socialized with instrumental values, we are bound to develop a partial understanding not only of our own role in society, but of society itself as a political community. If education appears to operate only for the stratification of children into employment categories, little wonder that they will be inclined to develop values and beliefs with self-interest, not the general interest, uppermost in mind.

The partiality of our outlook in modern society is further underwritten by the process of cultural impoverishment. According to Habermas, this is a function of the process of cultural specialization as identified by Weber. The differentiation of knowledge into specialist fields – such as the branches of science, politics and the arts – creates a culture of expertise in which our only option as individuals is to narrow down our outlook as far as possible, that is, to become members of one cultural elite or another. But as a result, we inevitably lose the interest and ability to address general questions in a more rounded way. Expert cultures are increasingly detached from the everyday praxis of social life. Where questions are raised which should concern everyone in society, we can only approach them from sharply differing perspectives, and with our own narrow priorities to defend. Weber certainly understands this. But he characterizes it as a consequence of rationalization *per se*. For Habermas, cultural impoverishment does not arise from a general growth of reason in modern society, but from the dominance of one particular dimension of reason within areas of society from which it should be repelled as alien and perverse. The key question for critical theory is whether such a debilitating process can be reversed. As I shall move on to discuss now, Habermas believes not only that it can, but that it will.

The normative potential of communicative reason

As I have already discussed, the concept of communicative reason can be regarded as an extension of the argument, formulated by the earlier critical theorists, that reason is grounded in human praxis. But Habermas provides an account of this connection which is both more substantial and more positive than anything that can be found in the writings of the Frankfurt theorists. The argument is inherently normative, because it suggests not only that the human capacity for communicative reasoning is already present in what we say and do, but that this capacity underpins a deep-rooted orientation towards universal values of freedom and justice. The key to Habermas's theory is not, therefore, that these values need to be drawn from the outside under the auspices of a transcendental project, but that they are already implicit in society. The task of critical theory is to enable them to be realized in full. Unlike the Frankfurt theorists and Foucault, however, Habermas maintains that the task can be fulfilled without fear of false and misleading affirmation. In effect, he abandons the idea of negation.

The essence of Habermas's normative argument can be distilled by considering two sentences taken from his Inaugural Address of 1965: 'What raises us out of nature is the only thing whose nature we know: *language*. Through its structure, autonomy and responsibility are posited for us' (1987a: 314, Habermas's emphasis). These sentences are worth rereading, because they contain the basic ingredients of the normative project which Habermas has pursued ever since. Two points merit particular scrutiny. First, the idea that language 'raises us out of nature' indicates that it is our ability to communicate linguistically that distinguishes us from animals, and reiterates Habermas's insistence on Marx's basic notion that interaction and cooperation should be on an equal footing with labour in the struggle to fulfil human potential. Second, the suggestion that it is the structure of linguistic communication – not the substance of what is said – which holds the key to human freedom signals Habermas's commitment to outlining *procedures* for a rational dialogue through which universal values can be agreed, not to deciding what those values might be. The second point, in particular, will be important when Habermas defends his argument against those who regard it as ethnocentric.

In very simple terms, Habermas's conception of critical theory as a normative project rests on the contention that there is an intrinsic link between the implicit but unrealized structure of linguistic communication and the political ideals of inclusivity, freedom and justice. This argument is derived from two main sources: ordinary language philosophy as developed by Wittgenstein and extended by Austin and Searle; and hermeneutics, particularly the work of Gadamer.[10] A brief discussion of these ideas, and the way that Habermas draws on them, should help us to understand more clearly his argument that the potential for what he calls the good and true life is already implicit in linguistic communication.

Wittgenstein's philosophy hinges around the concept of the language game. This consists of the rules and conventions which govern the language associated with a particular activity. The concept is important because it emphasizes the connection between language and forms of social life. That is to say, it suggests that language is not external to but an integral part of everyday human praxis.[11] Habermas uses this approach to emphasize that communication between speakers is not just about the world or our place in it. On the contrary, speech is a social activity in its own right.[12] This idea is also expressed by the distinction between pure and natural language. Whereas pure language is governed by abstract and external rules of grammar, natural language contains and reproduces its own conventions.

The notion of ordinary language is developed in the speech-act theory formulated by Austin and Searle. Quite literally, a speech-act is the action which is performed by and through speaking.[13] The concept of the speech-act is important for Habermas's argument because it focuses attention on speech itself, rather than on a more abstract idea of language. The form of competence needed in order to speak with others is of a different order than that which is required to use language in a more technical sense. For it is a form of social competence which entails, but is irreducible to, rules of grammar and syntax. Crucially, speech necessarily involves social interaction, and requires skills that are not just technical but normative.

According to Habermas, when we communicate verbally with others we implicitly advance the claim that our utterances are valid: not just in relation to the subject we are speaking about, but in relation to the social context in which we are speaking. The question of validity can be broken down into four main parts, which Habermas calls validity-claims: first, that we can be understood by our interlocutors; second, that what we are saying is (objectively) true; third, that we are being (subjectively) honest; and fourth, that when we are invoking certain values, we believe these values to be justified. Crucially, only the first of these validity-claims is really a matter of technique. The others involve our relationship to the world and, above all, to a social interaction as it is taking place. In short, they draw on the assumptions, values and conventions – the knowledge we need in order to participate in social life – that Habermas associates with the lifeworld.[14]

Habermas likens the knowledge that we have to draw on in order to communicate successfully with others to a 'culturally ingrained preunderstanding'. This notion is taken from Gadamer's concept of 'prejudgement'. In his theory of hermeneutics, Gadamer argues against the idea that interpretation is an objective process based on the rigorous application of abstract rules. For Gadamer, on the contrary, interpretation always and necessarily relies on prejudgements which are derived from our cultural background, or what he calls our 'historical life'.[15] Without this cultural background, we would have no basis for interpretation at all, merely access to what Gadamer calls 'dead meaning' (1989: 149). Crucially, our historical life is oriented not only to the past but towards the future. In other words, we tend to apply our interpretations to a specific purpose, namely, the maintenance of tradition. Our understanding of others is therefore both dependent on our cultural background, and guided by our interest in reproducing it.

Given that Habermas seeks to argue that linguistic communication contains the seeds of an idealized political community, the significance of Gadamer's argument should be clear. While the arguments of Wittgenstein and the speech-act theorists enable him to suggest that speaking is a social activity in its own right, Gadamer provides a basis on which to argue that the process of interpretation depends on our cultural background and outlook – or in other words, our lifeworld. But Habermas disagrees with Gadamer on a number of points. These are vital to his argument that the colonization of the lifeworld not only can but will be reversed.[16]

Habermas disputes the notion that the process of interpretation is necessarily guided by an interest in preserving tradition. When applied to the sciences, for example, a more complex picture emerges. While knowledge which is tied to the humanities and historical sciences may well be informed by an interest in maintaining tradition, this cannot hold good where the natural and social sciences are concerned. For Habermas, each of these other two realms of knowledge is guided by its own distinctive interest: to control nature in the case of the natural sciences, and to realize human freedom and autonomy in the case of the social sciences. He calls these knowledge-constitutive interests, and they can be defined as interests which guide and shape our pursuit of knowledge (1987a: 308).[17] This latter connection suggests that we should not simply seek to preserve our tradition or historical life but should be in a position to criticize it. Habermas draws an analogy between this process – which he calls critical self-reflection – at the level of society, and psychoanalysis as it affects the individual.[18] Linguistic communication – and more specifically, rational dialogue – is at the heart of both ideas. For Habermas, we should participate in a rational dialogue regarding our culture and historical life because it is up to us to reproduce that culture and continue that life in a selective way, not blindly and unquestioningly. He refers to this as the 'self-conscious appropriation of history' (1986: 243).

Two features of Habermas's argument against Gadamer are important for this discussion. First, while he largely agrees that culture and tradition shape our ability to communicate with others, he maintains that it is imperative that we also bring our culture and tradition under critical questioning. That ability is the focus of the second key feature of his argument. This concerns the linguistic and social competence which we require in order to enter into social relations. According to Habermas, this basic level of competence necessarily involves advancing implicit validity-claims in our dealings with others. It therefore contains all the ingredients of communicative reason. Thus, as Habermas states in his Inaugural Address, our interest in free and open dialogue with others – an interest which suggests a broader concept of a just and egalitarian political community – is 'not mere fancy' (1987a: 314). That is to say, it is neither wishful thinking nor an invention of theory, but is implicit to linguistic communication *as it already occurs*.[19] By his own reckoning, Habermas's strategy enables him to reaffirm the opposition between tradition and reason that Gadamer's philosophy denies, while also sustaining the argument advanced by the Frankfurt theorists that reason is not identical to positivism, that it is grounded in human praxis.

The process of critical self-reflection which the concept of communi-

cative reason supports is pivotal to what Habermas calls the rationalization of the lifeworld. Critical self-reflection is integral to the capacity
of the lifeworld to resist further colonization by the system. According
to Habermas, rational communication along the lines he suggests is
vital if we are not only to reproduce but to improve our historical life.
He insists that the argument is neither fanciful nor utopian, but merely
draws out a learning process which is already at work within the
lifeworld of modern society. In so far as that learning process is as important to human survival as economic and technological advancement,
it is inconceivable that its colonization will continue unchecked.
Habermas is also adamant that the principles of communicative reason
he outlines, in so far as they are inherent in any and all forms of linguistic communication, can be applied universally, irrespective of differences in the historical life of particular cultures. In other words, his
argument does not concern the substance of values and beliefs in
modern society, but rather the basis on which they come to be held and
the way in which they are reproduced over time. It is an argument
about process in so far as communicative reason literally involves
giving reasons for the beliefs we hold, and demanding that others provide reasons for their beliefs. Habermas maintains that the genuinely
rational society need be neither the privilege, nor a reflection of the
prejudices, of any specific culture. It is nothing less than the destiny of
our universal lifeworld.

Critical Discussion

Habermas's argument has attracted volumes of critical commentary.
The critics range from those who broadly share his convictions and are
seeking to iron out inconsistencies, to those who disagree fundamentally with his theoretical and normative approach. In this discussion, I
shall examine Habermas's theory in the light of the themes which have
been developed so far in this book. Two are particularly important.
The first concerns Habermas's synthesis of critical theory and systems
theory. While this enables him to explore the impact of instrumental
reason as a source of major problems of integration in modern society,
it arguably presents a rather narrow interpretation of the dimension of
society which he defines as the system. This raises difficulties when
interpreting the relationship between reason and economic life, and
also the role of law and the state, in modern society. The second theme
concerns Habermas's development of the argument that reason, in its
communicative form, is grounded in human praxis. If this approach is

to carry the normative significance which his project demands, the concept of communicative reason must be theoretically robust. Closer analysis raises severe doubts that it is.

A critique of functionalist reason?

Despite drawing extensively on systems theory in his account of the distinction between the system and the lifeworld, Habermas refers to his theoretical approach as a critique of functionalist reason. Implicitly, this is a critique of instrumental reason which follows on from the work of the Frankfurt theorists and therefore rejects the use of a narrow concept of reason to explain the operation of society as whole. Habermas's dualistic concept of reason represents a step forward from critical theory, however, in that it enables him to resolve the dilemma that I discussed in chapter 3: namely, between using reason as the basis for a theoretical account of modern society while simultaneously advancing a critique of the consequences of the growth of reason in modern society. Habermas's key point is that reason is ambivalent, not contradictory. That is to say, reason contains two dimensions which can grow within modern society in a complementary way. But in his critique of modern society, Habermas suggests that these two dimensions of reason are in conflict. This conflict is expressed by the internal colonization of the lifeworld.

By employing the distinction between instrumental and communicative reason to explain the problem of integration in modern society, however, Habermas probably goes too far. In effect, he replicates precisely the mode of functionalist reasoning that he seeks to avoid. Significantly, his account of the relationship between the system and the lifeworld is unilinear. Note that it is invariably the system which shapes the lifeworld. The lifeworld does not appear to shape the system. Indeed, his account of the operation of both money and the law suggests that it cannot. For example, money is important to Habermas's argument not only because it is a steering medium in the way that Parsons suggests. Money is a major force behind the internal colonization of the lifeworld. As such, it must be assumed that social relations involving money consist entirely of instrumental reason: they have no lifeworld or cultural dimension. Without making this assumption, the role of money in colonizing the lifeworld would make little sense. But closer analysis of Habermas's characterization of monetary relations suggests that they *must* have a cultural dimension, not least because money draws on lifeworld support for its value and legitimacy.

The linkage between money and the lifeworld is provided partly, though not wholly, by the state. The state issues money, and implements various measures to ensure its stability and to prevent counterfeit. Now Habermas agrees that the state, and therefore the circulation of power, require lifeworld support. Yet in distinguishing between money and power as steering media in the Parsonian sense, he argues that, unlike power, money 'needs no legitimation' (1987c: 272). There is plenty of room for confusion here. If Habermas is suggesting that money operates independently of the lifeworld, and that monetary relations are defined solely by the use of instrumental reason, this is an untenably narrow approach which contradicts not only the arguments of Simmel but others who argue that many instances of the use of money, and of the use of reason in conjunction with money, are replete with cultural or symbolic meaning.[20]

This difficulty has a broader significance for Habermas's theory because it suggests that the distinction between instrumental and communicative reason as he defines it tends to overstate the predominance of the former over the latter. Part of the difficulty stems from Habermas's insistence that the two dimensions of reason can be identified with particular institutions and social practices in modern society. Closer inspection of money alone suggests that they are more closely intertwined in *all* forms of social practice. If reason genuinely is ambivalent, this approach would make much more sense. The problem, however, is that it would contradict Habermas's analysis of the central problem of integration in modern society as he perceives it. His theoretical account of the internal colonization of the lifeworld means that the system must operate autonomously from the lifeworld. It would seem that Habermas has not distanced himself from systems theory to the extent that he would like us to believe.

A similar problem arises, and for broadly the same reason, in Habermas's account of the relationship between the legal system and the state.[21] One might reasonably imagine that the legal system straddles the system and lifeworld. On the one hand, the law has a societal function, that is, the function of social control. In that capacity, the law can be evaluated for its instrumental efficiency. On the other hand, the law must be legitimate, or valid, in order to be accepted and followed. Whereas the functionality of the law brings it closer to the system, the legitimacy of the law clearly requires lifeworld support. Habermas broadly agrees with this analysis. He even goes further to argue that, in practice, there is a fundamental tension in modern society between these two features of the law: its facticity on the one side, and its validity on the other. According to Habermas, the tension is inherent in the legal system because the law serves both as a sanction and as an expression of morality in society. But there is a further tension which operates around the law. This stems from the fact that the process of lawmaking or legislation (which is democratic, and therefore draws on the lifeworld) might be distorted by the exercise of power in the pursuit of instrumental goals (the system).

Habermas maintains that his theory enables us not only to understand but to resolve these difficulties. But in doing so, he implicitly concedes that the distinction between the system and the lifeworld is too rigid, that it suggests too narrow and too negative an interpretation of the functions of the state and, by extension, of the law. He nevertheless seeks to sustain the distinction between the system and the lifeworld in its basic form by suggesting that the legitimacy of the law derives primarily from its association with democracy (lifeworld) and the state (system), rather than from morality, which cannot be reduced to either. But this seems merely to presuppose what the argument sets out to prove, namely, that the legal system genuinely can operate, in conjunction with democracy and the state, in an inclusive way. In this respect, Habermas's argument probably takes him even closer to functionalist reasoning, because it suggests that a singular societal community is already in place, centred around institutions such as the law, which can ensure social integration right across even the most pluralistic society.[22]

The universality of the concept of communicative reason underpins Habermas's conviction that the political community he envisages is inclusive. But this raises another important question, namely, whether such a general concept of communicative reason does justice to its multifaceted role in modern society. As an account of linguistic communication, the four validity-claims outlined by Habermas appear to exclude important aspects of social interaction: for example, humour, bravado or rhetorical effect – all of which are likely to feature in any political discussion. If he is suggesting that these can be subsumed under the more general idea that, in communicating with others, we are implicitly seeking rational consensus, this raises more and bigger questions than it answers. They are, above all, research questions. Habermas does not appear to conceive them as such, merely taking for granted what his argument is intended to establish.[23]

Habermas has defended his account of communication by arguing that he is merely drawing on practical, everyday features of communication. As he remarks in an interview, 'I don't design the basic norms of a "well-ordered" society on the drafting table . . . I am referring only to the normative contents that are *encountered* in practice' (1994: 102, Habermas's emphasis). One might well ask where. Thomas McCarthy has sought to provide an answer to this by resorting to Garfinkel's studies in ethnomethodology. According to McCarthy, Garfinkel's research demonstrates that everyday communication does indeed exhibit a 'normative-structural bias in favour of maintaining the intersubjectivity of mutual understanding' (Hoy and McCarthy, 1994: 71). But ethnomethodology does not provide a theory of communication, merely a description of ordinary talk. Moreover, Garfinkel appears to reject the idea that there is an inherent normative structure to all instances of ordinary talk. On the contrary, he argues that the normative principles that are invoked through social interaction are contextual, that is, they are the 'ongoing accomplishments' of the particular setting in which the interaction takes place (Garfinkel, 1984: viii). McCarthy suggests that those accomplishments nevertheless do apply beyond the context of a particular interaction. They are 'presuppositions that function as regulative ideals' (Hoy and McCarthy, 1994: 72). But this merely corroborates the circularity which is already evident in Habermas's approach. Nothing that Garfinkel might have said can resolve this particular problem.

Habermas probably contributes to the argument of the Frankfurt theorists that a concept of reason can be derived from cultural and social practices. But in seeking to retain the idea of a universal form of reason, he prevents us from asking more detailed questions about what those practices are, their degree of uniformity, and the circumstances in which they arise. In effect, he builds a generalized model of modern society on what turn out to be precarious foundations. As a result, many of his arguments fall victim to the kind of inflexibility I earlier identified with the two classical theorists who work with a holistic concept of society. Just as the problem of empirical closure must arise in Marx's account of the development of capitalism by virtue of his theoretical approach, so Habermas's universalistic concept of communicative reason means that he has to assume away social and cultural practices that do not fit his general model. And where Durkheim seems bound to regard problems of social integration as mere instances of maladaption in respect of the organic development of society as he theorizes it, Habermas must regard specific forms of communication as mere distortions of the learning process which he attributes to the lifeworld. In each instance, the source of the problem lies with the inflexibility of the theories themselves. This is a function of the level of generality to which they aspire. But the difficulty also arises because these theories are intended to support an idealized notion of society, and I shall move on to this in the next part of this discussion.

The project of modernity

Habermas argues that the project of modernity originated with Enlightenment philosophers who sought to utilize the 'accumulation of specialized culture for the enrichment of everyday life' (1981: 9). He argues that the project is incomplete, and that it is the task of critical theory to bring about its fruition. In Habermas's hands, the project of modernity is closely tied to ideals of justice and egalitarianism. Moreover, his argument is underpinned by the conviction that such ideals can be realized on a universal level, and in a form which is genuinely inclusive. In a world which, so the postmodernists allege, is characterized increasingly by cultural pluralism and even a relativism of values, this is a bold and intrepid claim. The question is whether Habermas's theory, in its details, lives up to it.

Habermas's argument hinges on the contention that we have inflated the importance of instrumental reason in modern society, but not the importance of reason *per se*. He warns against allowing our increasing distrust of instrumental reason to lead us, whether fatalistically or ecstatically, into 'something wholly Other' (1987b: 8). If our misgivings towards instrumental reason are based on a belief that it is narrow, authoritarian and exclusionary, such disquiet can be accommodated by the concept of communicative reason. But it remains open to question whether the concept of communicative reason can embrace pluralism, and whether it is genuinely inclusive. These questions apply to two basic features of Habermas's approach. The first concerns the means that are advocated in his theory for achieving that enrichment of everyday life that was envisaged by Enlightenment philosophy. The second concerns the terms in which he characterizes the goal itself. The discussion here will focus only on the first question. For as I shall explain later on, the second takes us into the heart of postmodern territory.

For Habermas, communicative reason demands that we set aside special interests when engaging in dialogue with others. In short, we should bring to our political community only those questions which concern all of its members. The questions, in principle at least, must be universal. But it is important to ask precisely what comes under the category of special interests. Indeed, one wonders exactly how we are to decide what is in the general interest without preempting the entire discussion. Habermas's response to such questions is confusing and unhelpful. He insists that rational dialogue as he conceives it does not require participants to set aside their own culturally ingrained preunderstanding, but merely to bring that understanding into question. His argument is not that we should seek to create better norms and values, only that we scrutinize those we already have. (Presumably, then, that scrutiny is not meant to lead to the creation of better norms.) And he suggests that it would be pointless to engage in discussion 'without a horizon provided by the lifeworld of a specific social group' (1990: 103).[24] In other words, culture must always provide the context and background for rational dialogue.

This last point seems straightforward enough where only one culture, or lifeworld, is at stake. It is open to question, however, whether it makes sense when different and even competing lifeworlds are involved. Habermas's response to this line of questioning is hypothetical. He suggests that we should proceed *as if* dialogue were between equals. Now it is one thing simply to declare, or even to imagine or pretend, that a political community is egalitarian. To ensure that it is so is a different matter entirely. When our actually existing political communities are increasingly shaped and controlled by a centralized media industry, one is entitled to ask what exactly there is to be gained by pretending otherwise. Moreover, in any political discussion, prejudices that reflect differences of gender, class or ethnicity may well operate informally, whatever the extent to which, officially, they have been set aside.[25] For this reason, the crucial distinction between form and substance breaks down.

The important question raised here concerns whether communicative reason can provide a framework in which differences of culture within a political community can be accommodated, or whether they will inevitably be overridden. The problem is one of generality. Habermas maintains that we should hypothetically suppose that other participants in dialogue are on the same footing as ourselves. In other words, we should proceed on the assumption that we are dealing with some kind of generalized other. This other is disembodied, disembedded and, as far as the lifeworld is concerned, already displaced. As Seyla Benhabib has noted, rational dialogue as conceived by Habermas appears to be situated 'beyond historical and cultural contingency' (1991a: 4). Not only does it ignore the concrete circumstances that have affected participants; it demands that they themselves ignore those circumstances. Habermas asks that we assume what Benhabib calls an 'Archimedean standpoint' (ibid.), or what Young describes as 'the point of view of a solitary transcendent God' (1987: 62). Habermas's means for enriching everyday life bear a discomforting resemblance to authoritarianism.[26]

Habermas's defence is robust, but not altogether convincing. He claims that rational dialogue as he envisages it 'binds without unnaming difference', but that it also 'points out the common and the shared among strangers, without depriving the other of otherness' (1994: 119–20). But this is merely to reassert his original position. Suggestively, Peter Dews rallies on Habermas's behalf by presenting us with a choice. On the one hand we might opt for the 'trivialized technicality' suggested by critics who emphasize the implausibility of setting aside cultural differences in a political discussion. On the other, we are offered the 'grandiose arbitrariness' of those who suggest that there is no need to iron out such differences at all, that we should embrace and live with pluralism.[27] In an interview, Habermas claims that he presents the middle way between these extremes, a course in which 'modern life-worlds "come to meet us halfway"' (Habermas, 1994: 19).

The significant question, however, is whether we would actually *choose* to meet the modern lifeworld halfway. According to the postmodernists, we have exhausted the modern lifeworld in so far as it is dominated by a narrow and unyielding form of reason: economically, politically and culturally. For them, Habermas merely tries to extend and consolidate the kind of uniformity to which that form of reason has given rise. What we have, and what we should try to retain, is increasing cultural diversity, and a growing scepticism towards the economic and political systems that modern society has brought into being. For these critics, Habermas's suggested compromise with the modern project is both unnecessary and unwarranted. His continuing faith in the ideals of the Enlightenment is out of place in a world in which, increasingly, people have ceased to believe in the authority and legitimacy of one cultural perspective at all. What is to be gained by compromising with a culture which is defined by a form of reason in which we no longer have faith, and which contains ideals to which we no longer aspire? As Roger Scruton has witheringly said, postmodern culture is a culture of the inverted comma:[28] there is no single version of 'truth'; no universally applicable form of 'justice'; no generally agreed form of 'democracy'; and certainly no desire for a unified 'belief system'. In such hostile terrain, Habermas's project appears to be little short of reactionary. As I set out to explore that terrain in the next part of this book, I shall be asking whether that conclusion is justified.

Part III

Postmodern Social Theory

6

Reality in Retreat: Lyotard and Baudrillard

The concept of postmodern society implies a break with modern society. There are several different viewpoints, however, on exactly what such a break might entail. According to one view, postmodern society represents a new historical era, signifying a change which is just as radical as the transition from traditional to modern society. According to another, it signals merely a collapse or melt-down: not only of modern society but the modern project. This second approach is more common in the sociological literature. But it is not as negative as it first appears. The collapse of modernity is linked not only with the failure of modern ideas of progress and improvement, but with our release from the ideological straitjacket which, in the eyes of postmodernists, they imposed. If there is an identifiable postmodern project, it demands that we embrace cultural and political pluralism in a way that Habermas could never envisage. With this new project, however, come serious theoretical dilemmas. It is my aim in the following three chapters to explain what these are, and to ask how they might be resolved.

In sociological terms, the concept of postmodern society can be understood in terms of a process of de-differentiation, or contextualization. Whereas the development of modern society was characterized by a process of social differentiation, postmodern society arguably signals an inversion of this. In other words, the boundaries or distinctions created through social differentiation are blurred in postmodern society: for example, the boundary between high and low culture, between reality and the representation of reality on television (or in film, painting, literature), between politics and advertising, economic life and culture, production and exchange, artificial and human intelligence, or Western and Eastern systems of belief. This idea underpins the theme of fragmentation in postmodern social theory. The concept of de-differentiation suggests that it is no longer possible to conceptualize society as an integrated system, or totality, in the manner suggested by Marx and Durkheim.

In the first section of this chapter, as a means of providing a historical setting for the next three chapters, I shall discuss core features of postmodern society which enable us to compare it with modern society, before moving on to examine specific themes in the work of Baudrillard and Lyotard.[1] To some degree, this works against the grain. Postmodern social theorists tend to oppose the continuous, or narrative, approach to history which such a comparison might imply.[2] For example, Lyotard claims that 'rewriting modernity' is a more appropriate way of defining his work, for it avoids the kind of periodization of history suggested by terms such as pre or post.[3] Likewise, Baudrillard suggests that we inhabit not a distinctive historical epoch so much as some kind of perpetual present.[4] This theme is directly expressed in their theoretical arguments. Lyotard contends that modern conceptions of progress are ill-suited to a postmodern age in which the grand narratives of history have fallen into disrepair. Baudrillard writes of postmodern society as a hyperreal world in which the distinction between fact and fantasy has broken down, and in which history has come to an end.

In the second section, the normative arguments of Lyotard and Baudrillard will be discussed. Lyotard mounts an explicit challenge to Habermas's conviction that the good and true life represents a culmination of the rationalization of the lifeworld. For Lyotard, the goal of political dialogue should not be consensus but ongoing disagreement, a celebration of uncertainty and paradox. In his later work, he focuses on the predominance of the post-industrial system, particularly the impact of fragmented bits of information which have been generated by what he calls the computerization of culture. Baudrillard argues that fatal strategies such as silence and seduction are the only feasible response to the wall-to-wall simulations of postmodern society. Both are a form of ironic defiance, or what he calls intelligent subversion.

In the third section of the chapter, I shall evaluate these arguments, both from the viewpoint of modern social theory, and in their own terms. The discussion will be in two parts. First, I shall examine whether Lyotard's idea of the postmodern project genuinely has moved beyond the strictures of modern thought as he perceives them. Second, I shall ask whether the normative implications of Baudrillard's writing are consistent with his theoretical depiction of postmodern culture and society.

Postmodern Society

As I have already said, the concept of postmodern society is often understood to mean the society which follows modern society.[5] In the work of Lyotard and Baudrillard, however, the postmodern condition primarily refers to the demise or exhaustion of modernity as a project. Their work consists not of the announcement of a new social order, but of a call to re-evaluate what we thought we knew about the origins and development of the modern age. Nevertheless, it is possible to identify several important changes in Western society which form the backdrop to this assessment. I shall begin by doing so here, before moving on to discuss key theoretical ideas in the work of Lyotard and Baudrillard.

Post-industrialism, consumerism and democracy

Three interrelated themes provide historical background to the concept of postmodern society. The first is post-industrialism, which is closely connected to the concept of the information society.[6] An important component of postmodern social theory concerns the development and impact of forms of communication such as the global mass media and computing. The second theme is the growth of consumerism, which helps to explain why some postmodern theorists allege that exchange now plays a much more important role in economic life than production. The third theme is the apparent triumph of liberal-democratic capitalism in the wake of the Cold War. This idea lies behind postmodern arguments concerning the end of history and, paradoxically, the declining global influence of Western culture. Let me briefly discuss these themes now.

The concept of post-industrialism is an important precursor to the economic analysis which is implicit, though rarely explored, in postmodern social theory. Daniel Bell provides perhaps the most influential account of post-industrial society.[7] In basic terms, he argues that capitalist society has moved beyond its old industrial infrastructure. The analysis identifies five basic changes: a move towards post-Fordist production; the emergence of a new professional and technical occupational class; a growth in the importance of theoretical knowledge as a source of innovation and of policy formulation; an increasingly systematic orientation towards the future in the management of technology; and the increasing use of organizational and information theory.[8] Bell's analysis has generated wide-ranging debate.[9] The main argument against his thesis is that the changes he diagnoses indicate a process which is more akin to globalization, particularly the industrialization of lesser developed countries, than to any fundamental shift in the nature of capitalism *per se*.

Whereas Bell tends to be associated with a conservative or right-wing outlook,[10] two further analyses of post-industrialism come from the political left. Alain Touraine identifies post-industrial society with the emergence of a knowledge class which, because of its capacity for innovation, carries a significant degree of power. He suggests that student movements and public sector workers, detached from 'constraints of great production organizations' (1971: 68), are the major source of tension and conflict in post-industrial society. They are intolerant of experts whose direct involvement with the economic system allows them to force the pace of economic and technological change. André Gorz argues that the working class has been replaced by a post-industrial nonproletariat which consists of the poorly unionized employed and the unemployed.[11] While this new class grouping cannot fulfil a role which is functionally equivalent to the conventional proletariat, the non-working sector can still form a site for emancipatory politics. But if Touraine and Gorz offer a more radical interpretation than Bell of the concept of post-industrial society, they too are open to criticism for failing to place their analyses in global perspective. An extension of the international division of labour, after all, is arguably the most important underlying cause of the shifts they identify in the economic structure of advanced Western societies.[12]

Post-industrialism is an important precursor of the theme of consumerism in the analysis of postmodern society. For example, a key post-Fordist principle holds that stocks should be highly sensitive to sales. And as Bell notes, company budgets in the post-industrial economy tend to be spent less on research and development than on marketing and advertising. The analysis of consumerism, especially its connection with postmodern society, has been developed by Lash and Urry.[13] They argue that manufacturing has declined in the West because industrialization has accelerated in the Third World. At the same time, Western metropolitan centres have been weakened, and regional economies undermined, by industrialization in rural areas. As a result, cultural life in the West has become increasingly fragmented. Consumerism is an important feature of this. According to Lash and Urry, the consumption of goods on the basis of their symbolic value, or sign-value, has created a highly specialized market for consumer goods. Significantly, however, this tends to involve stylistic imitation, or pastiche, rather than invention. As a result, distinctions between styles from different historical periods or cultures are increasingly blurred. Lash and Urry suggest that the sheer complexity of imitation, interchangeability and manipulation of sign-values has led to a decentring of subjectivity: in short, our self-identity loses coherence. On the collective level, media such as television have broken down those symbolic systems which, traditionally, reinforced group identity along the lines of class, gender and age: 'The result has been, on the one hand, the creation of a sensibility conducive to the reception of postmodernist cultural objects, and on the other, the opening of possibilities for a more universalist and rational subjectivity' (1987: 299).

The pre-eminence of the theme of consumerism in contemporary sociology, particularly in the sociology of culture, rests partly on a belief that liberal-democratic capitalism is unlikely to be superseded. This belief draws on two basic arguments: first, that the market provides the most effective means of transmitting economic information; and second, that towards the end of the twentieth century an unprecedented number of countries can legitimately be described as liberal democracies. The political shifts in Eastern Europe during 1989, and the subsequent end of the so-called Cold War, provide an important context for both arguments.

Some theorists maintain, however, that the hegemony of liberal-democratic capitalism might well lead to something of a political malaise in postmodern society.[14] For example, Fukuyama argues that this hegemony signals the 'end of history', that is, the culmination of a deep historical logic.[15] According to Fukuyama, liberal democracy is based on the principles of liberty and equality, and is historically necessary because only this political arrangement can satisfy the innate human desire for recognition. The argument rests on the claim that the demand for recognition, and hence the desire for democracy, is irreducible to an interest in economic maximization. Pointing to the rapid expansion of Pacific Rim economies, he argues that democracy is not the most efficient form of political organization from the point of view of market capitalism.[16] Therefore the growth of liberal democracy cannot be explained in terms of economic necessity. At the same time, this culmination of history threatens to generate 'dissatisfaction *with* liberty and equality' (1992: 334, Fukuyama's emphasis).[17]

All three themes discussed here feature strongly in the work of postmodern social theorists. The concept of post-industrialism, together with the idea that consumerism now plays a significant role in shaping human identity and popular culture, lend themselves to the argument that capitalist society can no longer be understood in terms of the Marxist idea that the economic system, and therefore social change, are conditioned primarily by productive forces. Exchange, the 'symbolic' world of sign-values, is more important now than production, the 'real' world of machines and materials. At one remove, this reversal of the production paradigm underwrites a postmodern attempt to collapse the distinction between the real, or the material world, and the symbolic, the world of representation. With this comes one further significant theoretical contention, namely, that there is no obvious logic or pattern to historical development. At its extreme, this amounts to the view that history has been exhausted or foreclosed. These, then, are the basic ingredients of postmodern social theory. I shall move on now to examine their treatment in the hands of Lyotard and Baudrillard.

Lyotard on the postmodern condition

Although some critics allege that Lyotard writes only of the liquidation of modernity, his earlier work suggests that the postmodern condition offers something distinctive in its own right. The subtitle of *The Postmodern Condition*, 'a report on knowledge', reflects that book's chief purpose: to write 'a report on knowledge in the most highly developed societies' for the Council of Universities of the government of Quebec (1984: xxv). The book consists of a philosophical discussion of scientific enterprise and education. Lyotard suggests that in the computer age, boundaries between scientific disciplines, and between teachers and students, have been eroded. Computer technology enables students to obtain information independently of their teachers. From now on, he suggests, 'didactics can be entrusted to machines linking traditional memory banks (libraries, etc.) and computer data banks to intelligent terminals placed at the students' disposal' (p. 52). Underlying this assertion is a more general argument about the breakdown of modern approaches to the verification of knowledge. This provides the key to Lyotard's conception of the postmodern condition.

Lyotard's analysis fits in closely with the themes of post-industrialism and consumerism. He argues that post-industrial technology, particularly in telecommunications and computing, has shifted emphasis away from the intrinsic value of knowledge and towards an assessment of its role in achieving efficiency, or performativity, within organizational systems. Particularly in science, knowledge will increasingly be evaluated, and research undertaken, not on the basis of intrinsic merit but according to whether it can be translated into computer language. In short, knowledge will be broken down into bits and commodified.

The fragmentation of knowledge in postmodern culture is expressed more broadly by a widespread incredulity, which has its roots in the late nineteenth century, towards 'grand narratives' of historical progress (p. 37). According to Lyotard, the consequences of this are twofold. First, postmodern culture is characterized by relativism. The truth-claims of competing forms of knowledge, which Lyotard calls language games, cannot be evaluated in the absence of universally accepted criteria. Second, the postmodern condition is characterized by an increased awareness and acceptance of uncertainty. This is most sharply expressed in postmodern science, which focuses on 'such things as undecidables, the limits of precise control, conflicts characterized by incomplete information, "*fracta*," catastrophes, and pragmatic paradoxes' (p. 60). Lyotard does not entirely dismiss the notion of scientific advancement. He merely suggests that science does not progress incrementally but thrives on paralogy, that is, by taking unexpected, even deliberately unpromising turns and by resisting orthodoxy. He opposes the idea that the goal of science is to achieve greater levels of certainty about the world. Rather, to court *un*certainty will lead to a science which is genuinely inventive: 'working on a proof means searching for and "inventing" counterexamples, in other words, the unintelligible; supporting an argument means looking for a "paradox" and legitimating it with new rules in the games of reasoning' (p. 54).

Lyotard's argument at this stage might be taken to suggest an affirmative conception of postmodern society. He makes clear, however, that the postmodern condition is part of, not something which breaks away from, the modern era.[18] Later on, he appears to reject the concept of postmodernity altogether in favour of the notion of 'rewriting modernity', because 'neither modernity nor so-called postmodernity can be identified and defined as clearly circumscribed historical entities' (1991: 25). More than this, however, Lyotard moves away from a sociological interpretation of postmodern society and towards a philosophical investigation of its normative and aesthetic implications.[19] For a more sustained attempt to address postmodern society and culture, we must look to Baudrillard.

Baudrillard: modern and postmodern society

Much of Baudrillard's recent work, such as his writings on America, must be regarded as an expression, rather than a fully fledged theoretical analysis, of various facets of postmodern society and culture.[20] For this reason, his arguments are peculiarly difficult to summarize. It is in his earlier work, however, particularly his break with Marxism, that he formulates something closer to a theory of postmodern society. I shall examine that theory here, before moving on to discuss its elaboration in later books and articles.

Baudrillard's earliest work was undertaken within a Marxist theoretical framework. When understood chronologically,[21] however, his writing marks a steady retreat from Marxism. With *The Mirror of Production*, for example, he moves from supplementing Marx's theory towards superseding it altogether.[22] This stems from an analysis of the implications of the growth of consumerism for Marxist political economy. Initially, he suggests that Marxist theory should be broadened to account for the increasing significance of consumerism: 'Production and Consumption are one and the same grand logical process in the expanded reproduction of the productive forces and of their control' (1988c: 50). This entails reassessing the concept of need. Whereas Marx argues that basic human needs underwrite the use-value of material goods, Baudrillard contends that in the consumer society, the concept of innate human need is untenable.[23] Rather, consumer needs are constituted and expressed through forms of symbolic communication. Use-value therefore becomes a fetishized social relation. The idea that objects are useful because they answer basic or innate needs is an 'anthropological illusion' (1988c: 131–2).

Baudrillard revises the concept of use-value by turning to Saussure's work on the relation between the signifier and the signified in linguistic communication.[24] The signifier can be defined as a physical object, word, or picture. The signified is the mental concept which is indicated by the signifier. Saussure's central argument is that the relationship between the signifier and signified is arbitrary: in short, that there is no intrinsic or natural connection between a material object or word and the mental concept which represents it. Baudrillard uses this idea to collapse the distinction between the material world and the world of ideology or culture, and thereby develop what he calls a critique of the political economy of the sign. In Marxist terms, this strategy is intended to avoid characterizing culture as a 'surf frothing on the beachhead of the economy' (1981: 144). In the context of consumerism, this is important because it enables us to move beyond the idea that, in the last instance, commodities possess a use-value that answers innate needs. According to Baudrillard, the contrary is true. In the consumer society, our needs are brought into being by commodities, our desires constituted and shaped by them in advance.

This argument should be interpreted less as attempting to overturn Marxism, that is, as prioritizing the superstructure over the infrastructure, than as collapsing that distinction altogether. Baudrillard takes this strategy to its furthest extreme with the concepts of simulation and hyperreality.[25] Hyperreality can be characterized as a breakdown of the distinction between reality on the one hand, and the media through which reality is represented on the other. Recalling McLuhan's argument that the medium is the message, and also Benjamin's work on the significance of mechanical reproduction in art,[26] Baudrillard suggests that hyperreality is neither the medium nor the message but a third state which has no origin or object in the real world (1983b: 103). As the concept suggests, this state is literally more than (that is, is hyper) reality.[27] Like McLuhan, Baudrillard suggests that it is the form, not content, of the medium which is important. Because hyperreality disrupts conventional principles of representation, social theory must free itself from those principles. Both Marxism and structuralism fail in this respect, for they are derived from what he calls a hermeneutics of suspicion, which aims to expose the truth beneath a surface reality. For Baudrillard, there is no hidden or deep reality that can be uncovered by social theory. Instead, we must focus on the genesis of simulacra – that is, the way in which signs are transformed and translated into other signs – not the reality they conceal.[28]

Whereas Lyotard suggests that the main consequence of the information society is the fragmentation of knowledge into bits or chunks, Baudrillard's is a totalizing view. Television provides the sharpest illustration of this. Unlike cinema, television has no depth. Television is unable to differentiate between a range of images and emotions, which instead become a pure surface. The television image allows no space for a dialectic between the real and imaginary. Without this, it is impossible to conceive of the notion of an image at all. And it is from this that one's capacity to enjoy and be seduced by images at all should be derived.[29] Real life and television images thereby dissolve into each another.[30] The more television provides us with information, the less meaning we are able to give it. Television does not so much manipulate as constitute its audience as a mass. Thus for Baudrillard, 'mass(age) is the message' (1983b: 44).[31]

Perhaps the most controversial expression of the idea of hyperreality occurs in Baudrillard's argument on the Gulf War. In a series of three articles published by the French newspaper *Libération* in 1991, Baudrillard maintains that the Gulf War did not take place.[32] This was, he argues, not a real war but '*a simulacre* of a war, the only consequence of which is a *simulacre* of negotiation' (1993c: 207).[33] With apologies to Clausewitz, he defines this non-war as 'the absence of politics continued by other means' (p. 7). Some commentators have taken Baudrillard's argument literally,[34] that is, as a thesis about the actual existence of the

Gulf War.[35] Others suggest that the articles provide an important illustration of the concept of hyperreality, and that to read them in a literal way is to miss the point of that concept. This interpretation holds that the Gulf War was a non-war at least in the sense that the military relied on computer simulations of real events. This altered the character of the way events unfolded over time and the way those events were reported. Baudrillard argues, moreover, that the objectives of the United Nations and the United States government were never fully realized by the war, which 'went completely off the rails'. In short, this was a war without consequences. Given Baudrillard's remarks on specific aspects of the war, such as US government policy and negotiations within the UN, it makes little sense to read the piece literally. If it is a provocation, it is a deeply moralistic one.[36]

The concept of hyperreality is further illustrated by Baudrillard's work on America. He compares the urban and natural landscape of America to cinematography: 'If you drive round Los Angeles in a car, or go out into the desert, you are left with an impression that is totally cinematographic, hallucinatory' (1993c: 31). Disneyland is the perfect model of the hyperreal. Although designed as an imaginary world, as a contrast to the real world outside, Disneyland merely conceals the fact that Los Angeles, and America as a whole, are no longer real, but have all the qualities of hyperreality and simulation.[37] Much of Baudrillard's work on America is presented in the form of diaries, and this underlines the fragmentary quality of the writing.[38] There are echoes of Simmel in the way he records fleeting encounters with people and passing impressions of events. But whereas Simmel's accounts of urban life suggest the perspective of the city-dweller, Baudrillard's diaries reflect the gaze of the tourist. According to some critics, this accounts for the superficiality of his observations: not only does he focus primarily on tourist centres, he rarely digs beneath the surface of what he sees. For others, however, this is an exact expression of what Baudrillard means by hyperreality. Whereas the Frankfurt theorists write of a reality that has been reified by the culture industry, Baudrillard suggests that the media industry has driven reality mercilessly into retreat. But what is the historical significance of hyperreality? In what sense, exactly, is it postmodern?

Baudrillard's theoretical approach is set out more clearly in *The Transparency of Evil*. Here, the breakdown or liquidation of modern society is characterized as a bursting of limits. Baudrillard specifically refers to the erosion of boundaries between art and non-art, fact and fantasy, male and female, the economic and the political, and between the religious and the secular. This is a form of contextualization: 'Everything is sexual. Everything is political. Everything is aesthetic. All at once' (1993a: 9). In the economic sphere, for example, he highlights the contrast between the growth rate of financial networks on the one hand, and the level of trading in material goods on the other. Money now circulates within a hyperrealized, inaccessible space: it is 'our imagined economy' (p. 27).

Baudrillard characterizes the relationship between this hyperreal world and modern society as the implosion of modernity. In the first instance, this consists of an orgy of liberation: political, sexual, and aesthetic (p. 3).[39] But in any case, liberation has ceased to occur at all in any real sense. We can only simulate it, 'because all the goals of liberation are already behind us' (ibid.). This notion is pivotal to Baudrillard's conception of the way that modern society has characterized itself. The idea that this conception has come to an end is therefore vital to his view of postmodern society. The suggestion that modern processes, movements and even disciplines of thought are reaching their end recurs throughout his argument: the end of political economy – because we have an imagined economy now (p. 35); of anthropology – because technology means that we can no longer say whether we are people or machines (p. 57); the end of evil – because evil is everywhere, we no longer have anything to set against it (p. 85); and the end of history – because we lack notions such as responsibility, causality and meaning which are required to make sense of it (p. 91).

According to Baudrillard, the absence of a feasible alternative to liberal-democratic capitalism is bound to generate political inertia. History has been drained of energy. So, crucially, has normative social theory: at least in the sense of there being any connection between theoretical truth and political emancipation.[40] Like Fukuyama, Baudrillard suggests that history has come to an end: 'not for want of actors, nor for want of violence (there will always be more violence), nor for want of events (there will always be more events, thanks to the media and the news networks!)' (1994: 4). However, there is a revealing distinction between the end of history as defined by Fukuyama and by Baudrillard. For Baudrillard, the end of history is characterized by 'deceleration, indifference and stupefaction' (ibid.). Fukuyama, while conceding that such inertia is possible, places his argument in the context of a historical theory that all human societies have an inherent developmental tendency towards liberal democracy. Thus, while Fukuyama argues that history has reached its *goal*, Baudrillard implies that history has come to a *stop*.[41] This has important political consequences. For Baudrillard, the 'immense indifference' of the majority of Westerners towards history and democracy gives them a 'silent potency' (1994: 3).

To understand what this might mean, we need to consider post-modernity as a normative project.

Games and Seductions

The normative arguments put forward by Lyotard and Baudrillard do not outline an alternative to modern society and the modern project so much as explore the consequences of their exhaustion. On the face of it, Lyotard is the more direct exponent of a normative project. He sets out a framework for political dialogue, based on the motif of the language game, which contrasts sharply to that which is proposed by Habermas. Lyotard flatly rejects ideas of universal reason and object-ive truth: particularly any connection that the modernists assert between these ideas and political justice. By contrast, Baudrillard asks how we might live in and with hyperreality. His answer is that we must allow ourselves to be seduced by it. The most radical response to postmodern society is passivity. The arguments of both theorists hinge on their remarks about the peculiar nature of the social fabric – or what Lyotard calls the social bond, and Baudrillard the symbolic order – of postmodern society.

Lyotard: the postmodern social bond

Lyotard's normative argument in *The Postmodern Condition* rests pri-marily on a critique of Habermas.[42] This hinges on the claim that to believe that there is an intrinsic connection between truth, universal reason and justice is to espouse a form of political terror. This is a grave accusation. It derives from the contention that knowledge can be ad-vanced only by seeking out uncertainty and paradox, not by searching for a higher truth through universal reason. Lyotard deploys this idea to underwrite the case for a distinctive, postmodern conception of jus-tice and political freedom. He sets out by distinguishing between the normative goal that informs Habermas's argument and the method, or means, which he advocates for achieving that goal: 'The cause is good, but the argument is not' (1984: 66). Lyotard suggests that, in practical terms, political consensus in the form envisaged by Habermas could only ever be attained in a negative way. It can only exclude dissent, not actually realize universal agreement. Indeed, this appears to be as self-evident to Lyotard as it is self-evident to Habermas that the only de-fensible political regime is one based on consensus. In short, Lyotard appears to be suggesting that to look for consensus in a political community over basic normative principles is dangerous *in principle*.

As I have already said, the argument comes down to the way in which Lyotard characterizes the social fabric, or social bond, in postmodern society. In simple terms, the social bond can be characterized as the mechanism by which a society is held together. For Habermas, society is bound by a set of beliefs which are derived from dialogue and agreement. But these beliefs will only be valid – and the social bond they underscore will only be sustained in a just manner – if such dialogue is undertaken according to principles that are consistent with the concept of communicative reason. It is vital to understand that this argument is directed towards the process of dialogue, not its outcome: in other words, the form rather than content of communication. According to Lyotard, however, the distinction between form and content in Habermas's argument cannot be sustained, because the formal principles themselves are derived from Western values. The cultural specificity of Habermas's approach is merely disguised, not transcended, by his formal, rationalist language. This is not a just, but an ethnocentric, view of the good society.

Lyotard advocates a framework for dialogue which is designed genuinely to take account of cultural pluralism. He argues that this can only be achieved by consciously searching for dissensus, not consensus, in discussion. This normative argument is the corollary of his theoretical contention that, in science, knowledge can only be advanced through uncertainty. Lyotard thereby calls for an approach to political dialogue which respects 'both the desire for justice and the desire for the unknown' (1984: 67). In practice, this means that dialogue should consist of a series of language games. Language games do not follow a unified set of fixed principles. The rules are invented according to the circumstances of the game itself. Ethical judgements need not be derived from universally agreed rules. We must be allowed to 'invent criteria' (Lyotard and Thébaud, 1985: 17). Moreover, language games are incommensurable. They each consist of a distinctive perspective and a unique idiom. Thus, for Lyotard, the social bond in postmodern society is 'formed by the intersection of at least two (and in reality an indeterminate number) of language games, obeying different rules' (1984: 40).

According to Lyotard and Thébaud, political conflict in the modern world is resolved all too frequently by the forceful manipulation of a language game which is properly understood by just one of the parties involved. They refer to such instances as differends: they may involve, for example, workers who have to objectify their own labour when ne-

gotiating in the language of their employers; and the feminist movement whose challenge to the patriarchal idiom must be couched in the
language of that idiom.[43] Above all, they maintain that politics 'is not a
matter of science' (1985: 23). In short, questions of justice are not tied to
questions of truth. To imagine so is to court political authoritarianism.
Are we therefore to conclude that there is no connection between reason, truth and justice?

Some of Lyotard's best-known work in philosophy is concerned with
aesthetics and the avant-garde, and it is in this context that some sense
of the relationship between reason, truth and justice begins to emerge.
Aesthetic principles are expressed in his political writings in as much
as he outlines a conception of politics which is intrinsically connected
with the 'libidinal economy', or desire. For Lyotard, there is no such
thing as good or bad desire. By its very nature, desire is positive, affirmative and productive. So it is here, not through reason, that the
postmodern conception of truth must be derived.[44] We should as far as
possible be sensitized towards cultural and political perspectives which
are different from our own. In other words, we should respect alternative *desires* for truth rather than eradicate them through a bogus commitment to rational debate according to universal principles. This is an
explicitly relativist position which, on the face of it, represents the
starkest conceivable contrast to the concept of communicative action
espoused by Habermas.

Later on in his work, however, Lyotard appears to doubt that desire
can, after all, promise any kind of release from a post-industrial system
which reduces all human knowledge and culture to technological bits.
That system, he argues, persists under the name of a form of development which 'imposes the saving of time'. We move faster. But we forget just as quickly. Against this background, he contrasts the adult and
child. The developed adult is civilized, conforms to institutions, speaks
through reason, and seeks to escape from such misery only implicitly
through 'traces of an indetermination, a childhood' (1991: 3). The adult
is in this sense inhuman. By contrast, the child – during the earliest
stages of infancy – cannot speak through the civilizing form of language;
cannot calculate; and is insensitive to reason. But according to Lyotard,
to be infantile is to be eminently human: the expression of a delay to
the humanizing process which 'manifests to this community the lack of
humanity it is suffering from' (1991: 4).

This argument puts a slightly different complexion on Lyotard's critique of historical narratives. Whereas earlier he writes of our increasing incredulity towards them, later on he focuses on the functions of
narrative itself, particularly the way in which it breaks down informa-

tion into bits. The narrative is a technique, a means 'to store, order and retrieve units of information, i.e. events' (1991: 63). But the outcome of this process is to transform the emotive charge we attach to single events into something which supposedly has meaning for us. In so far as the narrative has a generalizing form, however, the information becomes anonymous and essentially meaningless. The immense potential of computer memory generated by the microelectronics revolution actually diminishes our own capacity to recall, because 'the body supporting that memory is no longer an earth-bound body' (1991: 64).

According to Lyotard, what we call civilization is therefore anything but. Not only the form of rational dialogue involved in Habermas's concept of political community, but the form of rational pedagogy involved in education, are terroristic and inhuman. The postmodern condition therefore consists of two forms of inhumanity: that of the post-industrial system, and that of the civilized adult with only memory traces of infancy. These inhumanities combine under the banner of development: couched in terms of economic competitiveness, liberal democracy, and even human rights. The driving force behind development is therefore not the maturation of civilization as the Enlightenment thinkers suggested, but the unrelenting logic of specialization: 'between two elements, whatever they are, whose relation is given at the start, it is always possible to introduce a third term which will assure a better regulation' (1991: 6). For Lyotard, the only means of resisting the inhumanity of development is to draw on and recover the (eminently human) 'inhumanity' of our infancy. What memory traces we have are a debt we owe to our childhood. For in the infant are distilled all the essential properties of humanity. But memory is not enough to interrupt the regularities of adulthood. For a recovery of our humanity, we must look to aesthetics.

Lyotard's argument helps to clarify, for the time being at least, what might be entailed in the postmodern project. Where modernity stands for a belief in progress towards a better society, the concept of postmodernity implies that there are no criteria – other than those that are culturally specific – against which such progress could be judged. While the project of modernity explores the connection between political justice and universal reason, postmodernity suggests that they are antithetical because universal reason could only ever be imposed arbitrarily by the powerful on the powerless. Where the project of modernity is derived from a theoretical conception of society as being held together by agreement over core values, postmodernity imagines a fluid community consisting of many incommensurable language games. And just as modernity is inexorably linked to the notion of collective emancipation, so the concept of postmodernity suggests that there can only be the emancipation of individual desire. Lyotard offers perhaps the clearest, and certainly one of the earliest, statements of the postmodern project. It is arguably Baudrillard, however, who is today most closely associated with postmodern social theory, even if he claims to reject that association himself. But he has a rather different project in mind.

Baudrillard: the politics of seduction

Baudrillard's normative argument hinges on the idea of reciprocity, which he explores in *Symbolic Exchange and Death*. This theme is important in the first instance because, in the consumer society, signs are exchanged not by virtue of what they represent, but on the basis of their exchangeability with other signs (1993b: 7). Signs have a reciprocal relationship only with each other, not with reality. The consumer-led, simulated society consists of signs which are 'conceived according to their very reproducibility' (p. 56). In the hyperreal world, nothing – not even the unconscious[45] – can escape simulation. All opposition is absorbed and 'disconnected from its own ends' (p. 4). To this extent, direct political subversion is impossible. If Baudrillard espouses a normative project, it claims to focus not on how to overcome hyperreality, but on how to live with it. It seems that he is searching for an antidote, that is, something which counteracts but cannot destroy the effects of hyperreality. This calls for a different kind of reciprocity from that entailed in the relationship between signs. It consists not so much of equivalence but of a form of challenge or defiance. To explain this, we must turn to the concepts of symbolic exchange and seduction.

Symbolic exchange is the antithesis of commodity exchange because it is reciprocal. In gift-giving, for example, the countergift 'abolishes power' in so far as it cancels out all further obligations (1993b: 49 n5). Likewise with seduction. Now one might reasonably imagine that seduction is anything but reciprocal. Not, however, as far as Baudrillard is concerned.[46] According to him, to allow oneself to be seduced is in fact the best way of *seducing*. In seduction, the subject and object are interchangeable, or reversible. In effect, they become each other. Seduction is therefore neither passive nor active. It is rather like a challenge or a game: 'an uninterrupted ritual exchange, an infinite escalation of the ante' (1990c: 101). To be seduced is not to surrender power to another. On the contrary, it is to empower oneself, because seduction involves a mutual challenge, a crucial element of defiance. It is the potentially endless processes of seducing and of being seduced – not their outcome or resolution – that are the basis for this.[47]

As a metaphor, seduction appears to be immoral, trivial and shallow. By contrast, capitalist production is based on control, because it seeks to regulate the flow of objects or commodities. Seduction can in this sense symbolize a reversal of capitalism. But it is also a reversal in another, more vital sense. According to Baudrillard, we have allowed ourselves merely to be fascinated by simulacra. It is as if we are possessed by an ecstatic stupefaction: an absorption with models, fashion and simulacra.[48] But fascination is not the same as seduction. To be fascinated by something is to be drawn into it. And it is to remain fundamentally passive: 'There's no defiance.' Fascination is a kind of ecstasy, a form of 'coagulation, proliferation of messages and signs'. By contrast, being seduced by the hyperreal is rather like reversing it, turning it against itself. Seduction must involve a moment of defiance: 'signs are received and immediately sent back.' With fascination there is no defiance, merely absorption. With seduction, there is 'always a game, a possibility of a game, and a very intense dual relation through defiance' (1993c: 85). The concept of seduction therefore suggests, in theoretical and practical terms, the power to collapse the idea that there is a distinction between the real and the imaginary, and therefore between the subject and object. This, after all, is what is sustained by Marx's analysis of reification, and by the Frankfurt theorists' commitment to negation. Seduction provides a motif around which, in theoretical terms, we can overthrow the language of representation on which those ideas depend. In practical terms, it provides a paradoxical means of defying the hyperreal in respect of which that language is no longer appropriate. Through seduction, both can be turned inwards and imploded.

Baudrillard characterizes seduction as a fatal strategy.[49] The concept of a fatal strategy is deliberately paradoxical: 'how could there be fatality if there is a strategy?' It is also self-consciously indeterminate: 'No one knows what a strategy is' (1990c: 188). But in very basic terms, a fatal strategy pushes something to its limits: to its fatality. But in doing so, it does not destroy but destabilizes. By definition, its outcome appears to be unforeseeable. Baudrillard characterizes this as an intelligent form of subversion. In order to understand a little more of what the concept entails, let me briefly consider one further instance of it: silence.

For Baudrillard, our silence in the face of hyperreality, our 'massive de-volition' or hyperconformism, may in fact constitute 'refusal by overacceptance'. This amounts to nothing less than 'a massive delegation of the power of desire, of choice, of responsibility' (1988c: 215–19).[50] It is, however, a paradoxical silence: not a silence which merely stops speaking, but a silence which 'refuses to be spoken for in its name'

(1983a: 22). Once again, defiance is key. This argument rests on a specific interpretation of the symbolic order of postmodern society. The fundamental purpose of that order consists of the 'over-production and regeneration of meaning and speech' (1983a: 109) in an endless network of simulacra. But its outcome is a catastrophe of meaning. The more information we have, the less meaning can be given to it. Baudrillard describes the potential of silence as 'the subversion of the media by the masses' (1990c: 86). It is a secret revenge against a system which berates the masses for not knowing what they want (whereas, according to Baudrillard, they have no desire to know); for not seeking power (but they have no desire for power); and for their stupidity and passivity (whereas, in fact, the masses are 'very snobbish'). The masses are snobbish because they have effectively delegated all designation of needs, all power and all activity to mediators. In their administration of the 'tedious business of power', the mediators merely relieve the masses 'for their greater pleasure, and to reward them with the spectacle of it' (1990c: 98).

Baudrillard's approach presents a significant contrast to the arguments of Lyotard. Lyotard advocates paralogy: the active and noisy pursuit of disagreement and paradox. Baudrillard counsels silence. As a silent mass, we are in the same double bind as children. As objects, we can rebel; as subjects, overconform. For Baudrillard, neither strategy has more objective value than the other (1983a: 107). But overconformity has a great deal going for it as a fatal strategy. In the simulated society, silence is itself a form of simulation 'of the very mechanisms of the system, which is a form of refusal and non-reception' (1983a: 108). Our silence has the potency of an absolute weapon. Its aim is not simply to mirror the system, that is, to reflect back an image without absorbing it, but to distort it. Whereas the metaphor of the mirror evokes the idea of 'opaque resistance', Baudrillard suggests that the metaphor of a black hole best captures the potency of silence: it 'inexorably inflects, bends and distorts all energy and light radiation approaching it' (1983a: 9). To embark on active resistance would be to act in accordance with the system. Silence, by contrast, is a form of provocation: a refusal to be a subject of the system. To be silent is therefore to go beyond alienation.[51]

Whereas Lyotard urges that we celebrate pluralism and difference, Baudrillard suggests that we have become a congealed and silent mass. For Baudrillard, a mass has no sociological reality because it entirely lacks 'attribute, predicate, quality, reference' (1983a: 5). Where Lyotard writes that persistent disagreement with others is vital to free and just political dialogue, Baudrillard writes of a mass in which there are no others: 'This is what makes the circulation of meaning within the mass impossible: it is instantaneously dispersed, like atoms in a void' (1983a: 6). Thus while Lyotard argues that the postmodern social bond thrives on difference and otherness, Baudrillard suggests that there is no postmodern social bond, at least in any meaningful sense. But both theorists, albeit in different ways, advance statements about postmodern society which present peculiar difficulties for sociology. I will address these difficulties in the critical discussion.

Critical Discussion

Lyotard and Baudrillard agree that the fundamental flaw in modern social theory is the belief that it is possible to understand society from an objective standpoint. But they advance this argument in rather different ways. I shall therefore discuss their work separately, although I shall compare and contrast their arguments and ideas wherever possible. Lyotard contends that the grand narratives which stem from this belief must give way to an acknowledgement that different cultural and political perspectives have equivalent value. Social theory can facilitate this. What it must not do is set itself up as an arbiter when these perspectives compete. No criterion exists, such as universal reason, against which the process of arbitration could proceed. In philosophical terms, there is no objective truth, no universal reason: merely several points of view, each with its own language. For Baudrillard, the failing of modern social theory is its search for a hidden logic or structure beneath the surface of social reality. In the hyperreal world, the logic of representation this implies has broken down. As sociologists, all we have to go on is pure surface. There can be no liberation in this world because the web of signs is all-encompassing, a total system which absorbs all resistance.

Both arguments express the conviction that in postmodern society, social theorists and philosophers are in much the same position as everyone else. For Lyotard, we all lack guarantees governing the truth or validity of our own outlook and convictions. Where disagreement exists, we have no choice but to participate: without believing for a moment that the disagreement can or should be resolved. Indeed, we should revel in the uncertainty of it all. It is the nearest we will get to justice. For Baudrillard, we can only reflect our condition back on itself without taking it in. Defy through seduction or silence and we will avoid being drawn into the wrong kind of political struggle – that is, the outmoded collectivist struggle – that the system demands and on which it will always thrive. Social theorists and philosophers, just like everyone else, must condemn themselves to silence and passivity. It is the closest thing we have to radicalism.

Of the two theorists, Baudrillard comes closest to following his own recommendations. As I shall explain in the first part of this discussion, Lyotard wavers at crucial stages in the argument, and therefore appears to fall back into a theoretical and normative position which is recognizably modernist. It remains open to question whether this is merely a failure of execution or an inherent failing of the postmodern project as he conceives it. As I shall note in the second part of this discussion, Baudrillard follows the logic of his own argument by formulating what amounts to a celebration of hyperreality. Yet by doing so, he offers a clear signal that a theory of postmodern society might well turn out to be a contradiction in terms. Each in their own way – Lyotard wavering, Baudrillard not – these pre-eminent postmodernists lead us fumbling towards the conclusion that a postmodern sociology may not be feasible after all.

Lyotard: modernist or postmodernist?

Two main themes dominate criticism of Lyotard in the sociological literature. First, his approach to political dialogue leads not to justice but to an unpalatable moral relativism. While he explicitly seeks to avoid the terrorism which, by his reckoning, is implicit in Habermas's theory, his argument achieves exactly the opposite. In effect, it rules out any distinction between authoritarianism and liberal democracy. Second, Lyotard is unable to support his normative position with consistent theoretical argument. Indeed, his attempts to do so draw him to a position much nearer to that of Habermas. This argument is closely connected to the first criticism, because it suggests that the more Lyotard seeks to avoid the less acceptable implications of his pluralist normative stance, the more he seems to retreat to a theoretical argument which is recognizably – albeit reluctantly – modernist.

One might say that Lyotard's normative argument tries to achieve a modernist goal, that is, universal justice, by postmodernist means, that is, pluralism and relativism. It is at least questionable whether such a combination can work. For some critics, Lyotard's position lacks clarity.[52] For others, it is deliberately ambivalent. For example, Benhabib suggests that the emphasis on experimentation in political dialogue suggests 'a post-Marxist radical, democratic politics'. But if language games are as incommensurable as Lyotard suggests, where should such a dialogue lead? The notion of incommensurability suggests that dialogue would be not only pointless but virtually impossible. Lyotard therefore invites not radicalism but 'moral and political indifference' (Benhabib, 1984: 122).[53]

To this extent, Lyotard is trapped in a theoretical dilemma. To set out his position as an objective and rational philosophy would be like putting forward an alternative, specifically postmodern, narrative, and therefore remaining firmly rooted in the terrain of Enlightenment thought. But at the same time, simply to ignore the notion of objective truth and universal reason altogether would be merely to abandon, not critically engage with, that terrain and therefore leave it untouched.[54] This dilemma is further expressed in Lyotard's normative arguments. In *Just Gaming*, Lyotard and Thébaud distinguish between two sets of criteria against which a normative assertion can be judged. *Lexis*, or rhetoric, refers to the way an argument is presented. *Logos*, or reason, refers to the substance of the argument itself. They suggest that these criteria have equal status, that is, that there will be injustice whenever there is asymmetry between them.[55] Yet this seems to contradict Lyotard's position in *The Postmodern Condition*, which is that the attractiveness of an argument, not its rationalism, should be the basis of political conviction. Now these two books were originally published in the same year, 1979. In the former, there appears to be implicit agreement that an argument *can* be judged according to rational principles which have been agreed in advance. In the latter, Lyotard's position is starkly against that of Habermas, and emphasizes contingency, relativism and difference.[56]

It remains open to question whether this represents inconsistency in Lyotard's position, or confirmation that the argument of *The Postmodern Condition* is simply unpalatable, suggesting as it does that political arguments are best judged according to the force or style with which they are advanced. Dews argues that the apparent concession to reason in *Just Gaming* sounds 'the death-knell of post-structuralism' (1987: 219). According to Jameson, however, the question is more complicated than this. Lyotard is not proposing a postmodern project which is distinctive from modernity. On the contrary, he is seeking to reaffirm 'the authentic older high modernisms very much in Adorno's spirit' (1991: 60).[57] This interpretation suggests that Lyotard regards the growth of information technology as a regeneration of modern society, and is merely seeking to avoid the technocratic language of post-industrialism – not the goals of modern society *per se* – when focusing on uncertainty and paradox in science: 'How he does this is to transfer the older technologies of aesthetic high modernism, the celebration of its

revolutionary power, to science and scientific research proper'
(Jameson's introduction to Lyotard, 1984: xx). As even Jameson concedes, however, Lyotard's political enthusiasm for paradox and uncertainty in science is at odds with the economic prospect of a monopolistic
information industry. That monopoly, 'like the rest of the private property system', is unlikely to be challenged through the kind of pluralistic dialogue that Lyotard recommends. Another way of saying this
might be that Lyotard requires a social theory in order more fully to
understand the prospects for the information industry. But he does not
even begin to provide one. His argument for opening up the data banks
has a hollow ring, not least because he provides not the slightest ink-
ling of how this might be achieved.

As I have already suggested, however, Lyotard's work focuses primarily on philosophical and normative, rather than sociological, aspects of the postmodern condition. One might therefore expect his
philosophical arguments to be more robust. In his critique of Habermas,
Lyotard suggests that the aspiration to establish universal procedures
for political dialogue will, in all likelihood, merely exclude individuals
and groups who are already marginalized. Significantly, however, he
has no serious difficulty with Habermas's basic idea: namely, that we
should develop a political structure in which all have an equal opportunity to speak. He only really disagrees with the notion that this can
be achieved through political consensus. But one might well ask how
Lyotard imagines that the freedom to participate – and disagree – in
political dialogue can be *upheld* without there being at least some form
of consensus regarding core principles: at the very least, about the process of dialogue itself. It is one thing to suggest that it is difficult to
arbitrate between different perspectives without compromising the
beliefs from which those perspectives are derived. It is quite another to
say that we should not even try. Moreover, as soon as it is suggested
that we should have a right to express disagreements and differences
of perspective – and, correspondingly, the obligation to respect the disagreements and differences of others – it becomes impossible to avoid
relying on principles that apply (and can be defended) above and beyond the context of dialogue itself.[58] Lyotard's advocacy of relativism,
or perspectivalism, consists of two basic arguments: first, that our
political structure should guarantee access to a limitless range of viewpoints; and second, that we should not seek to resolve differences between those viewpoints. It is the second of these arguments which leads
him to reject the concept of universal reason. Theoretically, that concept implies that philosophers can arbitrate between those different
viewpoints. Normatively, it implies that consensus is not only possible

but desirable. But these arguments do not fit together. Unless a political structure which guarantees access *to* all is agreed upon and defended *by* all, the freedom it provides might well be open to abuse. This is universalism by default, despite all of Lyotard's pronouncements to the contrary. Just because he opposes Habermas's argument for its universalism, it does not necessarily follow that he avoids it.

Habermas makes exactly this point in his defence of the project of modernity. Time and again, that defence returns to the distinction between procedure and substance: between an argument about *how* dialogue proceeds, and an argument about the *content* of what is discussed and agreed. Habermas rightly maintains that the discursive principles outlined in his theory concern only the process of argumentation. He suggests that, whatever the range of perspectives among participants to such a debate, principles of argumentation must come into play if any decision is to be made. These principles are not culturally specific: 'From the perspective of the first person, the question of which beliefs are justified is a question of which beliefs are based on good reasons; it is not a function of life-habits that enjoy social currency in some places and not in others.'[59] We seem to be facing an impasse.

If Lyotard's normative argument appears first to reject, and then re-admit, the commitment to universalism, his critique of modern historical narratives is hardly more successful. The idea that history has a deep logic – for example, a dialectical relationship between the forces and relations of production, or the process of rationalization as defined by a concept of universal reason – is restrictive. As I have argued in this book, social theories that are derived from this basic understanding of history tend to be inflexible. They are either unable to account for historical contingency, or almost bound to prejudge the significance of particular historical developments: contrast Marx and Durkheim on the phenomenon of class conflict or the forced division of labour. But there is a second serious difficulty here. The modern understanding of history is implicitly normative. It suggests an ethnocentric understanding of the advancement of society. Societies that are different from the basic historical model tend to be characterized as underdeveloped, and therefore as inferior.

Lyotard's critique of Habermas identifies this second difficulty with the narrative understanding of history-as-progress. But his rejection of modern social theory appears to have been based entirely on these grounds. In other words, he does not address theoretical difficulties in the interpretation of history *per se*. He offers nothing to replace modern social theory, merely the observation that we have lost faith with the narrative of progress. Indeed, he appears to be rejecting not so much one particular approach to social theory as the very idea of social theory itself. We might already have suspected that Habermas's argument unnecessarily conflates theoretical and normative interpretations of history by deducing a theoretical deep logic within the development of modern society which, it so happens, neatly coincides with his own – culturally specific – language of liberation. But Lyotard appears merely to commit the same error from another direction. By default, he rejects the very notion of social theory on the basis of a normative dispute with only one particular *type* of theory. This is tantamount to suggesting that if Habermas's theory is ethnocentric, all theories must be ethnocentric. From here, there is simply no way forward.

Baudrillard against theory

One might reasonably imagine that any suspicion that the postmodern project means an outright rejection of theory is unlikely to be eased by reading Baudrillard. If, as Bryan Turner argues, Baudrillard's arguments suggest the need for a new theoretical vocabulary which 'offers an alternative discourse by which the complexities of the new realm of postmodernity might be approached' (1993: 72), his work probably offers few clues as to what that vocabulary might contain.[60] As Barry Smart suggests, 'it is arguable whether a postmodern *social* theory can be generated from within the analytic vortex Baudrillard fabricates. Indeed . . . it might be more appropriate to classify his oeuvre as anti-social theory' (1993: 51–2). Bauman, meanwhile, describes Baudrillard's work as being primarily about decomposition: of modernity as a project and, above all, as a 'way of life' (1993b: 42). That way of life tends to be described by Baudrillard himself in terms of a caricatured distinction between the modernity of Europe with its aristocratic traditions, and the postmodernity of America, which has already realized the ideals of justice and freedom to which those traditions continue to pay lip-service (Baudrillard, 1988a: 77).[61] Baudrillard, meanwhile, tends to disagree that his arguments should be categorized as postmodern at all. Others support him in this. While Kellner characterizes Baudrillard as 'perhaps the first to organize . . . a postmodern social theory' (1988: 242), Gane counters that 'far from embracing postmodernism, Baudrillard's whole effort is to combat it' (1991a: 51). In effect, this suggests that the significant distinction to be drawn from Baudrillard's work is between modern society on the one hand, and radical, not postmodern, society on the other.[62] So which is the more accurate of these alternative accounts of Baudrillard's work?

If Baudrillard's work is meant to radicalize the project of modernity, it might seem relatively easy to anticipate what this means for social theory. Like Lyotard, Baudrillard appears to conflate his own rejection of modern social theory with a broader dismissal of the idea of social theory itself. His analysis of hyperreality contains an announcement of the death of the social. For Baudrillard, this must signal the end of sociology, because it 'can only depict the expansion of the social and its vicissitudes' (1983a: 4). Subsequently, he describes his work as that of 'a metaphysician, perhaps a moralist, but certainly not a sociologist'. This is an explicitly negative position, characterized only by an 'effort to put an end to the social, to the concept of the social' (1993c: 106). In any case, even if one accepts that Baudrillard has a point about the difficulties of theorizing hyperreality using established sociological concepts – which, after all, rely on a logic of representation that he regards as untenable – it is doubtful for many critics whether his normative argument genuinely can be described as radical. His work on symbolic exchange, replete as it is with references to primitive rituals associated with death, suggests the kind of Romanticism we have already found in the work of the Frankfurt theorists.[63] But, above all, it is the argument on seduction which appears to carry overtones not of radicalism but of passivity and conservatism.

Baudrillard relies on a curiously feminized interpretation of seduction. In his view, seduction is trans-sexual. This explains its potency. Seduction is about 'the fragility of appearance' (1990c: 101) and therefore seems capable of undermining masculine power not necessarily because it represents feminine power but because, like symbolic exchange and death, it opposes power relations in general. Crucial to this seems to be the idea that seduction is more of a game than a strategy. Seduction involves a moment not only of defiance but of irony: it 'makes use of weakness, makes a game of it, with its own rules' (1988c: 162). But by Baudrillard's own reckoning, seduction is a fatal strategy.[64] A fatal strategy has no predefined goal other than to provoke, to push something to its farthest extremes. The outcome is necessarily uncertain, because once something has been taken so far and there is 'nothing more to say', the only result will be destabilization (1993c: 82).

The concept of the fatal strategy is used by Baudrillard not only to characterize the potency of seduction, silence and death. It defines his own potency as a theorist. He describes his approach to theory as concatenation, that is, 'union by chaining or linking together' (*OED*). This depends on using concepts loosely, and thereby refusing to claim their 'conceptual tenor' (1993c: 56). More importantly, this approach is sustained by the argument that theory has the right to be untrue and arbitrary *as long as* it is provocative and radical. This is crucial to our discussion here. For Baudrillard, theory is a provocation, a challenge to the objectivity of things. It consists not of some deep or underlying search for truth or reality, but of story-telling: a chain of interconnected concepts that, like the black hole created by our silence, inflects and distorts its object and thereby resists being itself turned into a mere subject. This approach is premised on a rejection of the quintessentially modern connection between theoretical truth and political emancipation. That connection is derived from the distinction between reality and the representation of reality, and from a commitment to what Baudrillard calls the language of liberation. In his estimation, neither the distinction nor that language is viable in the hyperreal world of simulacra.

It remains open to question, however, exactly what role the concept of a fatal strategy plays in relation to Baudrillard's conception of theory as a provocation, and to his prioritization of radicalism over truth. It is difficult to accept that the notion of a fatal strategy is *merely* an arbitrary provocation, just an attempt to unsettle, destabilize and distort. It is all of those things, of course. But it is certainly not arbitrary. Baudrillard presents it as the *only feasible means* of reversing hyperreality. There is a tight consistency here. The normative recommendation to resist through silence and to defy through seduction closely parallels Baudrillard's self-appointed role as a fatal strategist.[65] One justifies the other. And that justification relies on a theoretical account of the collapse of the real. Baudrillard's theoretical and normative arguments are closely interwoven.

Baudrillard therefore appears to produce a theoretical basis for the concept of the fatal strategy, and the radical commitment it engenders, without being able to argue for it explicitly. Because, by the force of his own reasoning, he cannot do so. There can be little doubting that the fatal strategy, as Baudrillard describes it, contains the ingredients of a normative project: namely, of reversing hyperreality and thereby refusing to become its subject. There is a clear suggestion here of liberation. Fatal strategies are premised on the idea that the system, as Baudrillard calls it, already has built-in spaces for conventional forms of political resistance.[66] Our only alternative is to resist in less conventional ways, that is, to practise intelligent subversion. We therefore cannot dismiss Baudrillard's argument on the basis that he recommends that we do nothing. The problem is not, as many critics allege, that Baudrillard advocates silence. It is that his position relies on exactly the connection between theoretical truth and normative argument which he purports to reject.

One might well object to Baudrillard's normative strategy for what it entails. But we should hardly be surprised by it. And we should certainly not seek to deny that he has one. As a project, it follows inevitably from, indeed it is implicitly supported by, the theoretical concept of hyperreality. For all his rhetoric, Baudrillard seems to be caught within the modern theoretical enterprise that he associates with theorists such as Marx. At the very least, his standpoint is that of the grand, albeit ironic, moralist of the postmodern society. To this extent, he presents us with a stark choice. If we accept his theoretical argument concerning the collapse of the real, we must reject his normative strategy. For that strategy relies on a relationship with the world which, according to the theory, has ceased to be viable. But if we opt for the strategy, we must repudiate the theory. For that theory claims that it is arbitrary; tells us that the language of liberation is dead; and instructs us merely to provoke. The normative strategy outlined by Baudrillard is not arbitrary but supported by a theoretical rationale; it revives the language of liberation; and it seeks to reverse, not provoke. Paradoxically, it is the very consistency of Baudrillard's approach which leads to this contradiction: to advocate a fatal strategy is not equivalent to, indeed it excludes, the actual pursuit of one. Little wonder that the critics cannot decide whether Baudrillard is a modernist, a postmodernist, or a radicalized reincarnation of both.

Baudrillard runs up against much the same difficulty as Lyotard, but from another direction. Both theorists envisage a society in which it is possible to make up or invent the rules of political dialogue or theoretical argument according to our own purposes at a particular point in time: in short, as we go along. Likewise, both question modern interpretations of the nature of the social bond: Lyotard, because there is no need for a singular, overarching fabric or lifeworld that binds us together (our own language games are enough); Baudrillard, because the concept of the social no longer makes sense in the hyperreal world (which presupposes only the existence of a mass with no boundaries and no shape). But just as Lyotard has to presuppose the existence of general political guarantees without defending them in an explicit way, Baudrillard must assume that, to all intents and purposes, the major struggles of liberation have already been won in postmodern countries like America. Lyotard's position rests on political assumptions that he is unable to defend. Baudrillard's argument relies on historical assertions which fall back on the very notion of historiography he goes to such lengths to reject, and which, moreover, form the basis of a normative strategy that contradicts the self-proclaimed arbitrariness of the theory from which they are derived.

The work of Lyotard and Baudrillard is postmodern in so far as both theorists explicitly reject key features of modern social theory. Neither offers much by way of an alternative. But neither, in any case, successfully escapes those features that he finds most problematic in modern theory. Lyotard suggests that the historical generalities and grand narratives of modern thought are no longer tenable. The argument is entirely normative: those narratives are untenable because they are culturally specific and therefore potentially terroristic. But the alternative, paralogism, relies on the kinds of guarantees that those selfsame narratives were meant to uphold. The real difference for Lyotard, it turns out, is that he is unwilling to argue for them.

Baudrillard also rejects the modern version of history. More fundamentally, he dismisses the idea of a sociology which seeks to represent society as it is, just as he rebuts the idea that there is an inherent theoretical connection between truth and radicalism. For Baudrillard, the modern approach to the social must be thrown out, along with its vocabulary of collective political action. We are now a mass that has been seduced, and must continue self-consciously to allow itself to be seduced, by the seamless web of signs put out by the media conglomerates. Yet that very seduction holds the key to any resistance we might put across. And this, it emerges, is Baudrillard's normative project for these times, a strategy which rises irresistibly out of his theoretical account of the essence of the hyperreal. The only difference between this (postmodern) project and the modern project is that he cannot label it *as* a project: any more than he can verify the theory which informs it. If a genuinely postmodern theory is arbitrary, groundless and untainted by talk of liberation, Baudrillard is a long way from providing one. This is not a question of whether he wants his work to be characterized as postmodern, but of how he himself describes its purpose. For it is overwhelmingly clear that Baudrillard seeks to defy the postmodern condition. The problem is that he does so by advocating a normative project couched in a language, and with a critical function, whose strictures he claims to have left behind.

Critics of postmodern social theory customarily complain that it is a negative project, designed to undermine the principles of modern social theory without offering a viable alternative. In this chapter, I have tried to approach the question from a different angle, because it seems to me that Lyotard and Baudrillard are *in no position* to suggest an alternative theoretical strategy. In their defence, one might argue that neither has sought to do this, at least not in a systematic way. But that would be to rely on a serious misreading of their work. It is one thing to challenge the normative assumptions and theoretical arguments that are associated with modern social thought. Without doubt, both Lyotard and Baudrillard mount such a challenge. But it is quite another matter to escape the arguments and assumptions of modern social theory. In this latter and crucial respect, neither theorist really succeeds. For a more systematic and sustained attempt to move forward, the discussion must turn to the work of Zygmunt Bauman and Richard Rorty.

7

Society under Suspicion:
Bauman and Rorty

In chapter 6, I suggested that the arguments of Lyotard and Baudrillard should be read as a challenge not only to modern social theory but to social theory *per se*. Bauman and Rorty also set out a systematic critique of modern social theory and philosophy.[1] But in Bauman's case especially, a more constructive conception of postmodern theory and the project associated with it is advanced. He argues that modern social theory is characterized by a missionary zeal for objective truth which is inseparable from the ideal of technological progress. In its place, he advocates an approach to social theory and sociology which offers alternative interpretations of reality rather than a final or objective account, which emphasizes human agency as against structure or social totality, and which accepts that history has no underlying logic. In similar vein, Rorty argues that attempts in philosophy to formulate a language that mirrors nature have become demonstrably untenable in a postmodern, or what he calls a post-philosophical, culture. He urges that we formulate an approach to philosophy which has an ironic stance towards its own truth-claims, develop a culture which recognizes that its own belief-system is merely one among several alternatives, and participate in a form of political debate which is based on empathy for others, not absolute conviction derived from first principles. Some of these arguments may sound familiar from chapter 6. But in the hands of Bauman and Rorty, they are accompanied by a more sustained attempt to formulate a normative theory which acknowledges the implications of their theoretical and philosophical arguments.

In the first section of the chapter, I shall examine what we can learn from Bauman and Rorty about the contours of postmodern society.

Bauman identifies this as a society of the tourist and vagabond. It is without roots, lacks historical trajectory, and above all, has no clear economic and political shape. Bauman argues that we need to develop distinctive sociological concepts and modes of explanation that will enable us to characterize postmodern society as more than simply the antithesis of the modern age. Rorty's view of postmodern society is implied, rather than spelled out, by observations which derive from his central philosophical thesis about the need to develop a post-philosophical culture. He argues that we inhabit an age in which, more clearly than ever, there is no grand project oriented to the advancement of society as a whole. His primary concern is that we develop a philosophical and political language, or vocabulary, which is appropriate to this condition. In short, we must dispense with binary oppositions, such as that between the rational and the irrational, or between the absolute and the relative, which support an erroneous belief in first principles. According to Rorty, if there is an outcome to the development of modern society, it consists not of a reasoning and scientific, but rather a poetic, culture.

In the second section of the chapter, I shall discuss the normative arguments entailed in Bauman's concept of postmodern ethics, and Rorty's notion of a post-philosophical culture. Both theorists advocate a political framework which embraces pluralism and does not seek to advance universal values, such as justice or equality, in abstract terms. Dismissing Baudrillard's concept of seduction as morally indifferent, Bauman argues that postmodern social theory must incorporate normative considerations from the outset. He outlines the basis for a postmodern conception of the relationship between ethics and morality which combines the absence of centralized authority with heightened autonomy for the individual. Rorty's normative framework also emphasizes pluralism and individualism. He argues that the balance between the public and private dimensions of contemporary society should be adjusted. While irony and self-questioning will always be confined to our own private space as individuals, we must take a more sceptical and pragmatic stance in any dialogue concerning public standards and ideals. This argument is exemplified by his distinction between movement politics and campaign politics.

In the third section of the chapter, I shall explore difficulties and inconsistencies which arise in the work of Bauman and Rorty. The discussion will be in two parts. In the first, I shall ask whether Rorty's normative argument is consistent with the philosophical principles that underwrite it. In the second part, I shall explore Bauman's conception of the way forward for postmodern social theory, and ask whether it presents a viable enterprise.

Pluralism and the Postmodern Condition

Of the two theorists discussed in this chapter, only Bauman is specifically concerned with the sociological analysis of postmodern society.
Initially, he does not suggest that there has been a break with the modern age, but maps out ways in which important features of modern
society have been exhausted. Modern society has reached its limits, and
it is our realization of this that defines the postmodern condition. That
realization, however, has helped to create a society which is altogether
distinctive, and which must therefore be addressed theoretically in its
own terms. Rorty identifies a crisis of representation in contemporary
culture and social thought which is crystallized by the failure of Western philosophy to fulfil its project of mirroring essential properties of
the world.

Limits of the modern, freedom of the postmodern

According to Bauman, postmodern society cannot merely be regarded
as a break with the past because we lack the historical perspective against
which such a break might be understood. Instead, we face a situation
in which 'our journey has no clear destination' (1991: 244).[2] Bauman is
much clearer than Lyotard and Baudrillard, however, in seeking to explain how this condition has arisen. An important component of his
explanation is the collapse of socialism in Eastern Europe. For Bauman,
the struggle between capitalism and socialism was integral to the narrative of modern society. Without this, we seem to be at a crossroads,
'with one road which contains both capitalism and socialism together,
married forever in their attachment to modernity, and another road
which is still hard to describe' (1992b: 222). But primarily, it is our realization of the limits of modern society that holds the key to the
postmodern condition. In the first instance, the postmodern condition
signifies a society which has become increasingly self-conscious. But
more than this, whereas modern society imposes limitations on human
agency, postmodern society promises liberation. This calls for a new
approach to social theory: a theoretical emancipation that breaks away
from the concepts of progress and universalism that are associated with
modern social theory.

Like Baudrillard, Bauman establishes a close connection between
postmodern culture and the information age. He agrees that postmodernism is a media-driven culture of excess. It is chaotic, fragmented
and fleeting. And it is a culture characterized above all by individual-

ism and pluralism. In postmodern society, the human world consists of many different sites of authority, with no clear hierarchy. As a consequence, we have lost access to supposedly objective accounts of the world. All we have left are our own individual interpretations. More broadly, the pre-eminence of Western culture has been superseded. If modern society was centred around the state, and on relations between states, postmodern society consists of fluid and fleeting forms of association: each defined by its own activity, language, interest and outlook. Modern society mistakenly saw itself as progressing towards the realization of universal reason, whereas in fact it merely 'gave birth to the multitude of uncoordinated and self-guided (local, parochial) rationalities which turned into the principal obstacle to universal rational order' (Bauman, 1995: 25). I shall be returning to this point later on, because it provides important clues as to how social theory might now move forward.

The process of fragmentation in postmodern society is closely associated with the privatization of life. According to Bauman, ideas of community and society have shifted in status: from a guarantee of mutual security, to an apparent burden and bane. The ideal of joining forces for the collective good is in terminal decline. This is a 'new strain of the electoral-apathy virus' (1995: 272). The malaise signals frustration no longer with a specific project or ideal, but with the very idea that we – as a society – should pursue any projects or ideals at all. In place of public debate over particular concerns, individuals merely push for an increasing number of rights which guarantee legal redress. But the outcome may well be a stultifying moral indifference.

In postmodern society, consumerism – much more than work – now provides the link between individual lifeworlds and society itself. The pursuit of profit has effectively been replaced by the pursuit of pleasure. But if anything, this has merely strengthened capitalism: instead of repression and control, the rhythm of the system is dictated by the pleasure principle.[3] The ideological hegemony of capitalism has therefore been superseded by a cultural heterogeneity. Variety, not uniformity, defines the logic of postmodern culture. This is a triumph for the market: not only as a mode of organization but as an idea: 'Cultural authorities turn themselves into market forces, become commodities, compete with other commodities, legitimize their value through the selling capacity they attain' (1992b: 52).[4]

Bauman nevertheless rejects the argument that the postmodern condition is characterized simply by a sense of decline. On the contrary, postmodern society is 'an aspect of a fully fledged, viable social system which has come to replace the "classical" modern, capitalist society'

(1992b: 52). It must therefore be theorized in its own terms and according to its own logic. The fragmentation of culture in postmodern society, and the dissipation of objectivity that characterizes the postmodern worldview, has far-reaching consequences for social theory. The concept of the social system is the first casualty. But this concept is especially difficult to replace because the aim of providing an objective account or model of society has been discredited. Instead of trying to analyse the postmodern condition, sociologists have tended merely to express core features of that condition through a form of mimesis, or mirroring, in their concepts and practices. Sociology has itself become pluralistic, fragmented and subjective, giving voice to a range of cultural perspectives. Although Bauman agrees that sociology must play a role in revealing, interpreting and embracing cultural pluralism, he does not accept that this rules out seeking a more unified approach to postmodern theory than has been formulated thus far.

Among the revisions of social theory suggested by Bauman, perhaps the most important is that we must dispense with the concept of society. In modern social theory, society tends to be characterized as a structured space which is unified, organized, and bounded by the nation-state. This approach has always generated difficulties when seeking to understand the space beyond and between nation-state societies. But in the contemporary age, this has ceased to be merely an irritant and has become a disabling theoretical flaw. According to Bauman, we no longer inhabit a world organized according to dominant cultures or economic systems, but live rather in a 'social space populated by relatively autonomous agents who are entangled in mutual dependencies and hence prompted to interact' (1992b: 61). In place of society, we must therefore conceptualize a non-societal space with no central authority, no core value system and no unitary organization.[5] The reality of the postmodern world is 'much more fluid, heterogeneous and "under-patterned" than anything the sociologists tried to grasp intellectually in the past' (1992b: 65). It is vital that social theorists present this not as an aberration from modern society, but as distinctive. It is a system, of sorts, in its own right. In the postmodern world, we no longer have recourse to modern social theory – not even as our antithesis.

Post-philosophical culture

Rorty's philosophy is similar to that of Bauman in so far as he too is concerned with the question of limits. But whereas Bauman writes of the limits of modern society *per se*, Rorty's argument focuses on limitations to what can be *known* about the world we inhabit. For Rorty, the problem for contemporary social thought is not so much that modern society has reached its limits, but that we have no means of knowing what those limits might be. There is no philosophical language in which we could know for certain that modern society, and modern culture more broadly, are at an especially high or low point on some imagined developmental trajectory. Likewise, there is no language in which to compare modern society and culture with non-Western alternatives, because, equally, there is no basis for deciding what the limits or advantages of such alternatives might be. Modern philosophy and social thought, much more than modern society itself, must acknowledge this. The language of historical breaks cannot be sustained.

Rorty's argument is rooted in a critique of philosophical foundationalism, and I shall discuss this here only in as much as it relates to the core themes of this book. In philosophy, foundationalism refers to the notion that our knowledge, or our beliefs, rest on indubitable foundations.[6] According to Rorty, this notion is expressed by the fact that, since Descartes, Western philosophy has focused around the aim of formulating a language which mirrors nature, that is, a language structured according to the world as it inherently is. For Rorty, the aim has always been misguided. It falsely supposes that the world has intrinsic properties. That supposition suggests that the world was created by a divine being 'who has something in mind, who Himself spoke some language in which He described his project' (1986a: 6). One way or another, we can never know this, any more than we might know the nature of truth or the nature of human beings. Even science has no privileged access to certainty. Despite its impressive range of applications, science is on no surer a footing than literature.

By carefully unpacking Rorty's argument, it should be possible to grasp the significance of what he is saying for philosophy, and relatedly, its implications for social theory. In very basic terms, Rorty contends that it is impossible ever to be certain that our descriptions of the world are accurate. On closer scrutiny, this assertion might actually mean a number of different things.[7] First, it could mean that we cannot think about the world independently of our descriptions of it. Second, and further, it might be taken to mean that the world is open to alternative forms of description, to different interpretations. But as Bernard Williams has claimed, Rorty seems to be taking a position which is more radical still, that is, that the real world does not present itself to us in a form that would enable us to *arbitrate* between alternative descriptions of it. In short, there is nothing beyond those descriptions against which their validity can be tested. All that can be said is that the descriptions we have are a product of time and place, 'formed through historically localized tradition' (Williams, 1990: 27). It is no less important, however, to grasp exactly what Rorty is *not* saying. Although he might seem to imply that there is no such thing as an independent reality, he does not in fact go quite this far: 'To say that we should drop the idea of truth as out there waiting to be discovered is not to say that we have discovered that, out there, there is no truth' (1989: 8).

As I have already said, Rorty's argument is significant for our understanding not only of philosophy but of science. He suggests that science possesses no overriding claim to truth: and by extension, that scientific progress cannot be understood in terms of the ever-increasing proximity of scientific theories to a true, accurate representation of the world. In this context, Rorty invokes the work of Thomas Kuhn, the philosopher of science.[8] Indeed, Rorty's remarks about scientific progress run into similar questions to those which have been raised about Kuhn's own work. Rorty characterizes the various branches of human knowledge, and the various human cultures, as vocabularies. Now, for paradigm in Kuhn's work, we might read vocabulary in that of Rorty. The concept of vocabulary is similar, also, to the notion of the language game which is used by Wittgenstein and, later, by Lyotard. For Rorty, a vocabulary serves as a framework through which particular statements or sentences[9] about the world – chunks of facts, as he calls them – make sense to us. He argues that truth 'is simply a compliment paid to sentences seen to be paying their way'.[10] Moreover, the various vocabularies we have used, and which are used in other cultures, are incommensurable. For example, we might try to compare 'the vocabulary of ancient Athenian politics [with] that of Jefferson', or 'the vocabulary of St Paul as against that of Freud', but 'it is difficult to think of the world as making one of these better than another, of the world as deciding between them' (1986a: 3). Crucially, Rorty suggests that thought cannot reach into a world beyond language: language – our vocabulary – is all that we have. We therefore should not seek to justify our beliefs on the basis of their correspondence with the natural world, or the world as it is. The only justification we should seek for our beliefs is that it is 'good for us' to hold them. From this, it follows that we should dispense with those beliefs only when something better – or more good for us – is available. In short, knowledge can be justified only on pragmatic grounds: it has no foundation beyond or beneath this.

Rorty's chief objection to the Western philosophical tradition concerns the pursuit of general rules about what constitutes true knowledge. As Charles Taylor notes, this was the 'bad practice' of developing 'some conception of what knowledge and validation *had to be*' (1990: 264, Taylor's emphasis). According to Rorty, there is no such thing as objective knowledge, but merely varying degrees to which beliefs are shared by others. This is not to suggest, either, that beliefs that are widely shared are in some sense more true or objective than those that are not. Rather, we should dispense with notions of truth – and above all any attempt to arrive at some theory of truth – altogether. Rorty's argument is not so much intended to imply that philosophical foundationalism is wrong as that it is futile: attempts to justify beliefs with reference to foundations in the real world will simply lead us back onto the terrain of language.

This brings the discussion back to one central question: can the world arbitrate between our linguistic descriptions of it? As Williams points out, Rorty is effectively advancing two basic propositions, one more controversial than the other. The first proposition concerns the question as to 'whether the success of science invites or permits any interesting description of what the success of science *consists of*' (1990: 29, Williams's emphasis). The second proposition concerns whether it is possible to deduce from the previous success of science 'any general methods to secure its future success' (ibid.). As Williams notes, the second question is basically a matter of rational procedure. It is the first which raises the more fundamental problem of the relationship between scientific theory and the world. And it is on this first point that Rorty's argument is significant, for he denies that this relationship is meaningful in the case of science, any more so than it is in respect of literature, poetry or the arts in general.

Now this might be taken as a blanket denial that there is any difference between fact and fiction.[11] But Rorty professes not to be a sceptic. Nor, by his own reckoning, is he a relativist.[12] According to him, he is a realist who is committed to theories – such as behaviourism, naturalism or physicalism – which 'help us to avoid the self-deception of thinking that we possess a deep, hidden, metaphysically significant nature which makes us "irreducibly" different from inkwells and atoms' (1980: 373). He therefore accepts that reality exists. And he acknowledges that one description of reality may be judged better than another. However, 'better' in this context cannot refer to some deep-seated sense of encapsulating an external truth, 'out there' in the world itself. Rather, 'better' – for Rorty– refers to our own specific purposes in a particular place and at a particular time. All we can reasonably think of where the world itself is concerned, he argues, is that it consists of 'reality-under-a-certain-description' (1980: 378). From the point of view of social theory, this assertion has far-reaching political and cultural implications, because ultimately, Rorty's arguments provide the basis for recommendations as to how best we might live our lives.

Rorty suggests that the one legitimate task of philosophy and social thought should be to interpret the world in as many ways as possible, not to strive for a singular, authoritative account. A culture without such an account is a culture without philosophy. In place of philosophy, we should turn to literature, which can provide us with thick descriptions of our own and other cultures. Such descriptions will enable us to empathize with others, but not to judge them: 'novels and ethnographies which sensitize one to the pain of those who do not speak our language must do the job which demonstrations of a common human nature were supposed to do' (1989: 94). If there is a 'crisis' in modern culture, it is precisely this: we have come to recognize that, after all, our systems of knowledge and our cultural artefacts have not followed a line of progression towards greater truth and perfection. They are arbitrary. Cultural pluralism is merely the symptom of this. On the other hand, pluralism represents a crisis only if we regard different belief systems as being in conflict, and turn to philosophical argument in search of a resolution. Philosophy should not seek to provide this because it cannot do so. Conceived in such a way, we no longer have any need for philosophy. All that we can do is learn to live in our post-philosophical culture.

Withdrawing from Society?

Bauman and Rorty agree that postmodern or post-philosophical culture is characterized by the absence of any authorized account of history, and by the erosion of dominant belief systems. Their normative arguments focus on the consequences of these developments. They suggest that it is at the level of human agency that the postmodern project must be framed. In line with this, they contend that morality is essentially a private matter. If the work of Lyotard and Baudrillard marks a retreat from reality, the arguments of Bauman and Rorty signal a withdrawal from society as a political and normative space.

Postmodern ethics and morality

Bauman argues that universal reason cannot provide the foundations of an emancipatory critique of contemporary society. Quite simply, we have ceased to be convinced by the authority of reason to legislate our moral affairs. The vacuum left must be filled by a sociology which offers alternative and competing interpretations of our historical condition.[13] Moreover, the postmodern environment is inhospitable to critique because it contains insurmountable obstacles to collective political action. This suggests a need to withdraw from public space, from state politics and from national society.

Bauman disagrees with the notion that the postmodern project hinges on maintaining and supporting plural lifeworlds, or communities. Indeed, he even denies the normative relevance of communities altogether. Unlike the nation-state, communities have no institutional support. Instead, they require 'shrill, high-pitched, vociferous and spectacular declarations of faith' (1995: 277).[14] It is up to individuals to take moral responsibility for themselves, not hide behind notional communities. In modern society, bureaucratic organizations bypassed the need for individual moral responsibility by adhering rigidly to instrumental reason: bureaucracy 'strangles or criminalizes moral impulses; business merely pushes them aside' (1995: 264). In postmodern society, the notion of community circumvents moral responsibility by differentiating between moral standards as applied to us and as applied to them, to those who belong and those who do not.

Nevertheless, Bauman is set against the idea that the fragmentation of culture and identity in postmodern society should merely be mirrored in its normative project. Although sociologists can no longer talk of a unified social system, or even of society in any coherent sense, this does not rule out developing a unified normative strategy in social theory. The key to establishing an ethics for the new age lies with the rediscovery of shared responsibility and collective well-being: not under the modern guise of universality or uniformity, however, but in a postmodern form which acknowledges the fragmentation of culture and enables us to 'reforge that polyphony into harmony and prevent it from degenerating into cacophony' (1995: 284). In order to achieve this, it is vital to understand that individual moral autonomy on the one hand, and collective ethical responsibility on the other – which, in modern society, tend to be translated as the tension between individual and state – do not contradict but presuppose each other. This need not mean adhering to generally applicable principles derived from universal reason. In their modern guise, such principles provide only an illusory certainty, excusing us from making difficult moral choices that may under certain circumstances contravene the principles themselves. In order to live with fragmentation, we must accept that uncertainty is not a temporary condition but a permanent fact of life. This requires the coalition, not separation, of public and private realms, or ethical and moral concerns. For neither is thinkable without the other.

Bauman's argument homes in on the relationship between private morality and public ethics. We must accept that human beings are morally ambivalent, that is, neither intrinsically good nor inherently bad. There is no publicly derived guarantee of human conduct, and to believe that there is can only result in 'more cruelty than humanity, and certainly less morality' (1993a: 11). Morality is also non-rational. Moral questions cannot be answered by recourse to universal reason, nor subjected to means–end calculation, because morality does not entail the sense of reciprocity that such a calculation would imply. Moral dilemmas therefore cannot be resolved by resorting to ethical principles. Moral impulses tend to be contradictory and uncertain: the outcome of moral actions is not always satisfactory. But while there are no universal foundations for morality, it cannot be reduced to local custom or tradition. We should therefore seek neither to impose an ethical code on personal morality from the outside – an approach Bauman associates with modernity – nor to embrace moral relativism. For morality can disrupt and undermine social order, while at the same time providing the 'raw material of sociality and of commitment to others in which all social orders are moulded' (1993a: 13). A theory of ethics should cultivate private morality, sustaining its vitality without allowing it a completely free rein. It must acknowledge that morality is a precondition of selfhood: 'I am moral *before* I think' (1993a: 61, Bauman's emphasis). In short, we do not have to surrender some aspect of our selves in order to become moral. Morality is a prerequisite, not an outcome, of empathy with others. To understand this is flatly to contradict the modern perspective which contrasts the natural to the social self.[15]

Bauman therefore reverses Durkheim's conception of society as a moral and constraining force: 'we live in society, we *are* society, thanks to being moral' (ibid.). He argues that the postmodern condition is marked by a suspicion towards the notion that the moral competence of individuals depends on the existence and well-being of society.[16] In all likelihood, it is even the reverse that is true. The moral competence of the individual derives from everything that the project of modernity has sought to eradicate through the application of universal reason: the passions, the emotions, non-rational thought, drives, sympathies and loyalties. Against this background, postmodernity must signal the re-enchantment of the world.

Bauman seeks to undermine the self-image of modern society as a rational and just world. As expressed through the project of modernity, this amounts merely to the 'practice of parochialism under the mask of promoting universal ethics' (1993a: 14). Postmodernity has always been a thorn in the side of modernity. But this does not mean that modernity should be superseded by a new parochialism, that is, a form of relativism. It is one thing to diagnose or identify a condition of moral relativization in postmodern society. It is quite another to support and express that condition in social theory.[17] Bauman therefore warns against 'the twin errors of representing the *topic* of investigation as an investigative *resource*, that which should be *explained* as that which *explains*' (1993a: 3, Bauman's emphasis). To express this in another way, social theorists must not lose sight of the distinction between 'what humans do' and 'what they think they are doing or how they narrate what they have done' (ibid.). But while he resists the association of postmodernity with relativism, Bauman does not seek, either, to replace the ethical code associated with modernity with an alternative, postmodern version. On the contrary, he suggests that ethics should no longer be given such pre-eminence. The relationship between morality and ethics, as it is conceived in modern philosophy and social theory, should be revised. This calls for a repersonalization of morality which entails 'returning moral responsibility from the finishing line (to which it was exiled) to the starting point (where it is at home) of the ethical process' (1993a: 34). By stark contrast, discursive procedures such as those outlined by Habermas merely bracket away moral impulses and emotions.

Bauman argues that in all human societies there are two basic logics of integration: socialization and sociality. These logics compete. Socialization perpetuates rules and identities. Sociality emphasizes uniqueness, not commonality. In modern society, socialization had primacy over sociality, regulating our freedom to choose between different identities by medicalizing or criminalizing anything marginal. In effect, morality was privatized. The postmodern project must seek to regenerate sociality: not in order to replace the logic of socialization, but so as to provide a proper counterweight to it. Socialization still holds the key to reproducing social structures without which daily life and history would be impossible. Yet it has its costs, stifling creativity and suffocating individual autonomy. These costs can be reduced by placing a much greater emphasis on sociality. The process has already begun with the decline of the state.

According to Bauman, the state has ceased to function as a viable totality. It is losing the capacity to remain economically solvent, to provide a full range of cultural and spiritual resources, and to defend its borders against military attack. The process of globalization is one important cause of this: national economic policies are increasingly prey to external forces, cultural influences now transcend state borders, and national armies are virtually incapable of acting alone effectively.[18] But more than this, nation-state governments are no longer able to service any obvious needs in the lives of their constituents. And in any case, we as individuals no longer have the stomach for a politically managed society. Bauman agrees with Michel Maffesoli, the French postmodern social theorist, that national cultures are being replaced by neo-tribes which consist of a much more spontaneous and ephemeral sense of community.[19] Global communications media are vital to the formation of neo-tribes. But they also account for their short life expectancy. Single media events take on global, albeit brief, significance. As such, they provide a focus for 'counter-structural collective sociality' (Bauman, 1993a: 142).

The emergence of neo-tribes is problematic, however, for personal morality. Whereas the modern process of socialization banishes moral autonomy to the private sphere, the counterstructural sociality of neo-tribes merely provides a channel for emotions that are properly the basis for moral action. Global communications media are cancelling out spatial distance, drawing individuals closer together across vast spaces. Forms of industrial technology expose us increasingly to the risks and consequences of processes and events that occur on the other side of the world. But this interconnectedness has not been matched in moral terms. Global media and technology have created a social proximity 'as measured by the reach of human action', while failing to achieve moral proximity as measured 'by the reach of moral responsibility' (1993a: 219). Bauman uses the concepts of the vagabond and the tourist to describe this condition. Both are unsure of their natural place while being more open to experiencing what is around them. Both are extraterritorial: the tourist by choice, the vagabond not. The vagabond is the alter ego of the tourist, the rubbish as opposed to the tourist filth (1997: 94). They are the two halves of postmodern society. Both move through others' spaces. In so far as they do so as strangers, tourists and vagabonds share no moral responsibility. But in postmodern culture, they are no longer confined to the margins of society. They have turned into 'moulds destined to engross and shape the totality of life' (1995: 242). Never has the need for moral autonomy been greater. Never has the opportunity to attain it seemed so remote.

Bauman's normative argument has an ambiguous relationship with the postmodern theories of Lyotard and Baudrillard. He disagrees that there is no place in postmodern sociology for moral debate. Sociology can and should address normative questions. But he seems to hold out no greater prospect than Lyotard and Baudrillard that such questions can be resolved by theory. To attempt to do so would be return to the outmoded modern belief that morality is a matter for something like a universal reason. But in so far as we are all now either tourists or vagabonds, Bauman appears to hold out little hope that the repersonalization of morality can be achieved. As a theorist, all he seems able to do is to express scepticism towards 'socially conventionalized and rationally "founded" norms', while insisting – but *merely* insisting – that 'it does matter, and *matter morally*, what we do and from what we desist' (1995: 250, Bauman's emphasis). If postmodern society seems to be a heartless world, Bauman stages a boldly emotive attack on its moral ramifications.

Rorty: politics beyond reason

Rorty's normative argument urges that we live with the consequences of post-philosophical culture. It hinges around the notion of contingency: as applied to language, the self, and community.[20] Rorty broadly agrees with Lyotard that our language games, or vocabularies, are incommensurable. But instead of seeking to set up a game or competition between different vocabularies, he argues that we should learn merely to think of our own vocabularies in a more ironic way.[21] To Rorty, irony is primarily a means of expressing doubt towards the truth-claims which are implicit in those vocabularies. In short, we must believe less vehemently in them. The more it is understood that normative vocabularies cannot be grounded in philosophy, the less likely it is that, in cases of conflict between cultures, there will appear to be some deeper reality or truth at stake.[22] After all, those who are 'always aware that the terms in which they describe themselves are subject to change, always aware of the contingency and fragility of their final vocabularies, and thus of their selves' should never be quite able to take themselves so seriously (1989: 73–4).

For Rorty, thick description in literature, not philosophical debate – however self-consciously playful – is the only way to deal with cultural pluralism. We should seek not uncertainty and paradox, but empathy. Reason cannot provide a philosophical foundation on which to justify normative principles.[23] According to Rorty, Habermas's claim that free and rational discussion will produce one right answer to moral questions rests on the untenable idea that there is a relation between the 'ahistorical essence of the human soul and moral truth' (1991a: 176). If there is such a thing as moral progress, it consists not of a gradual unveiling of universal rights and values through the use of reason, but of

a more practical, local and contingent form of solidarity within communities. It is not that a philosophical justification for consensus is un-
desirable. It is simply unattainable. There is no inherent connection
between communication, truth and moral progress. All we have available are incommensurable vocabularies. To move from one vocabulary
to another is not something we can decide according to universal reason.[24] Whatever Habermas might say, the better argument cannot be
established with any certainty through rational debate. We can only
establish which vocabulary is more attractive to us under given practical circumstances. This applies to philosophy as much as to any system of belief.

Rorty's argument hinges on the view that our vocabularies, belief
systems and values are contingent. They cannot be derived from universal philosophical criteria. Any philosophical argument that contains
themes such as moral progress or political advancement implies, even
if it does not explicitly advance, particular assumptions about human
nature. But questions about human nature or selfhood cannot be
answered by philosophy. For example, Habermas suggests that all
human beings possess an inherent capacity to participate in free, open
and rational debate, and above all, to accept the outcome of such debate. This is to presuppose that we are not self-interested: or more precisely, that a convergence of some common purpose might neatly
coincide with our private purposes.[25] According to Rorty, human nature has no inherent structure. Like language, it is contingent: 'The process of coming to know oneself, confronting one's contingency, tracking
one's causes home, is identical with the process of inventing a new language – that is, of thinking up some new metaphors' (1989: 27). We
therefore cannot move any closer towards an idealized model of a political community by trying to answer questions about ultimate human
needs or characteristics. The answers we do arrive at will merely reflect
our needs at a particular time. There is no central faculty, or self, which
can be deduced from or reduced to reason, and from which that community could be derived.[26]

Having argued that both language and selfhood are contingent, Rorty
applies this theme further to the notion of social solidarity. He agrees
with Habermas that free and open debate is desirable. He also agrees
that consensus, not disagreement, probably offers the best means of
holding a political community together. But he denies that this view
can be justified by philosophers, and above all by recourse to the concept of universal reason. As he says of his debate with Habermas: 'Our
differences concern *only* the self-image which a democratic society
should have and the rhetoric which it should use to express its hopes'

(1989: 67, Rorty's emphasis). According to Rorty, political consensus is relative to a particular belief system and therefore cannot transcend culture in the way Habermas envisages. The notion that the political views of different cultures will eventually converge – which is what universalism amounts to – is untenable once the contingent status of our vocabularies is understood. Cultural pluralism is inevitable, and can be accommodated only by greater levels of empathy.

Rorty's normative argument can be defined as liberal pragmatism. It rests on a particular view of the social bond. For Rorty, a political community cannot be strengthened merely by claiming that its beliefs are grounded in reason. It is enough to know that people agree that particular beliefs and values are attractive under given circumstances and at a given point in time: 'What binds societies together are common vocabularies and common hopes' (1989: 86). In broad terms, this argument – like that of Bauman – demands a recasting of the relationship of public and private life. Rorty states that, in the ideal liberal society, 'the intellectuals would still be ironists, although the nonintellectuals would not' (1989: 87). The rest of us would adopt a dual stance which he describes as 'commonsensically' nominalist and historicist, especially where our final vocabularies are concerned, because 'I cannot imagine a culture which socialized its youth in such a way as to make them continually dubious about their own process of socialization' (ibid.). Nominalism entails acknowledging that our vocabulary is merely a collection of words. That vocabulary may appeal to us, but it does not follow that it represents a deeper truth or hidden reality. Historicism refers to the ability to think of ourselves, and our ideas, as contingent. This does not mean that we should abandon our beliefs, but that we take them less seriously, particularly in relation to the (different) beliefs of others.

So what of the intellectuals? According to Rorty, philosophy 'has become more important for the pursuit of private perfection rather than for any social task' (1989: 94). In other words, irony is a private matter. And only a society in which we are free, privately, to express doubts towards our final vocabularies should be regarded as genuinely liberal. The thick descriptions of other cultures provided by literature can sensitize us to alternative perspectives. But we need go no further than that in seeking out some unattainable rational consensus. Where Habermas writes of rational argumentation over normative principles, Rorty envisages a literary conversation about alternative points of view. Habermas contends that the goal of rational discourse should be universal consensus. Rorty counters that the aim of literary conversation should merely be to increase our awareness of and empathy towards other perspectives. But the argument is couched in pragmatic rather than analytical terms. As Rorty concedes: 'I am going to try to make the vocabulary I favour look attractive by showing how it may be used to describe a variety of topics' (1989: 8–9).

The practical ramifications of Rorty's vision of political discussion in a liberal society are spelled out further in *Achieving our Country*. Here, Rorty is explicitly critical of the 'tenured radicals' of the European Left, whom he dismisses for the futile exercise of seeking political advancement through what he calls high theory.[27] In place of this, he advocates engaging in the 'civic work' of building, or achieving, a greater sense of nationhood. For Rorty, the greatest danger of globalization is in creating a 'cosmopolitan upper class' which has no greater sense of community with workers than the early twentieth-century capitalists had with their own immigrant workers. The nub of the argument, however, is expressed by a shift which Rorty identifies in American political association: from movement politics to campaign politics.[28] To be a member of a movement requires some sense that there is a broader objective, such as moral progress or social advancement, that invariably outreaches and outlasts more immediate and practical questions. Implicitly, this is to believe in a narrative of perfection, rationalization and historical teleology. But it is also to make 'the best the enemy of the better'. Rorty objects to the totalizing approach to change which this implies, for it assumes that 'things must be changed utterly, so that a new kind of beauty may be born.' The rise of campaign politics is undermining that belief. Campaigns are rooted in the particular. They are oriented to improving a specific situation in a feasible way. Campaigns are uninhibited by the need to place practical questions in broader perspective. Campaign politics is a politics of the fragmentary. It emphasizes difference, not uniformity. And it is the quintessence of liberal pragmatism.

Critical Discussion

There is a degree of consistency between the normative arguments of Bauman and Rorty. They seem to agree that morality cannot be grounded in philosophy or social theory. They also agree that the concept of universal reason cannot provide fail-safe answers to ethical questions. And they concur that we should place greater trust in a private sense of morality. Yet neither appears to be particularly at ease with the relativization of values and beliefs which is associated with the postmodern condition. Rorty explicitly denies that his position is relativist: he merely refuses to advance his vocabulary for any other reason than that it is attractive. Bauman explicitly (and vehemently) opposes relativism: but he neither denies that the process of relativization has been underway in society, nor suggests that relativism can be countered by any theoretical argument. In both cases, then, normative arguments seem to have been advanced as a question of private morality more than anything else. In this critical discussion, I shall ask whether this is enough.

Dangers of pragmatism

Rorty's normative argument is based on the notion that humans are capable of redescribing themselves in any number of ways according to whatever vocabularies are available to them. Where moral judgements are concerned, he describes the self as a 'network that is constantly reweaving itself'. This reweaving takes place 'in the hit-and-miss way in which cells readjust themselves to meet the pressure of the environment' (1983: 585). Society cannot and should not impose rules on that process. It is for this reason that Rorty prefers the notion of politics as literary conversation, rather than Habermas's argument that political discussion should proceed according to fairly strict rules of engagement.

Rorty's characterization of post-philosophical culture is deliberately formless.[29] But it raises the question as to whether a literary conversation as loose and unstructured as he envisages really can provide an adequate means of sustaining liberal democracy. Merely to encourage us to share different cultural perspectives may not be enough to guarantee that cultural differences can be embraced without initiating a struggle for power: precisely the kind of struggle that Rorty is anxious to avoid.[30] Indeed, he seems to be caught in a vicious circle. For even a literary conversation requires some shape, some set of rules, in order to amount to anything more than a chaotic free-for-all which is more likely to generate, not eradicate, the struggle for dominance among different cultural perspectives.[31] But to envisage such rules would be to undermine Rorty's central point, that is, that the moral point of view derives from nothing more than individuals describing and redescribing themselves according to a language which they find useful or advantageous under given circumstances.[32] The assertion that political communities are contingent seems to be merely that: an assertion, not an argument supported by any kind of social theory. But in any case, he cannot support the assertion theoretically in so far as to do so would be to replicate the modern approach to philosophy from which he seeks to escape.

This, then, is a self-imposed trap. As Charles Taylor notes, Rorty seeks to 'jettison the old epistemological view without espousing another one' (1990: 273). In effect, he moves from suggesting that political and cultural intolerance tends to be underpinned by philosophical disagreement, to a wholesale rejection of philosophy itself. But this leaves the argument in mid flight. To accept it could only ever be an act of faith.

There are not only serious doubts concerning whether Rorty's normative arguments can lead to the kind of political community he envisages; one might also question the goal of liberal pragmatism itself. Nancy Fraser suggests that Rorty's approach hinges on a combination of romanticism and pragmatism. Romanticism implies an image of the creative genius who is the 'source of all significant historical change'. Pragmatism, on the other hand, conjures up the image of 'technical competence and public-spiritedness' (Fraser, 1990: 304). In Fraser's view, Rorty confines each stance, respectively, to the private and public domain in seeking to combine cultural innovation and social justice. But in doing so, he outlines a political community in which solidarity can only be achieved by excluding internal opposition altogether.[33] In short, Rorty's political community consists of hearing, but not necessarily of listening to and engaging with, alternative points of view. He describes this as 'continuing the conversation of the West' (1980: 394). One might also describe it as a potentially restrictive, anti-liberal approach which inhibits those, such as women and ethnic minorities, who may regard themselves as excluded from public discussion from the outset. Rorty's response to such criticisms is suggestive.[34] Given that a literary conversation has no clear form but is – by definition – free of conflict, the only solution to this difficulty would seem to be a form of separatism. According to Rorty, minority conversations might be accommodated by clustering them together in separate enclaves that each guarantee freedom of expression.[35] But again he seems caught up in the logic of his own argument. As a form of liberalism, this seems curiously ghettoized.

The notion of campaign politics compounds these difficulties. Whereas political campaigns may in some instances appear to be partial, self-interested and even myopic, Rorty regards them – by definition – as essentially practical and realistic. But is a political system consisting only of campaigns, not movements, necessarily liberal? Or might it lead to social exclusion? Significantly, the argument for campaigns in place of movements has gained support from Bauman. He acknowledges that the concept of campaign politics might appear to have been tailor-made for a contented majority, and might therefore exacerbate rather than reduce existing levels of social exclusion. After all, campaigns need resources and thrive on timely alliances. But according to Bauman, Rorty is fundamentally correct in his argument that movement politics is invariably based on assumptions about the moral and ethical development of society which turn out, through experience, to be either invalid or unattainable: 'For all we know today, history does not seem to run towards "just society", and all attempts to force it to run in this direction tend to add new injustices to the ones they are bent on repairing' (Bauman, 1997: 68).

Bauman's defence of the distinction between movement politics and campaign politics is consistent with his own theoretical argument that society requires both socialization and sociality in order to sustain its historical life while nourishing individual creativity and moral autonomy. The problem, however, is that it is not consistent with the theoretical position outlined by Rorty himself. As I suggested earlier on in this discussion, Rorty seems to deny that anything *other* than sociality is required in order to maintain the historical life of society. According to this view, our communities are as contingent as our vocabularies, and as empty of content and regularity as his concept of the constantly rewoven self. (Which, incidentally, seems to lack the moral fibre which nourishes and sustains Bauman's conception of the self.) Rorty's advocacy of campaign politics instead of movement politics merely replicates the flaw which Bauman correctly identifies in the latter. The concept of campaign politics rests on a theoretical understanding of solidarity which – *for all we know* – may not turn out to be true. It is not difficult at all to establish that the idealized models of society which tend to be proposed in modern social thought have not been realized. It may even be possible to say that they never will be. But to leap from this conclusion to the assertion that the political community we have is contingent, and requires no protection whatsoever from society or ethical principles, requires no less than a theoretical account of how social solidarity is achieved and reproduced over time. Unlike Bauman, Rorty does not even come close to providing such an account. Once again, all we have to go on is faith.

Postmodern theory?

Both Rorty and Bauman express a deep suspicion towards society as a moral force. But they have rather different reasons for doing so. In Rorty's case, liberal pragmatism means working with whatever tools and resources, whatever words and concepts we have to hand. This stems from an acceptance that liberal-democratic society has largely coincided with, although can by no means guarantee, the peaceful

coexistence of cultures. It is merely that there is no deep or hidden structure within society that can explain this. For Bauman, the postmodern
condition marks a loss of faith in the ideal of society which is rooted in
the phenomenon of genocide: the mass destruction of one culture or
race by another. The modern era was 'founded on genocide, and has
proceeded through more genocide' (1993a: 227). Bauman rejects the idea
that the public always has primacy over the private, and ethics over
morality. But this raises difficulties for the relationship between theoretical and normative arguments in his work.

According to Bauman, modern social theory tends to support an
idealization of society which confuses social integration with social control. In practice, there will always be a risk that such an idealized model
of society lends itself all too readily to a political regime which excludes,
oppresses or even murders those who do not fit in. The connection
between the concept of society and the function of social control is derived from universal reason. Taken to an extreme, it was responsible
for the holocaust.[36] Genocide is not a barbaric and irrational departure
from the civilizing tendencies of modernity and the advance of reason.
It is a logical extension of that advance: an expression of tendencies not
towards higher levels of civility but towards a greater degree of social
control. Modern sociology – and its master concept, national society –
have unwittingly served that end. They were 'brought into being by
the encounter between the awesome task of management of social processes on a grand, societal scale and the ambitions of the modern state,
made to the measure of such a task' (1992b: 76). What, then, should
replace modern social theory?

For Bauman, modern social theory consists of concepts (such as society, totality and system) and metaphors (such as progress) that are inappropriate to the postmodern condition. He cites empirical features of
that condition as evidence for this. For example, the blurring of boundaries between nation-states has meant that what goes on in the space
between societies is as important as what happens within society. But as
I argued in chapter 1, the totalistic notion of society is not merely a topic
of investigation in modern social theory but is integral to its modes of
explanation, that is, to the causal relationships identified in connection
with specific social phenomena (such as class conflict in Marx's work, or
individualism as characterized by Durkheim) and, more broadly, with
the dynamics of social change. As Bauman suggests, it is the supposed
regularity and patterned character of social interaction in modern society which has supplied 'the semantic field for sociological concepts'
(1992b: 62–3). The first requirement of postmodern social theory must
therefore be to develop an entirely new semantic field.

As Bauman observes, postmodern sociology has thus far sought merely to imitate or reflect the postmodern condition. Instead of representing or modelling that condition, postmodern sociology consists of mimesis. Cast in such terms, social theory cannot explain, but can only signify the postmodern condition. Postmodern sociology codifies postmodern society 'through the isomorphism of its own structure' (1992b: 41–2). In other words, a fragmented theory has been used to interpret a fragmented society. The use of mimesis in social theory is consistent with the crisis of representation in postmodern aesthetics, and with the pluralism of values that characterizes postmodern culture in general. But for sociological purposes, it is unhelpful and unconstructive. Bauman is aware of the lack of clarity in postmodern social theory towards important analytical questions. He agrees that postmodern sociology lacks a theoretical core, that it merely offers multiple and competing interpretations of a given state of affairs rather than trying to explain how it has come about.

At this stage in the discussion, it is worth reiterating the distinction between relativization and relativism. Relativization can be defined as 'the action of making relative; the fact or process of being made relative' (*OED*). Relativism refers to 'a name given to theories or doctrines that truth, morality, etc. are relative to situations and are not absolute' (*OED*). In the context of postmodern theory, Bauman argues, these concepts must not be confused. Relativization is a process that can be understood theoretically, that is, its causes examined and explained. By contrast, relativism is a normative stance which suggests that various beliefs about the world, and about social and political arrangements within it, cannot be evaluated according to objective or rational criteria.[37] Crucially, relativization and relativism do not necessarily presuppose each other.

Bauman agrees that the objective of sociology in postmodern society should be to relativize existing interpretations of reality. By its very nature, sociological knowledge must be ephemeral, for the discipline is a 'transient activity' which is 'always engaged with current, topical issues' (1992b: 216). But expressed in these terms, it remains doubtful that postmodern theory is possible at all. Bauman nevertheless insists that the postmodern condition should not be viewed merely as a variant of or deviation from modern society – as if it were a distortion of all the basic principles of the normal state of society *per se* – but as altogether distinctive. In short, postmodern society should be modelled in its own specific way. Thus for society, read sociality; for patterned interaction, read Brownian motion; and for totality, read 'a series of randomly emerging, shifting and evanescent islands of order' (Bauman, 1992b: 189–91).

According to this view, there is one key feature of modern social theory that its postmodern successor retains: namely, the idea that a theory in some way represents, or models, social reality. To repeat, the reality to be modelled is merely 'more fluid, heterogeneous and "underpatterned" than anything the sociologists tried to grasp intellectually in the past' (1992b: 65). This solution is closely linked to Bauman's proposal to resolve the relativist dilemma thrown up by the postmodern condition. For this, he draws on a distinction between two forms of reason, legislative and interpretative. The concept of legislative reason is derived from Kant, and suggests that universal rational principles should form the basis of a tribunal which seeks to make a judgement between competing points of view. In its wake, modern sociology – particularly in the hands of Durkheim – has been set up as a critique of common sense in order to design a foolproof model of society which can eradicate social conflict. The notion of interpretative reason stems from Dilthey, and finds its 'most radical, uncompromising expression in the work of Richard Rorty' (Bauman, 1992b: 126). According to Bauman, the role of interpretative reason consists of mediation, not judgement. It enables us to regard pluralism not as 'a regrettable yet temporary and in principle rectifiable inconvenience' but as 'the constitutive feature of being as such' (1992b: 132). In short, interpretative reason is compatible with pluralism. It can help us to accommodate other perspectives alongside our own, and therefore to abandon our dangerous desire to iron out cultural differences.

To suggest that reason can mediate between different perspectives implies that reason is distinct from culture. Yet, as Bauman argues, reason is itself pluralistic, contextual and contingent. If the postmodern condition signifies anything at all, it is the realization that human reasoning does not assume an identical form within or between different cultures and practices. Bauman's argument suggests that reason is part of, not separate from these cultures and practices. It is no less multifaceted than the perspectives which, according to Bauman, interpretative reason is designed to mediate. If he is correct when he argues that modern social theory has been unable to accommodate 'parochial rationalities', it follows that reason itself must be regarded as a source and vital component of pluralism, not as something beyond or above pluralism which can be held up and sustained in order to mediate it.

It therefore seems doubtful that the concept of interpretive reason could fulfil the mediating role envisaged by Bauman unless the argument lapses into a form of ethnocentrism by default. The theoretical consequences of this would be harsh. If human reasoning genuinely is pluralistic, this should be a topic of investigation for sociology, not an organizing framework for our social theories. The problem is not whether, but *how*, that topic should be approached. Unless the theoretical model to which Bauman refers is much less general and ambitious than its modern counterpart, it is difficult to imagine how it can provide the focus for the reflexive, transient sociology he envisages. For example, it is unclear how such a model might be evaluated, that is, against which (or against whose) version of reality, and according to what criteria. This suggests that we do not require alternative, postmodern theoretical models. Rather, it implies that we should abandon the notion of modelling society altogether.

Despite his suspicions towards the concept of society and public ethics, Bauman appears to be wedded to the notion that sociology has an overarching role to play in sustaining, if not exactly guaranteeing, the pluralism which characterizes postmodern culture. He is held to this notion by a concept of interpretive reason which is intended to straddle different perspectives. He is critical of the association between universal, legislating reason on the one hand, and an overly managerial and oppressive societal regime on the other. This leads him to reject the modern understanding of sociology. There is much to learn from his analysis. If it is argued that the belief in the possibility of reaching universal agreement about core values is untenable, that universal reason no longer provides sufficient guidelines for understanding the development of society in a general way, and that we live in an increasingly fragmented, global society in which different value systems are alleged to have equal validity – it probably follows that to theorize such conditions in a general way is no longer feasible. It is for this reason that, as I said in the introduction to this book, the debate between modernity and postmodernity expresses a basic division over the nature and aims – indeed the possibility – of social theory itself, much more than it represents competing versions of social reality.

The postmodern reaction to modern social theory, even in the hands of Bauman, appears to be confused. As I have argued in the last two chapters, in postmodern – no less than modern – social theory, a grand conception of the range and scope of social theory itself seems to have been conflated with its subject-matter, namely, modern or postmodern society. Some postmodernists are well aware of this. They are even inclined to celebrate it. Bauman seeks to avoid it. But while he is justifiably critical of the universalism of modern social theories on normative grounds, he might well be mistaken in leaping from this criticism to a full-scale rejection of the explanatory aims of modern social theory. As I have argued in earlier chapters, it is not so much the mission to explain, but rather the explanatory *range* to which modern social theory aspires which has been a source of profound difficulty when seeking to apply its concepts and categories to the world around us. Perhaps these explanatory aims can be isolated, untethered from the more grand but less sustainable aim of providing a self-contained normative project. If social theory is seen as a tool of research, universalism may well be an acceptable and feasible aim in as much as it means that our concepts are sufficiently precise to lend themselves to comparative research. But if this is a goal that the modernists fail to realize, it is one that the postmodernists hardly even begin to pursue. For such a broader-based approach, which claims not only to have moved the focus away from national society but from social theory as a self-contained normative project, we must examine the arguments of Anthony Giddens and Ulrich Beck.

8

Modernity Renewed: Giddens and Beck

Giddens and Beck acknowledge that modern society has reached its limits. But in their view, the project of modernity has not imploded; it has been radicalized and renewed. Far from being confronted by the exhaustion of modernization, we are in the midst of its second wave. This account therefore differs in important ways from the analysis of both modern and postmodern society. Against the postmodernists, Giddens and Beck reject the theme of de-differentiation in favour of the concept of globalization. Against the modernists, they employ a concept of reason that emphasizes its role not as a driving force behind increasing certainty in our relationship to the world, but as a source of methodical doubt. Yet they repudiate what they see as the relativism of postmodern social theory so as to advocate a global framework for politics. This argument is advanced largely on pragmatic grounds, as the only means we have to address questions and problems which are indisputably global in scope. Giddens and Beck therefore retain the universalism of the modern project. But they do so for empirical, not theoretical, reasons.[1]

Giddens and Beck define the renewal of modernity as reflexive modernization, and I shall discuss this concept in the first section of this chapter. For both theorists, contemporary society is distinguished by an ever-closer, politically malleable relationship between global and local forces. They accept that the project of modernity has not been fulfilled, but advance a different interpretation of the implications of this for contemporary society and social theory. According to their view, reason has spun off from its original anchorage in certainty to be institutionalized in a reflexive form. This has generated an unrelenting process of accelerated change in society, with unforeseen side-effects.

In the second section of the chapter, the discussion will move on to the normative arguments advanced by Giddens and Beck. They flatly reject the idea that contemporary Western society is characterized by a widespread sense of political inertia. On the contrary, we are confronted by compelling opportunities for reinventing politics: not only for society but for self-identity. Both theorists urge that we move beyond classical modern political dichotomies – such as left versus right, and state intervention versus market freedom – without descending into the morass of relativism and neoconservatism which, they allege, characterizes postmodern thought.

In the critical discussion, two themes will be explored. Both are crucial to the way in which Giddens and Beck seek to distance themselves not only from postmodernity but also from classical modernity. The first concerns their interpretation of the concept of reason and its relationship to the modern project. The second concerns the project of reflexive modernity, particularly its relationship to sociology. Both theorists help to clarify important questions which have been raised so far in this book, particularly the difficulties posed by the relationship between theoretical and normative arguments in modern and postmodern social theory. I shall examine the way in which they seek to resolve these difficulties.

Reflexive Modernization, or the Two Modernities

The concept of reflexive modernization revolves around two themes. The first is the concept of reflexivity. In the writing of Giddens, the concept derives from his earlier work on structuration theory, and is used later on to explain the institutional logic of contemporary society. Beck provides a slightly different interpretation of reflexivity, and this will have an important bearing on the critical discussion later on. But they are in agreement over the basic premise that reflexivity has been institutionalized in contemporary society, transforming not only its structure but individual self-identity. This transformation is examined in terms of a second theme: risk. Giddens and Beck argue that we live in a risk culture which has radical implications in all areas of society: above all, for our personal relationships and political and economic institutions.

Reflexivity

Reflexivity is defined by Giddens as 'the monitored character of the ongoing flow of social life' (1984: 3).[2] The concept refers to the way in which we monitor social action as participants, therefore making a difference to – or what he calls constitutively altering – its character in a dynamic and ongoing way. The theory of structuration is developed in order to explore the relationship between social structure and human agency. This is sometimes referred to as the dilemma between objectivism and subjectivism in sociology.[3] Giddens now describes structuration theory as a methodological precursor to his work on reflexive modernization. The discussion here will focus initially on that connection, before moving on to some differences in Beck's interpretation of the concept of reflexivity.

The idea of structuration refers to the way in which social relations take on a structural, or patterned, character over time. Giddens sets out from the idea that sociological explanation must interpret social action in a way which takes account of the agent's point of view. For this reason, the concept of structure must be characterized in a way that includes social practices, not just institutions. He therefore rejects the rather static understanding of structure as being like the girders of a building. Social systems are dynamic, that is, they consist of the reproduction of social practices over time. It is the process of reproduction, not the fact that society is somehow external to agents, which gives those practices a structured or patterned appearance.

The key to Giddens's explanation of this is provided by the concept of rules. We are all familiar with the notion that the relationship between society and the individual is mediated by norms. According to Giddens, this idea is problematic because it implies that norms, and therefore the social system, merely constrain us or push us to act in particular ways. But the systemic properties of society should also be regarded as enabling, that is, as resources we can draw on in order to see certain actions and social practices through. Giddens defines these resources as rules. In a similar way to the concept of the lifeworld, rules basically consist of the stock of knowledge we need to enter into social interaction, and to respond to various social circumstances. Rules, not norms, make up the systemic properties of society. The concept of reflexivity is important to this argument because the use of rules as resources enables individuals to monitor, and thereby reproduce over time, patterns of social action. In this way, the structural properties of society are not consequences of social relations. They are the medium by which those relations are possible. In a very basic way, if rules consist of knowledge, the idea of reflexivity describes the way in which, by drawing on that knowledge, we also reproduce it. According to Giddens, society constrains the individual only in so far as there are gaps in our knowledge, for these gaps may give rise to social action which has unintended consequences.[4]

While Giddens maintains that his argument in the theory of structuration addresses ontological questions – that is, it seeks to rework 'conceptions of human being and human doing, social reproduction and social transformation' (1984: xx) – the approach also has important ramifications for understanding the nature of social change and political transformation. He suggests that all social action, in so far as it entails reflexive monitoring, is potentially transformative. In his analysis of power, for example, there are echoes of Foucault when he argues that there is no logical connection between power and conflict, or between power and inequality. In other words, power is not inherently oppressive. Of course, the exercise of power may in some instances have constraining properties, but fundamentally it is a medium of human agency, not an obstacle to it.[5]

The relationship between power and the structural properties of society is characterized by Giddens in terms of structures of domination. These rely on two kinds of resources, allocative and authoritative. Allocative resources are material resources such as the natural environment. Authoritative resources are non-material, such as the hierarchy within an organization. This distinction approximately corresponds to Marx's distinction between the infrastructure and the superstructure, but Giddens rejects the notion that one kind has priority over the other, for authoritative resources are 'every bit as "infrastructural" as allocative resources are' (1984: 258). Both kinds of resource are not fixed but expandable. The transformative potential of social action lies with our ability to garner these resources. Giddens therefore portrays society as having, in principle at least, a greater level of plasticity than either Marx and Durkheim would suggest. He rejects the notion that history has an underlying logic that can be deduced theoretically. Above all, his approach emphasizes the importance of conceptualizing power relations from below in terms of human agency and patterned social practices, not from above in the guise of large-scale structures and institutions.

The concept of reflexivity is developed further in Giddens's analysis of contemporary society. From the outset, he rejects the idea that there has simply been a break with modern society. The major transformations associated with the development of modern society are still working themselves through, but in such a way as to 'radicalize and globalize pre-established institutional traits of modernity' (1991: 2).[6] This analysis draws extensively on the arguments of both Marx and Weber.[7] Giddens contends that modern society has four main institutional dimensions: capitalism, industrialism, state administration and military power. In Europe, during the earliest stages of the development of modern society, these institutional dimensions were closely interrelated. None of them should be identified as singularly, or even primarily, responsible for the development of modern society.[8]

The idea of reflexive modernization addresses the relationship between modern society and its radicalized counterpart. According to Giddens, there has been an increased separation of time and space, that is, greater levels of interaction between processes and events occurring far away from each other, or what he calls action at distance. That distancing of time and space has been spurred on by disembedding mechanisms which enable social relations to be lifted out of particular settings. These mechanisms include symbolic tokens such as money, and expert systems which operate independently of the experts who created them. As a consequence, reflexivity has been institutionalized. That is to say, the process of reflexive monitoring has become the defining organizational feature of institutions right across contemporary society. As a result, our institutions – and even our self-identity – have become subject to a ceaseless process of change.[9] From the subjective point of view, this is profoundly unsettling. Reflexive modernization resembles a runaway juggernaut, always threatening to veer out of control. It is the principle of reflexivity, and the constant monitoring it implies, that generate this sense of uncertainty.

Building on this analysis, Beck characterizes contemporary society as a second wave of modernization, or the 'rationalization of rationalization' (1995a: 134). The first wave consisted of industrialization. But industrialism has been subject to the same ruthless demystification that it had previously unleashed on the premodern world.[10] The second, reflexive process of rationalization is more self-conscious, radical and extensive than the first.[11] We no longer live in a society of industrial production but in one of industrial consequences: the latter is the 'oversized and negative mirror image' of the former (1995a: 139).[12] Beck agrees with the analysis of postmodern society only to the extent that industrial society is in decline. But industrialism has not merely been replaced by the clean technology of microelectronics and an expanded service sector. Its decline has occurred in a way the classical modernists could never have imagined, 'via the back stairs of side-effects' (1992a: 11): without planning, and without revolution.[13]

Although Giddens and Beck place the concept of reflexivity at the heart of their analysis of contemporary society, they do so in slightly different ways. For Giddens, reflexivity consists of the appropriation and reproduction of knowledge in everyday social practice.[14] Knowledge is therefore a resource for social action, while also changing its character.[15] For Beck, reflexivity consists of gaps in our knowledge, which he calls unawareness. Unawareness is not, however, merely a question of what we do not know, but of our *inability* to know: 'This is not the expression of selective standpoints, of momentary forgetting or of underdeveloped expertise, but precisely the product of highly developed expert rationality' (1998: 94). In this sense, unawareness is an unintended consequence of the first wave of modernization. Beck argues that the side-effects of industrialism – pollution, genetic engineering, new social movements – have propelled us into a conflict of knowledge where the competing claims of experts run up against our own local knowledge and experience. The conflict is not merely about what we know, but how. In short, it is a conflict of rationalities.

Giddens and Beck agree that modern society has reached a point where established parameters for analysing social change should be revised in a radical way. In so far as reflexivity has been institutionalized, every dimension of contemporary society has been placed under unrelenting and intensely critical scrutiny by its own members. But this is not the well-ordered and teleological process of critical self-reflection envisaged by Habermas. It is an experimental society. For Giddens, history 'has no teleology' (1990: 154). For Beck, we have been placed unwittingly in the position of having to make decisions for ourselves rather than rely on politicians, experts or underlying forces to make them for us. The future is unprecedently open-ended: it is 'our aporia and our project'. As a result, 'social analysis must start afresh from its foundations, and on its methods of diagnosing the age' (Beck, 1995b: 5). That analysis must begin with the phenomenon of risk.

Risk

According to Giddens, the disembedding mechanisms that characterize late modern society – expert systems and symbolic tokens – generate their own distinctive forms of trust and risk. These systems are an unavoidable part of our lives. We cannot choose to opt out of them. From air traffic control, through food production, to the generation of electricity, we are exposed to the risks generated by these systems whether or not we use them directly. We therefore have no choice but to cultivate a specific form of trust: not the form of trust one develops from face-to-face encounters or in personal relationships, but an anonymous and spatially extensive trust which is constantly in the background of our everyday lives.[16] This is necessary because the risks we face daily are distinctive to our age. They are not natural risks. Neither are they risks to which some people are exposed merely by virtue of their actions or where they choose to live. They are inclusive. We cannot choose whether or not to take them.[17] And they are manufactured, contrived by our expert systems.

The analysis of risk culture, or the risk society, is undertaken most extensively by Beck. He refers to the inclusivity of manufactured risk as the universalization of hazards. Manufactured risk is not stratified. No longer is there a connection between the level of our exposure to particular risks and our degree of wealth or power. For example, the risks associated with food production connect everyone together in so far as food chains 'dip under borders' (1992a: 36). The threat of thermonuclear war or the risk of leakage from nuclear power stations do not recognize distinctions between social classes, races or continents. Manufactured risks have no boundaries. Their likelihood is incalculable, their consequences irredeemable: they are 'distorted objects, ambiguous and interpretable, like modern mythological creatures' (1995a: 26). But manufactured risk is also knowledge dependent. For example, risk management is inherently speculative. Of necessity, it demands that we imagine non-existent, future occurrences as a basis for making decisions or passing legislation. To this extent, there is a degree of fatalism involved. Science plays a dual role here. On the one hand, the exploitation of scientific knowledge by industry increases our exposure to risk. But on the other, it is primarily through science that we are able to identify a level of risk at all. Science thus provides the means for overcoming threats for which it is partly responsible (1992a: 163).[18] For this reason, scientific knowledge has a new ambiguity, as both 'enlightenment *and* anti-enlightenment, truth *and* concealment, liberation from inherited constraints *and* confinement in self-created objective constraints' (1995a: 51).

The identification and management of risk is as much a political problem, however, as it is a scientific exercise. For risk has not only been manufactured but politicized. In the political sphere, the definition and calculation of risk is loaded with the conflicting claims of interest groups and affected parties. But more than this, it is increasingly delegated to experts who bypass or preempt the democratic process, leaving a technocratic structure – or what Beck calls subpolitics – which has the 'political privilege of defining, bindingly for one and all, the conditions for survival in scientific-technological civilization' (Beck, 1995b: 118). Subpolitics takes place outside or beneath the formal democratic arena. Special interests are pursued primarily through the media and the judiciary. This engenders a fragmentary approach to political debate, 'breaking open and overcoming the selective interpretation of universally valid basic laws piece by piece' (1992a: 199). It is also a reflection

of the economic decline of the state: not only in terms of welfare pro-
vision, but in the sense that governments simply cannot afford public
inspection on an extensive scale. The sovereignty of the nation-state is
therefore being undermined by the 'global exchange of pollutants and
toxins and the accompanying universal health threats and natural destruction' (1992a:189). More broadly, this marks a shift away from mass
political parties and towards debate over single issues: something akin
to Rorty's political campaigns. This is a politics which is unusually sus-
ceptible to fashion and cultural difference. But it is not pluralism. Rather,
the loosening of traditional alliances has made way for conflict based
on ascribed characteristics such as race, gender and age. Different group-
ings attempt to gain political advantage by focusing on such characteristics in order to enforce social exclusion.[19]

This takes the discussion on to the broader ramifications of risk culture. Giddens and Beck agree that it is not only institutions that are
affected by risk, but all dimensions of social and personal life: from the
global to the local level. Globalization is defined by Giddens as 'the
intensification of worldwide social relations which link distant localities in such a way that local happenings are shaped by events occurring many miles away and vice versa' (1990: 64). According to Beck,
globalization means, 'among other things, that the walls of distance
break down and that strangers and strangeness are increasingly caught
in the horizon of one's life' (1998: 133–4). Thus, for both theorists, globalization is not a process which goes on over our heads but is inexorably bound up with the localities in which we live. In this sense,
globalization is dialectical: events at one extreme may produce diver-
gent or contrary occurrences at the other. The process of globalization
therefore has a nervous and erratic character: not just at the level of the
global system but in local and personal dimensions of social life.[20] On
the one hand, our everyday lives are increasingly influenced by events
that take place on the other side of the world. On the other, our local
activities can themselves be globally consequential.[21] In this latter respect, self-identity has itself been transformed by the process of reflexive modernization. Let me briefly discuss the main features of this
transformation.

According to Giddens, globalization has led not to the relativization
of values but to a world in which there are no 'others'. Our knowledge
of the world at large is enhanced by electronic communications media:
we inhabit a 'unitary framework of experience' (1991: 5). Moreover, the
insecurities we face as individuals tend to unify rather than divide us.[22]
Thus the perspective and outlook of different cultures has not become
increasingly plural but, if anything, more singular.[23] To this extent,

human experience is subject to the same process of reflexive modernization as modern institutions: 'the reflexivity of modernity extends into
the core of the self' (1991: 32). But expert knowledge has been appropriated by individuals in a way that has reconstituted their daily lives:
in relation to sexuality, health and spirituality. For example, psycho-
therapy expresses the dislocations and uncertainties that encapsulate
the subjective experience of reflexive modernization. In sexuality, the
appropriation of therapeutic ideas, combined with the increasing separation of sexual relations from reproduction, strike at the very meaning
of intimacy. One major consequence of reflexive modernization at this
level is a striving for intimate relationships which prioritize emotional
and sexual fulfilment over longevity.[24] Women, particularly, have been
empowered.[25] But not only the quantity and accessibility, but the sheer
range of information available to us has opened up our personal lives
to constant scrutiny. Because expert knowledge is not grounded in tradition, there is no real guidance on which alternatives to adopt, or how
to evaluate them. The openness of the future therefore presents us with
both opportunities and threats.

Beck's analysis runs parallel to that of Giddens. He argues that we are
only at the beginning of a liberation from feudally ascribed sexual roles.
In contemporary society, there is a profound tension between the demands of employers and the requirements of family life and personal
relationships, and it has been heightened by structural changes in the
labour market. We are having to be increasingly inventive in the way
that tension is handled. It is a tension that cannot be resolved, for example, within the parameters set by traditional roles in the nuclear family
or even the organization of professional childcare. In these and other
respects, individuals are increasingly compelled to invent their own bi-
ographies.[26] Moreover, the globalization of media means that we are 'potentially having to take a continued stand' on global issues (Beck, 1992a:
137). In this way, modern culture is at last catching up with the economic
changes which took place at the time of the industrial revolution. Hitherto, modern society consisted of a combination of a modern economic
structure with a largely traditional cultural system. But the removal of
limits and securities provided by traditional and class structures means
that individuals are 'confronted with themselves as the pivots and hinges
of their own lives' (1995a: 40). The consequences of increased individual
autonomy are not only social but psychological. What were once regarded
as social problems are increasingly being perceived as indicators of personal inadequacy, anxiety and neurosis.

Giddens and Beck maintain that far from being culturally impover-
ished by the specialization of knowledge, as Habermas claims, or cata-

pulted into a culture of narcissism, as Christopher Lasch has suggested, we have greater opportunities to become experts ourselves.[27] Quite literally, we are being propelled towards taking a more inventive and imaginative approach to the construction of our social identity.[28] But the culture of risk has undermined modern preconceptions not only of ourselves but of the relationship between the social and natural world. Environmental hazards do not signal the destruction of nature by society, but have blurred irretrievably the boundary between them. Nature has become a human artefact. If anything, our increased proximity to nature has desensitized us to the risks associated with our relationship to it.[29] If social theory has a feasible normative project, it is not only to resensitize us but to explore entirely new ways of constituting ourselves as a global political community. The transformation of self-identity will be at the heart of this process. But inclusivity must be its premise, not its outcome. That project will be discussed in the next section of this chapter.

Reconstituting Politics

Reflexive modernization has wide-ranging normative implications. The project of modernity is no longer viable. It relies on a teleological understanding of history which cannot take account of contingency. It is formulated from a position above, or outside of, society: whereas contemporary society has reinvented itself, and will continue to reinvent itself, from below. The task of social theory today must therefore not be to provide final answers to the ethical questions which confront us; it must be to facilitate the process by which individuals and communities can search for those answers themselves. But we should resist the postmodern call for pluralism. It is inappropriate to the global condition. That condition can be addressed only by harnessing the capacity for continual renewal which is brought into being by reflexive modernization. That capacity consists of generative politics. It recasts social reflexivity into a framework for political dialogue which is multifaceted and local, and which builds on the universal questions raised by our inclusive culture of risk. In this discussion, I shall consider those questions first, before moving on to examine the concept of generative politics.

Globalization, tradition and contingency

The normative argument developed by Giddens and Beck rests on a critique of the project of modernity, particularly of the restrictions it places on our understanding of social change. Both theorists suggest that the central plinth of the modern project consists of an idealization of society that is untenable in a world which is under constant renewal. Social theory must play an integral role in the process of critical self-reflection that reflexive modernity implies. But this is a considerably more affirmative and experimental approach than tends to be associated with critical theory.[30]

Giddens characterizes the project of reflexive modernity as utopian realism. Because of the sheer pace and unpredictability of social change in contemporary society, we need to 'balance utopian ideals with realism in much more stringent fashion than was needed in Marx's day' (1990: 155). Utopian realism hinges on the idea of reflexive monitoring. According to Giddens, the role of social theory should be to appraise alternative futures against a rigorous and critical analysis of present-day society. Given that the reflexive monitoring of action constitutively alters the process of human praxis, it follows that the very propagation of alternatives 'might help them to be realized' (1990: 154). He therefore seeks to combine an open-ended interpretation of the developmental trajectory of modern society with a sharp-eyed assessment of the feasibility of alternatives. After all, while history is certainly not teleological, we cannot just 'bend it readily to our collective purposes' (1990: 153).

According to Giddens, the project of reflexive modernity is alert to the ever-changing character of reflexive modernity; it is aware that deep-rooted moral commitment can be dangerous in a risk culture; it looks beyond national society; and it is concerned not only with liberty but with quality of life. But perhaps the most important feature of this project is the refusal to ground it in theoretical or philosophical imperatives. For to do so would be to construct a static, inflexible and potentially authoritarian model of the idealized society which is unable to cope with contingency and pluralism. But Giddens does not agree with postmodernists, either, who suggest that the only alternative to normative universalism is relativism. Like Bauman, morality for Giddens is in many ways intuitive: 'some things are clearly noxious and other things clearly desirable and . . . it isn't necessary to ground them in order to proclaim this to be so' (1982: 72). If there are compelling moral concerns that underpin the normative argument of Giddens, they are derived from an empirical understanding of reflexive modernization and the consequences of risk culture. For a more detailed understanding of what those imperatives might be, the discussion must turn briefly to the notion of detraditionalization.

Reflexive modernization is marked by a process of detraditional-

ization. This does not mean the disappearance from society of traditional beliefs and practices. In some instances, it may even signal their
reappearance. But in a post-traditional society, they play a very different role than before. Traditional practices are retained, or reappear, only
in so far as they can be articulated and justified. As such, they cease
being traditions in any conventional sense. They are no longer left un-
questioned, but are reflexively monitored.[31] According to Giddens, even
religious fundamentalism fits into this picture. It consists of a dogmatic
assertion of tradition that would be unwarranted in any other world:
'Fundamentalism tends to accentuate the purity of a given set of doctrines, not only because it wishes to set them off against other traditions, but because it is a rejection of a model of truth linked to the dialogic
engagement of ideas in public space' (1994: 6).

Beck's analysis is broadly consistent with this. He argues that where
individuals were once propelled from feudal and religious certainties
into industrial society, they are now being thrust from the relative
security of industrial society into the tumultuous uncertainties of risk
culture. Industrial society provided at least some sense of assurance.
But in the relationship between society and nature, in family structure,
in faith and class consciousness, all secure parameters are being de-
pleted in the post-traditional society. This entails a process of individualization, but not in the sense of atomization, or what Durkheim calls
individuation.[32] Neither is it individualism in the Durkheimian sense.
Individualization in risk culture is a form of compulsion. None of us is
exempt. It is therefore, necessarily, a form of inclusion. If the project of
reflexive modernity is to be universal in its scope, this specific form of
individualism will be its source.

The universalism of reflexive modernity is identified explicitly by
Giddens. According to him, 'this is probably the first time in history
that we can speak of the emergence of universal values' (1994: 20). So
what are these values, and from where exactly do they derive? Habermas
is the other theorist discussed so far in this book who writes explicitly
of a convergence of values on a universal plane. He anticipates a convergence of values on the strength of inherent and universal features of
communicative reason. For Giddens, there is no need of anticipation.
Convergence is already underway. And it does not need to be supported by philosophical argument. On the contrary, it is integral to reflexive modernization, and above all to the monitoring process it entails.
For above all, there has been a convergence of *fear* worldwide. According to Giddens, this has been generated by the 'collective threats which
humanity has created for itself' (ibid.). By definition, contemporary
society is an energetic society in which individuals and groups are more

or less compelled to take a vigorous stance towards their own quality of life. Because threats to that quality of life are global in reach, that stance must itself be global. Life politics is a politics of lifestyle which concerns how, both as individuals and collectively, we should live in a world 'where what used to be fixed either by nature or tradition is now subject to human decisions' (1994: 15). By necessity, we have reached a stage beyond privatism. We can no longer avoid active political engagement.

In similar fashion, Beck argues that the project of modernity was characterized by a form of industrial fatalism, in which the rate and direction – and above all the outcome – of social change were regarded as broadly predictable.[33] The project of reflexive modernity is not predictable. The political response to risk culture goes through two basic phases. In the first, we are more or less aware of the negative side-effects of industrialism, but continue to seek solutions from inside the industrial paradigm. In the second, that paradigm is set aside altogether and the struggle begins for access to decision-making over the definition of risk, its prevention and accountability for its occurrence. At this point – somewhere between psychological repression and hysteria – the 'institutional earthquake' of reflexive modernization 'enters into consciousness and action' (Beck, 1995a: 87). The impact of risk and danger in late modern society clarifies the connection between our own individual circumstances and much broader, collective concerns: 'It may be incidents such as the planned highway in the vicinity of one's own back yard, the worsening school situation for children, or the atomic waste storage dump being built nearby which cause aspects of a "collective fate" to penetrate into consciousness' (1992a: 134). As a result, we will unite around a 'grand ecological consensus' which focuses on the 'ethics of self-limitation' (1998: 151).

It is important to grasp what is at stake in these arguments. The convergence of values is empirical. It is based primarily on fear. Thus, in the first instance, it is also negative. But for Giddens and Beck, the commonality of fear has a reverse side: namely, what Rorty might call common hopes, and therefore a common vocabulary. For Beck, that vocabulary is primarily ecological but threatens to spread into other areas such as welfare and health. For Giddens, the vocabulary is about the sanctity of life, human rights, the preservation of species and care for the future. Unlike Rorty, they do not suppose that we have chosen this vocabulary merely because it is attractive. We have not chosen it at all. The universal vocabulary of fear they identify stems from our propulsion into a universal culture of risk. These theorists do not, therefore, have to invent or impose the universal values they claim to have identified. They exist. They do not need to anticipate convergence on the basis of a theoretical teleology. That convergence is upon us. Amidst all the uncertainty and fear that has been created by the culture of risk, we are in a position where we have no choice but to reinvent politics.

Generative politics

From the subjective point of view, reflexive modernization is an ambivalent process. On the one side, the experience of living in late modern society is profoundly unsettling and potentially alienating. On the other side, the institutionalization of reflexivity has presented us with unprecedented opportunities to shape the future: our self-identity, our personal relationships, and global processes and institutions. The idea of generative politics is drawn directly from this ambivalence.

According to Giddens, socialism has ceased to present us with a viable form of political and economic organization because it is appropriate only to the world we have left behind. Socialism is based on a cybernetic model of society which suggests that it can be managed and controlled only by a higher-level intelligence such as the state.[34] In its view of history, socialism is heir to the Enlightenment, focusing on the struggles and activities of individuals, not on the will of some transcendent force. But those struggles do not only take place between groups as a consequence of exploitation. They are primarily a struggle to dominate nature, manipulating it for the purpose of human advancement. While this combination of industrialism and central control might have been a reasonable basis for the earliest stages of economic development in modern society, it is irrelevant to contemporary society. Giddens therefore agrees with Hayek's critique of central planning: local, not central, sources of information are vital to the functioning of markets. But in the wake of reflexive modernization, they are also important to the functioning of society as a whole.

The decline of the state is pivotal to this analysis. That decline is not merely economic, that is, a function of the increasing power and reach of the multinational corporation from outside. It is political: a function of increasing social reflexivity both within and across national societies. According to Beck, the interconnectedness of individual circumstances with global risks threatens to bypass the national state altogether: while 'governments (still) operate within the structure of nation states, biography is already being opened to the world society' (1992a: 137). As Giddens argues, those concerns are as much about quality of life as they are about freedom. They concern questions of self-identity, ecological decay, gender and race: 'They are reactions to, and engagements with, a world precisely where tradition is no longer traditional, and nature no longer natural' (1994: 91). How, then, might politics be reinvented in a way that dips underneath the borders between national societies?

According to Giddens, the reinvention of politics hinges on the decentralization of political power. To increase the autonomy and recognition of individuals and local collectivities is not only morally imperative; it is a very practical means of capitalizing on the flow of information generated, from the agent upwards, by the process of reflexive monitoring.[35] The concept of generative politics refers to the fostering of active trust within the political community: active, in the sense of being constantly produced, monitored and negotiated. Generative politics is a politics of contingency (the openness of the future) and locality (our reflexive appropriation of knowledge). But it must also be addressed to wider concerns, because under the impact of globalization, the discursive space in which political questions can be addressed has become more extensive: 'The revolutionary changes of our time are not happening so much in the orthodox political domain as along the fault-lines of the interaction of local and global transformations' (Giddens, 1994: 95). The idea of generative politics therefore reflects an attempt to elude the classical dichotomy between market and state. The capacity of individuals and groups to constitute and reproduce themselves as political communities is crucial to this. Generative politics 'works through providing material conditions, and organizational frameworks, for the life-political decisions taken by individuals and groups in the wider social order' (1994: 15).

Beck's argument about the reinvention of politics also focuses on developments which take place both beyond and beneath the arena of nation-state government. Key here is the notion of subpolitics, which I defined earlier in this chapter as the politics of technocracy. According to Beck, subpolitics relies on secular faith in progress. Paradoxically, however, the dominance of experts over political decision-making will be undermined by technology itself. In particular, advances in information technology can help dismantle large bureaucracies by decentralizing labour and bringing information to individuals in an unmediated form.[36] A society which is increasingly conscious of the unintended consequences of industrialism, and which is increasingly flexible in its occupational structure, is simply incompatible with centralized decision-making.

The normative arguments laid out by Giddens and Beck seek to redefine the concepts of democratic participation and political dialogue.

They disagree with Fukuyama's argument that democracy answers an underlying desire for recognition in the human psyche or spirit.[37] In Giddens's view, the increasing worldwide hegemony of liberal democracy is a direct result of reflexive modernization. That process is inherently democratizing in the way it reorganizes everyday social practices. But it has occurred largely outside the formal political arena. Reflexive democratization is capable of destabilizing, not just reinforcing, liberal democracy. It leads to what Giddens calls dialogic democratization, and therefore to the establishment of interconnections and forms of exchange which are vital for generative politics.

According to Giddens, dialogic democracy – or democracy through dialogue – differs from liberal democracy in a number of ways. Whereas liberal democracy focuses on values and institutions, dialogic democracy emphasizes the importance of process, discussion and debate. To this extent, it is similar to the notion of deliberative democracy developed by David Miller.[38] But whereas Miller's conception addresses the formal political arena, the idea of dialogic democracy moves beyond it. Once again, the justification for this normative argument is empirical, not philosophical. One major consequence of reflexive modernization is rising discontent with liberal-democratic institutions: not, as the postmodernists suggest, because of a political malaise, but as a consequence of heightened social reflexivity combined with a greater awareness of inclusive risks. Giddens maintains that the process of reflexive democratization is already underway in four main areas of the post-traditional order:[39] personal life, social movements, economic organizations, and the international arena. But it is the democratization of interchanges between these dimensions, not just a transformation within the dimensions themselves, which is most significant. For example, ecological problems are already being addressed at all four levels.

Giddens and Beck characterize reflexive modernity as a politics not only of loss and decay but, above all, of recovery and renewal. Far from being exhausted, the project of modernity as they conceive it has been revitalized. That revitalization is partly a question of energy. But it is primarily a question of dispersion and expansion. For Giddens and Beck, a self-conscious, or reflexive, modernity does not signal a withdrawal from society as Bauman would suggest, but the expansion of political association across societies. Modern society has indeed been placed under suspicion, but in a way that has led to universal, rigorous and active scrutiny of the unintended consequences of its growth. In effect, we are being remoralized. The ramifications of this are volcanic, at all levels of society. By definition, reflexive modernity is precarious. It has no obvious underpinnings, no enduring guidelines, and gains no foundational support from philosophy. The project of reflexive modernity therefore runs in close parallel with the process of reflexive modernization itself. Sociology must be, indeed it cannot avoid being, an integral part of the radical and undercutting self-interpretation of modernity. But this connection cannot be characterized as reflection or mimesis in the way that many postmodernists suggest. It must be conceived as reflexive involvement. To this extent, sociology must itself be reflexive. Social theory must subject its assumptions to persistent scrutiny and methodical doubt. It is with that connection in mind, and in that spirit, that we turn to the critical discussion.

Critical Discussion

Giddens and Beck argue that our response to reflexive modernity should not only be to reject the teleological understanding of history which characterizes the project of modernity, but also to recognize that the privileged status of Western culture has largely evaporated.[40] This argument relies on a particular interpretation of the concept of reason which is universal but which, nevertheless, does not preempt normative discussion. This concept raises a number of questions about the relationship between theoretical and normative arguments in the work of Giddens and Beck. Two themes are particularly important. The first concerns the relationship between reflexivity and reason, and its implications for the project of reflexive modernity as Giddens and Beck conceive it. The second concerns the anti-foundationalist tenor of reflexive modernity as a project, and of reflexive sociology as a discipline.

Reason and doubt

The concept of generative politics rests on a specific interpretation of the concept of reason as the basis for scepticism rather than certainty and control. This interpretation underpins the idea of reflexivity. In their normative arguments, Giddens and Beck envisage a form of democracy through dialogue – or dialogic democracy – which has been made not only possible but inevitable in the wake of reflexive modernization. Dialogic democracy shares important features with Habermas's concept of communicative reason. But the latter is advanced in a rather different way. It might therefore be instructive to consider the extent to which Giddens and Beck manage to avoid the pitfalls associated with Habermas's normative argument. As I discussed in chapter 5, one of the main problems raised by the concept of communicative reason concerns the question of pluralism. Giddens largely agrees with Habermas that democracy through dialogue can build on and extend, rather than destroy, cultural pluralism. But the crucial step in the argument, and the key to a clearer understanding of the concept of generative politics, stem from two crucial areas where he departs from Habermas.

Habermas's notion of communicative reason emphasizes two vital points: first, that the way in which we advance validity-claims when communicating with others implies a basic orientation to participate in open dialogue; and second, that this is bound up with a further orientation to reach consensus. The theory of communicative action outlines a set of formal procedures through which both aims can be fulfilled. Habermas argues that these procedures need not be imposed from outside or above, but have been derived from inherent features of communication itself. Giddens takes a somewhat different view.

Giddens's normative strategy depends on two basic arguments: first, that there has been a convergence of fear which, in turn, rests on and signifies a set of convergent values; and second, that social reflexivity, as it actually occurs, suggests formal properties of dialogic democracy. As with Habermas, the distinction between form and content is vital to this approach. In and of itself, methodical doubt – like Habermas's concept of discursive justification – does not entail imposing one's own values on others. It involves only the exchange, scrutiny and justification of values. For Habermas, this is enough to ensure that the concept of communicative reason can be allied, not opposed, to pluralism. But according to his critics, the distinction between form and substance breaks down for two reasons. First, the idea that dialogue will or even must proceed towards an overarching consensus is unwarranted, and threatens to disfigure not only the outcome but the process of dialogue itself. As a result, the concept of communicative reason may turn out to be restrictive and exclusionary, not open and inclusive. Second, the formal procedures for dialogue which Habermas outlines are in fact an expression of a culturally specific point of view, because they demand that we take up a hypothetical stance in dialogue with a generalized model of the other. In other words, participants must set aside what is most particular about their own outlook as a condition of participation, and the distinction between form and substance can no longer be sustained. How, then, does Giddens seek to avoid these difficulties?

In respect of the first difficulty, he argues that methodically to doubt not only one's own values but the values of others does not necessarily have to lead to agreement but may lead merely to greater levels of mutual tolerance: 'dialogue in a public space provides a means of living along with the other . . . whether that "other" be an individual or a global community of religious believers' (Giddens, 1994: 115). He therefore accepts that open dialogue is valuable in its own right and for its own sake. But he disputes the view that universal consensus should necessarily be the *outcome* of such dialogue, and rejects Habermas's argument on account of its 'transcendentalism'. He also rejects Habermas's justification for the formal procedures which the ideal speech situation entails. According to Giddens, the basic principles of dialogic democracy are already at work in contemporary society. They are called social reflexivity, and have emerged from the process of interminable, methodical doubt that has exploded from the vortex of reflexive modernization. Thus they need not be deduced from theoretical argument at all. There are echoes of both Rorty and Lyotard here. In one respect, this comes closer to the position of Rorty than to that of Lyotard, because it draws the theme of empathy from the former while avoiding the principle of jousting, or gaming, which seems integral to the concept of paralogy as espoused by the latter. But in another respect, Giddens's position is closer to Lyotard, in so far as he urges critical engagement rather than the kind of ghettoism into which Rorty's literary conversation so easily descends.

The second difficulty which I raised above concerns the problem of how others in dialogue are perceived. Giddens does not address this question explicitly. But his implicit answer seems to be that the difficulty does not really arise. After all, new forms of solidarity are emerging on the strength of a convergence of fear. He therefore seeks to avoid the arbitrary, or wilful, connotations of an argument such as Lyotard's, which favours language games. But while he largely agrees with Habermas that universalism is an objective which we must uphold, Giddens suggests that it does not need to be argued for in philosophical terms. This takes the discussion back to the distinction I raised earlier on in this chapter: namely, between dialogue which is designed to achieve convergence, and dialogue which stems from and builds on it. Whereas the concept of communicative action falls into the first category – and therefore poses somewhat sharper questions about procedure – the notion of dialogic democracy comes under the second. In effect, the project of reflexive modernity is underpinned by a rejection of idealized models of the good society in favour of the rigorous analysis and evaluation of transformations that are already underway, that is, a reflexive sociology.

The normative strategy outlined by Giddens can be examined critically on two counts: the first concerns the concept of reflexivity and its relation to reason; the second addresses the reflexive role of sociology in relation to social reflexivity and dialogic democracy. I shall consider only the first point here, and move on to the second in the next part of the critical discussion. Giddens describes the second wave of modernization as a refutation, not a realization, of the 'Enlightenment prescription of more knowledge, more control' (1994: 4). But elsewhere he approaches the concept of reason from another angle, suggesting that 'the guiding principle of our age is methodical doubt, having its origins in Cartesian philosophy' (1994: 252). The second approach implies that reflexive modernization signals a triumph for, not a contradiction of, that guiding principle. From earlier on in our discussion, we know that the principle of methodical doubt is closely linked with our capacity to appropriate and reflexively monitor knowledge. But what exactly does Giddens mean by *more* knowledge – in greater quantity, or more accurate? He does not say directly. We can, however, arrive at a reasonable inference by examining more closely the connection between knowledge and control. It is important to do so because it sheds light on exactly why he objects to the Enlightenment project.

Giddens is critical of the Enlightenment prescription of control on much the same basis that he rejects socialism as any longer providing radical solutions to the problems of our age. In so far as socialism is premised on the idea of controlling society through a centralized intelligence such as the state, it is inappropriate for a world where information is increasingly gathered, and subjected to methodical doubt, from below. The theoretical corollary of this political argument recalls a theme which I have sought to explore throughout this book, namely, that general models of society of the kind suggested by Marx, Durkheim and Habermas are inflexible and unhelpful for sociology. But they are unhelpful and inflexible not only in their normative implications, as Giddens suggests, but because they tend to obstruct the formulation and rigorous pursuit of research questions which can enable us to know *more* about – and to understand more *accurately* – the world around us. The problem of inflexibility derives in each case from a *conflation* of a theoretical model with an overarching normative project which aspires to an idealized conception of the good society: not from the substance of the normative project itself.

In principle, one might imagine that these two strands in modern social theory – the mission to discover, and the desire for perfection – can be prised apart. There can be little doubting that Weber thought so. Giddens appears to suggest that they cannot. This much, at least, is implied by his assertion that 'the reflexivity of modernity actually subverts reason, *at any rate where reason is understood as the gaining of certain knowledge*' (1990: 39, my emphasis). The beginning of the second clause of that formulation, 'at any rate', implies that there might be a caveat, that is, that the concept of reason might be interpreted in another way. And that other way is supplied by Giddens himself, both in his Popperian interpretation of a science in which nothing is certain – 'In the heart of the world of hard science, modernity floats free' – and in his argument that the guiding principle of our age is methodical doubt. But if radical doubt is integral to the concept of reason, from where does its connection with certainty derive? It derives, according to Giddens, from the Enlightenment obsession with control. And that obsession, in turn, is rooted in the desire for perfection, in our striving for the good society. It is therefore an objection to the normative project with which the concept of universal reason has been associated, not the concept itself, which is the real basis of Giddens's critique. But only a conflation of that concept and that project could ever give rise to the formulation that reason is *equivalent to* the gaining of certain knowledge. If the idea of certain knowledge means anything, it suggests the kind of unquestioning cosmic system which Giddens and Beck associate with tradition. But it certainly is not an idea that necessarily invokes the concept of reason. In his critique of the Enlightenment project, Giddens appears to reproduce its most problematic feature. If anything, reflexive modernity does not subvert but clarifies the dual role of reason not only in contemporary society but in modern and postmodern social theory, that is, as the basis both for theoretical argument and an idealized model of society. Giddens's argument seems unwittingly to underwrite the case for separating these two applications. So one further question remains: Does the idea of a reflexive sociology make this possible? I shall turn to this question now.

Reflexive sociology

Giddens and Beck argue that sociology has a vital role to play in contemporary society. Like Bauman, they suggest that by necessity it is a transient and reflexive discipline. It is located within society, as an integral part of the way that society interprets itself, and dynamically reproduces itself, over time. Like Bauman again, they urge sociology to invent new concepts and modes of explanation that will enable us to analyse the major transformations that have taken place in modern society without remaining caught up in unyielding theories which presuppose the integrity of national society as a system, suggest a deterministic understanding of the relationship between economic life and culture, and obscure the multifaceted interconnections between human agents and social structures in contemporary society. Whether advanced by Bauman from a postmodern perspective, or by Giddens and Beck from the vantage point of reflexive modernity, these arguments suggest a constructive way forward for a social theory which is rigorously analytical, which facilitates research and which is genuinely reflexive. But what of the connection with reflexive modernity as a normative project?

As I discussed in chapter 7, Bauman implores us to repudiate the relationship between the discipline of sociology and the managerial control of society from above. As sociologists, we should sensitize others to different perspectives, not seek to impose a singular perspective from above or outside whose primary aim is control and advancement. The one key problem with Bauman's formulation is that he continues to view interpretive reason as a noble mediator between cultures – and therefore implicitly retains its association with a normative project of *some* kind – rather than as a means of discovery and a basis for systematic doubt. Giddens and Beck draw out and underline the interconnection between reason and doubt. This informs their conception of a reflexive sociology. Yet in aligning that conception so closely with a much larger normative project, they threaten to undermine the single predominant quality which a reflexive sociology must possess, namely, analytical flexibility.

One important aspect of a reflexive sociology as Giddens and Beck conceive it is that its research agenda cannot be generated entirely from within, that is, dictated by some internal logic of the kind that Adorno is so against in his arguments on theory and aesthetics, or on the basis of an Archimedean standpoint such as that rejected by Foucault in his interpretation of historiography. Now if this is taken to imply that sociology should address itself to practical questions and problems, or at least take these into account when seeking to discover more about the world around us, there is nothing here to which one might reasonably object. Weber's argument adds up to much the same thing, although he is at pains to explore how tensions are bound to arise in this context. Giddens and Beck do not share Weber's fatalistic despair about core features of the rationalization of modern society. Neither, quite frankly, do they demonstrate his explanatory ambition to compare different societies and cultures. In their hands, sociology is not placed at the service of an existing practical agenda. Nor is it meant merely to facilitate or mediate that agenda. It appears to have been designed to lead and to shape it. Their ambition, it would seem, lies in another direction: all the way back towards the project of modernity.

Giddens goes to some lengths to argue that the agenda of questions which has been formulated in the theory of reflexive modernization can be drawn from an empirical understanding of contemporary society. After all, this is vital for his case against transcendentalism. But some important differences emerge between the approaches of Giddens and Beck which place such a claim under serious doubt. For Giddens, social reflexivity refers to the active, dynamic and looped appropriation of knowledge: by looped, I mean the way in which that knowledge feeds back into the process by which it is appropriated. For Beck, by contrast, reflexivity is about the cultivation of unawareness. Against this background, Beck is scathingly critical of modern sociology: which, he argues loftily, 'has skidded into an unproductive consensus that now prevents it from even perceiving the great social upheavals and challenges, much less considering them creatively in an effort encompassing the entire discipline' (1995a: 112). That unproductive consensus stems from earlier theories of classical modern society and now embraces post-industrialism, the work of the systems theorist Luhmann, and even the arguments of Foucault on the disciplinary society. According to Beck, the problem is that these theories provide us with concepts and modes of explanation which are either undermined by new empirical data, or otherwise place that data under intolerable strain by force of the demand that it still fit outdated concepts. In this view, the difficulty arises from a suffocating proximity between theory and research: 'The social sciences are being run over by developments that, according to their own categories and concepts, really ought not to exist' (1995a: 114).

One is inclined to ask, however, just why Beck himself continues to interpret these developments in terms of concepts and categories that appear merely to reinvent or invert those which he claims to reject. In place of the concept of tradition, for example, he writes of detraditionalization and post-tradition: both of which bear close comparison with Weber's idea of disenchantment. Instead of modernization, he employs the notion of reflexive modernization, which he also calls 'the Enlightenment of Enlightenment'. And he replaces the notion of industrial society with the concept of industrial consequence society. Like Bauman, Beck calls for completely new concepts which might enable us to identify the distinctive properties of contemporary society in relation to what has gone before. But unlike Bauman, he seems unable to avoid presenting contemporary society in a way which suggests that – after all – it is merely antithetical to, not entirely different from, modern society. We seem to be reinventing the wheel.

Beck is adamant that we are in no position to foresee the consequences of risk culture. He might have added that we never *have* been in an especially strong position to understand future developments in a precise or subtle way. He is just as resolute in arguing that the risk culture in which we live is difficult to explain: 'Anyone who has an explanation for the present day is suspicious' (1998: 141). So we can safely draw two conclusions, at least: that we inhabit a world which is difficult to explain, and that this is a world in which prophecies are unreliable. That much, at least, might always have been foreseen. But the key problem with modern social theory is not necessarily that its concepts and categories are outdated as Beck suggests, but that we are in a poor position to establish even *whether* they are. This difficulty arises not because of a proximity between theory and research, but from the rift that inevitably arises when the concepts and categories of the former are inflexibly allied to a broader-based normative project: exactly the kind of enterprise that has been outlined by Giddens and Beck. Of course, the closeness between their arguments can be overstated. While Giddens boldly asserts that the convergence of values is already upon us, Beck appears to deny that we are in any position to judge, at least in as much as we lack the conceptual tools with which to make such statements. Giddens's argument seems to have been forced by a rigid theoretical requirement to distance the concept of dialogic democracy from the philosophical transcendentalism which he associates with Habermas. Beck's circumspection is underwritten by an empirical sensitivity, but also by what comes across as a rather dogmatic frustration with the outdatedness of modern social theory as he perceives it.

What draws these approaches closer together is the normative project of reflexive modernity. As in the preceding chapters of this book, I have sought to evaluate that project not on normative grounds, but in terms of its implications for and relationship with social theory: and above all for what it tells us about the way forward from the debate between modernists and postmodernists. For different reasons, Giddens and Beck clarify the need more clearly to separate the theoretical and normative aims of social theory. Albeit unwittingly, Giddens makes a powerful case for retaining the concept of reason as an analytical tool, and he underlines the potential of an association between theory and methodical doubt when allied with rigorous empirical enquiry. That case is blurred, however, by his insistence on its normative implications. Whatever else might be said about Giddens's normative arguments – and much might be said for his critique of cybernetic models which derive from an idealized concept of society – their continued proximity to the project of modernity is clear enough. Beck identifies the problematic relationship between social theory and sociological research. He underlines the difficulties presented by unwieldy concepts and categories. But by suggesting only that these should be replaced in kind, rather than analysed in conjunction with a much more fundamental investigation into the role of theoretical concepts and modes of explanation in research, he only threatens to make matters far worse. But in any case, as I have sought to demonstrate in this book, the problem is hardly new. It is as established as the discipline of sociology itself. In the concluding discussion, I ask how it might be resolved.

Conclusion

The question as to whether we now live in a modern or postmodern society cannot really be answered in a meaningful way, because to do so would be to rely on the kind of theoretical generalizations that I have sought to reject in this book. The distinction between modern and postmodern society does, of course, raise important issues. But these are best dealt with through empirical research, not general historical narratives. They include, in no particular order: the relationship between consumerism and social identity; the impact of new media and information technology on social life; the future of work; specific features of the local/global axis, such as economic life, financial markets, the media, religion, politics and national identity, and leisure and entertainment; the problem of environmental decay; and the fate of nation-state society. Of course, social theory should seek as far as possible to facilitate the process by which such questions are addressed by sociologists. At its core, however, the debate between modernists and postmodernists is about different versions of social theory, not different versions of social reality. It is a dispute about theoretical style, theoretical ambition and theoretical territory. In the preceding chapters of this book, I have addressed the debate in these terms. I shall now retrace the steps of my argument in order to draw together its main strands and to propose, albeit in a provisional fashion, a compromise.

The arguments of Marx and Durkheim have overshadowed modern social theory in two basic respects. First, they conceptualize society as a totality, that is, an integrated system. This approach has been sustained not only by theorists such as Horkheimer, Adorno, Marcuse and Foucault – who regard the modern social system, because of its totality, as an abhorrent constraint on human freedom and dignity – but also by Habermas, who envisages the development of modern society as progress towards the perfection of the relationship between the system and lifeworld. The second reason for the influence of Marx and Durkheim over the development of modern social theory stems from the fact that their arguments are at the same time an idealization of the good society. Both theorists tie the theorization of modern society inexorably to a normative project which prophesies its ultimate stability, integration and equality. I want to suggest that this vision of history as progress has remained pivotal in social theories of modernity ever since.

In this book, I have sought to question both features of modern social theory. The concept of society as a totality deadens our capacity, as sociologists, to cope with contingency and specificity within and across national societies. Moreover, it threatens to undermine our ability to understand whether national society itself is in decline. In this form, social theory all too readily turns into a generalizing monolith of interconnected concepts that are difficult to break down for the more specific and practical purpose of empirical research. As far as the second key feature of modern social theory is concerned, I have argued that theoretical and normative aspects of sociology should not be conflated. For to do so is to equate social theory rather too closely with prophesying.

The Frankfurt theorists raise serious normative objections to Enlightenment thought, and in particular to the claim that reason provides a neutral, objective and autonomous guide to social and political thought and practice. Yet, as a consequence, these theorists implicitly reject the enterprise of social theory itself. In calling for a return to a state of harmony between humanity and the natural world, based on the liberation of impulses and drives, their strategy offers little by way of a constructive alternative to modern social theory. Foucault takes up from where the Frankfurt theorists leave off. But he only compounds their basic position. Like them, he objects to Enlightenment thought primarily on normative grounds. He seeks a theoretical conception of history which emphasizes discontinuity, not progress, and an empirical interpretation of history which draws out non-rational phenomena. But his analysis of power/knowledge in modern society tends to reinforce, not undermine, the modern conception of society as a totality, because his concept of power is so general as to be applicable to almost all forms of social relation.

Habermas provides a more affirmative approach to the project of modernity. In his hands, the concept of reason is built up into a duality and used to construct a concept of the lifeworld that is underpinned by an understanding of history as ethical progress. But Habermas's project is grounded in an understanding of human communication which, on closer analysis, proves to be rather thin. His normative vision is not only unrealistic but, in all likelihood, ethnocentric. In the final analysis, his attempts to deal with the question of pluralism are unconvincing, as is his account of the good society which, as Bauman observes, resembles something which is hardly more robust than a university seminar. And his theoretical account of the social system is derived from a narrow interpretation of economic reasoning which tends to gloss over the complexity of the relationship between culture and economic life. Compared with Marx on this specific question, Habermas's argument represents something of a backward step. The concept of the social system is meant to serve as a general model of society. But as such, it services a broader-based normative project which, on closer inspection, turns out to be somewhat meaningless.

The postmodern case against modern social theory consists of two main strands. First, postmodernists reject the concept of society as a totality. Some even dismiss the concept of society altogether: to favour either the notion of sociality or, more strongly, an emphasis on agency before structure. Second, and above all, they oppose the normative idea that the development of modern society will culminate in the achievement of consensus around core values, beliefs and political procedures. This argument spurns the concept of reason as an emancipatory force. But rather unnecessarily, it also discards the use of reason as an explanatory tool in social theory.

Lyotard and Baudrillard defy the logic of representation which, by their reckoning, characterizes modern social theory. They argue that the social world cannot be modelled, and agree that the general narratives of history which are associated with modern social thought have lost credibility. But neither theorist successfully escapes that logic of representation. They end up simply denying that there is a social reality which can be represented at all. Taken to extremes, this strategy would leave us with no sociology worthy of the name, because the discipline would no longer have an object of study in any palpable sense. In normative terms, they retain ideals associated with the project of modernity. But they do so only by default. Lyotard's concept of gaming and Baudrillard's notion of the politics of seduction turn out on closer scrutiny either to require or to reproduce ideals associated with the project of modernity. In their arguments, however, neither theorist is willing or able to justify them.

Bauman and Rorty outline a more constructive approach to replacing modern social thought. Both theorists emphasize the need to address, not gloss over, pluralism and fragmentation in contemporary society. Their solution is to envisage social theory and philosophy as participants in an ongoing conversation or dialogue about the world, not as observers who seek to provide a privileged account. This approach has significant normative implications. Both theorists suggest that the role of social theory and philosophy is to provide alternative accounts of the world. This would be to uphold pluralism. According to their view, sociology should not seek to represent reality so much as reflect multiple realities which are continually changing. They might well have added that a pretty effective way of achieving this is by thoroughgoing comparative research. Both Rorty and Bauman refuse to embrace the belief in relativism which, in their view, characterizes postmodern thought. But in the end, the contradiction this generates with their theoretical argument proves difficult to resolve.

Giddens and Beck hope to transcend the dichotomy between modern and postmodern social theory. Their strategy has three basic components. First, they are committed to universal values. But this commitment is pragmatic, not grounded in a universal concept of reason. It is also contingent, based on their interpretation of the consequences of the globalization of risk. Second, their approach to the concept of reason, and its impact on society, emphasizes its importance not as a means of knowing the world with certainty, but as a perennial source of doubt towards what we think we know. They do not deny the significance of reason in the modern world, but neither do they conceptualize reason in such a way that it is meant to guarantee cognitive and moral progress. Third, both theorists tend to use core theoretical concepts rather than large-scale, generalistic theoretical models. Their account of globalization highlights the interconnection between specific processes at the global and local level, and rejects notions of society as a global system.

Critical analysis of these arguments suggests, however, that the work of Giddens and Beck remains rather closer to modern social theory than they might have intended. The use of globalization as a justification for universalism can appear as a form of foundationalism by default. Their concept of reason is usefully abstract, and emphasizes doubt rather than certainty. But neither theorist conceives of reason as grounded in human praxis, and therefore as localized and culturally specific. As a result, their argument that universal agreement is vital if we are to address global risks provides few clues as to how differences of perspective, and the pluralism of values, might be accommodated. In normative terms, the arguments of Giddens and Beck sometimes resemble the prophesying tone identified with modern social theory. The concept of reflexivity needs to be refined if we are to distinguish between different forms of organization, distinctive political systems, various forms of media technology and a range of economic activities. To suggest that all of these forms of social relation are reflexive is rather unhelpful when seeking to understand, in a more precise way, the uneven dynamics of globalization. One might say, of course, that the more detailed operationalization of such concepts is a task for research, not social theory. But this merely reopens a chasm between theory and research which, so I have suggested in this book, needs to be narrowed.

In a very basic form, I want to propose a tentative compromise, or middle way, between modern and postmodern conceptions of social theory. The compromise has two strands. First, we must jettison the project of modernity: primarily for theoretical, not normative, reasons. That project can only be sustained by a theoretical approach which generalizes historical outcomes and cannot deal with contingency. We must move away from the prophetic understanding of history which informs modern social theory, above all because it interferes with the usefulness of theory itself. Social theorists cannot be prophets. And whatever Rorty might say, they are certainly not poets. But they might make half-decent problem-solvers. That, however, would depend on the construction of useful theories. This takes us to the second strand of my suggested compromise.

What are useful theories? Bauman argues that we need new theoretical models that can cope with postmodern pluralism, uncertainty and flux. I would suggest that we reject the notion of theoretical modelling altogether, in favour of heuristic concepts and modes of explanation that can facilitate rather than obstruct empirical research. Theories in and of themselves cannot represent the world. And whether the world is defined as modern or postmodern is too sweeping a question to be answered with models. In all of its generality, it is quite possibly a question that we should not be asking at all. Theory must be used as a tool which enables us to arrive at accounts of social reality which strive as far as possible to be accurate. If social reality is as complex and pluralistic as the postmodernists suggest, this approach to theory suggests not just the best, but the only way of grasping such complexity. All the postmodernists have tended to do is replicate that complexity: which all too often comes out as muddy confusion.

In the debate surrounding reason, we tend to be presented with a stark choice: between reason and non-reason, between Enlightenment thought and neo-Romanticism. But several of the theorists discussed in this book suggest that our use of reason is bounded by culture, by society, by politics and by locale. I would propose that we follow this through. In social life, the use of reason is multifaceted and multidimensional. Reason cannot straightforwardly be opposed to culture because they are intertwined, shaping each other in a way which is ongoing and contextual. Both the Frankfurt theorists from the perspective of modernity and Bauman from that of postmodernity suggest there is no singular, generalized version of reason which can be applied across different societies and social contexts. Moreover, they argue that reason is grounded in, not the grounding for, social and cultural practices. For them, reason is contextualized and specific, impossible to generalize in a single definition. Habermas agrees that reason is grounded in human praxis. Indeed, this is arguably among the most significant insights that he provides. But he goes on to employ this argument to formulate exactly the kind of universal concept of reason – albeit on normative grounds, it must be said – which both the Frankfurt theorists and Bauman rightly reject.

At the beginning of this discussion, I argued that modern social theory has been overshadowed by the work of Marx and Durkheim. Postmodern social theory, by contrast, tends to have drawn primarily on the arguments of Weber and Simmel. There are two basic reasons for this. First, in the eyes of postmodernists, both theorists prioritize human agency over social structure. Second, they grapple with the complexity of reason from the outset. But in both respects, the postmodern interpretation of the arguments of Simmel and Weber may be slightly misconceived. Of course, these theorists do not agree with the concept of society as a totality. This need not mean, however, that they do not acknowledge that social forces can in some way and under certain circumstances constrain human agency. Both Simmel and Weber, in important areas of their work, analyse social structures and social institutions. Moreover, they are at pains to distinguish between the concept of reason and its impact on culture, and the use of reason in their own arguments about the social world. This is a distinction which postmodernists do not even recognize.

What distinguishes the arguments of Simmel and Weber is not only their approach to the concept of society. Nor is it just their ambivalence towards the impact of reason on modern culture. It is, most importantly, their stance towards the aims, the scope and the explanatory range of social theory. For both theorists, a heavily qualified account of the capacity of social theory is combined with a painstaking attention to detail in their accounts of the social world. Both theorists reject the generalizations found in the work of Marx. For them, theory is an abstract tool for sociological research, not a generalized model of society itself. This conception of theory underlines the real value of their work in the context of the debate between modernists and postmodernists.

Let me briefly expand on the distinction between generality and abstraction. A social theory that provides a generalized model of society must, above all, be inclusive, that is, it should *represent* as many cases as possible. By contrast, to conceive of theory as an abstract tool for research, as I have suggested here, is to call for concepts that do not include a range of cases but can be *applied* to them for clarification and comparison. As I argued in chapter 2, the first approach suggests a tendency to skate over specificity, or at the very least to regard it as less significant than commonality. The second approach, however, can highlight specificity without necessarily excluding commonality. In a world in which, the postmodernists allege, societies are increasingly pluralistic and fragmented, abstract concepts are needed so that we can analyse the complex and shifting forms of sociality and organization without seeking to mirror them with general models. If the world genuinely *is* without form as the postmodernists allege, just about the last approach we should take is to construct equally shapeless social theories. On the contrary, we require more incisive research questions. Such questions can only be arrived at by using and analysing concepts in a rigorous way: not by assembling rigid theoretical models as the modernists would have it, nor by producing a seamless web of interpretations as the postmodernists invite us to do. The postmodernists suggest that we should substitute unyielding theoretical structures with layer upon layer of interpretation. I would propose another solution: the analytically rigorous construction of heuristic concepts. Such concepts do not represent social reality in a general way. They are meant to be applicable to, and useful when addressing, specific research questions.

It is significant that those who disdain the association between theory and a universal concept of reason – that is, the Frankfurt theorists, Foucault, and the postmodernists – do so largely on normative, not theoretical grounds. At the same time, those who advocate a normative concept of universal reason, primarily Marx and Habermas, do so because, they argue, it can be grounded theoretically: in a philosophical anthropology according to Marx, and in an understanding of the inherent features of human communication in Habermas's view. Giddens and Beck effectively buck this trend. They argue for universalism on pragmatic grounds. And although they do so in relation to an interpretation of the consequences of the growth of reason for modern society, their understanding of reason emphasizes its role as a force for increasing doubt and uncertainty in our relationship to the world, not greater levels of certainty. Against this background, their normative argument is informed not by theoretical foundations but by a genuine practical concern that the core questions and problems we now face in a political sense are global in their dimensions, and must therefore be addressed at this level. A heuristic concept of reason which emphasizes its role as a basis for methodical doubt, as Giddens suggests – and which does not seek to represent its role in human praxis in the general way that is suggested by reflexive modernity but enables specific cases to be compared – is something that social theorists might usefully develop. It would also enable us to retain the analytical use of reason, as a basis for methodical doubt, at the heart of our social theories without this becoming caught up with our topics of investigation.

I have suggested that we dispense with the notion of social theory as an overarching normative project. But this does not mean that social theory should inhabit a moral vacuum. This would be implausible and unpalatable. And in any case, to argue that we should cease addressing ourselves to universal normative questions need not suggest, as Rorty and Bauman make clear, that morality is unimportant: it means merely that morality is perhaps best conceived in the personal context where, according to Bauman, it properly resides. And where public affairs, or ethics, are concerned, Giddens certainly has a point when he remarks that certain practices simply *should* appear noxious to us. What, from a moral or ethical point of view, lies between these extremes rests as much with the problem-solvers as with the prophets. Much more immediate and practical questions – about organizing our political systems, about forms of social exclusion and their consequences for social identity, and about asymmetries of wealth and power – are questions which, as Weber might say, involve the analysis of alternative means in relation to ends or goals which have either been agreed or are taken for granted, and therefore do not require the deeper logic of philosophical argument.

The normative project of modernity, and its counterweight, postmodernity, have proved to be a distraction from focused and sustained consideration of questions about the nature, the aims and the explanatory capacity of social theory. This may be part of the reason why sociologists – and sociological textbooks – tend to treat theory and method as separate entities, not as mutually intertwined sets of questions and problems. Certainly, few of the theorists considered in this book, with the notable exception of Weber – and, intriguingly, Giddens, who regards structuration theory as the methodological basis of his theory of reflexive modernity – take up methodological questions as worthy of consideration in their own right. But, above all, I have sought to emphasize the distinction between theoretical and normative questions through the organization of this book. If one significant conclusion can be drawn from what sometimes appears to be the rather trite positivist mantra about distinguishing between fact and value, it is perhaps that when we equate social theories as models of society with normative projects which advocate a future path of the development of society, we tend to do neither with conspicuous success. The second side of this equation pulls the first out of shape (Marx and Habermas), misrepresents it (postmodern theory), or even suffocates it (Foucault and the Frankfurt theorists). The distinction between problem-solvers and prophets is undoubtedly a caricature. After all, the theorist who resembles the problem-solver most closely, Max Weber, is certainly not averse to making prophecies. Significantly, however, he neither builds up his theory on the basis of such prophecies, nor extends it in order to sustain them. But like all caricatures, the distinction between problem-solvers and prophets has been formulated to make a point.

The point is this. If the primary task of the social theorist is to formulate concepts, categories and modes of explanation which may prove useful (or be proven wrong or unhelpful) through research – in simple terms, if the aims of social theory are informed by the drive to discover and understand more about society – this task comes closest to the notion of problem-solving. The task might well be better served by formulating theories which are heuristic, which provide abstract tools rather than general models. If the preferred task of social theory is to prophesy, on the other hand, there seems to be no outstanding need to disguise this in the form of, and above all as derived from, a general explanatory model of society – not least because the model appears to serve no real purpose other than that of supporting, or appearing to ground, the prophecy. To refer to social theorists as problem-solvers may appear limited. (But that might well say more about contemporary social theory than it says about anything else.) The purpose of doing so, however, is to suggest that social theory should set itself more feasible goals, bring itself more closely into the practical remit of sociology, and move unequivocally into the compass of social reality. If the debate between modernity and postmodernity signals anything at all, it indicates just how far we have strayed from feasibility: from that remit and from that compass.

Notes

Chapter 1   Modernity and Society

1   The most comprehensive selections of writings for these two theorists arguably remain Marx, 1977, and Durkheim, 1972. Other selections, which provide
a slightly different range of material, or which tend to be more specialized,
include Durkheim, 1973, 1975, 1979, 1985 and 1986; and Marx, 1986. For critical discussion of Marx's work, I would single out the classic Avineri, 1986;
Elster, 1986, and Cohen, 1978, for their clarity; and McLellan, 1995, for its empathy and authority. On Durkheim, Lukes, 1975, remains indispensable, although see also the succinct Giddens, 1978. For an examination of the work of
both Marx and Durkheim – and also Weber – Giddens, 1971 (2nd edn 1994),
remains unrivalled; although for a slightly easier approach, see Hughes, Martin and Sharrock, 1995. For those seeking clarification of difficult Marxist concepts, or an explanation of some of his key arguments, Bottomore, 1991,
provides an invaluable reference.
2   In basic terms, the philosophical anthropology seeks to describe the most fundamental or essential features of human existence and social life. For a more
detailed discussion of this, see Avineri, 1968, esp. ch. 3.
3   As Avineri notes, 'human consciousness could operate according to the new
epistemology only if the obstacles in its way in present society were eliminated' (1968: 69).
4   *Homo faber* refers literally to the idea of the human being as a maker of tools.
More broadly, it can refer to the making of both things and self.
5   In order to explain this principle, Durkheim uses the analogy of living cells:
'The living cell contains nothing but mineral particles, just as society contains
nothing but individuals; it is obviously impossible, however, for the phenomena characteristic of life to exist in the atoms of hydrogen, oxygen, carbon, and
nitrogen' (1972: 69). For further discussion of these ideas, see Durkheim, 1953,
1975 and 1994. This approach is of course crucial to the methodology behind

Durkheim's study of suicide, see Durkheim, 1952.

6   For a fuller explanation of this concept, see Durkheim, 1972: 264–8.

7   This is explained in more detail in Smith, 1986, book 1, ch. 2.

8   The most extensive study of reification by Marx is contained in Marx, 1970.

9   For a concise summary of the FRP thesis, see Elster, 1985: 156–61; and, more extensively, Fine, 1984; and Fine and Harris, 1979.

10 See Marx and Engels, 1992.

11 For example, Elster suggests that it is possible to envisage an automated economic system where 'goods would be transferred between firms and from firms to consumers according to well-defined notional prices, yet no labour would enter into the production of goods' (1985: 140). He adds that it cannot be assumed that technological progress will always be labour-saving (p. 159). In short, the two key assumptions contained in the FRP thesis – first, that only labour produces profit, and second, that technological progress will reduce labour – are somewhat flawed.

12 For a discussion of this, see Durkheim, 1984; and for a brief selection of key passages, Durkheim, 1972: 141–54.

13 Durkheim does engage with classical economic theory, urging the development of an economic sociology (see Swedberg, 1987: 25). Unlike Marx, however, his argument is not with the technicalities of economic theory but with the idea that the principles of economic explanation can be applied to broader sociological questions.

14 While the details of Marx's economic arguments in this context are contained in Marx, 1956 and 1982, the broad thrust of his approach is tightly laid out in the famous 'Preface' to Marx, 1981. Both Marx, 1977 and Marx, 1986 contain the key passages of this text.

15 These ideas are studied in much more detail in Durkheim, 1976.

16 For a broader discussion of this idea, see Lukes, 1975, ch. 17.

17 This argument can be found in Durkheim, 1992.

18 For a fuller description of this, see Mandel's introduction to Marx, 1982: 77 n81.

19 This is the view taken forcefully by Cohen, 1978: 353.

20 These quotations are from Durkheim, 1984, and are cited in Lukes, 1975: 164–5.

21 This definition is taken from Bottomore, 1991.

Chapter 2   Modernity and Reason

1   Selected writings for these theorists include Simmel, 1964; but most notably, Simmel, 1971. For Simmel's methodological and epistemological writings, see Simmel, 1980; and for more recent translations of his writings on modern culture, Simmel, 1997. For Weber's methodological writings, see Weber, 1969; for the famous essays on science and politics as a vocation and other important writings, Weber, 1991; and more generally, Weber, 1978b. Frisby offers the finest and most accurate discussions of Simmel's work in Frisby, 1992b; see also Frisby, 1985 and 1992a, although Levine's introduction to Simmel, 1971 is also illuminating, while Poggi, 1993, offers a clear and concise critical sum-

mary of *The Philosophy of Money*. On Weber, see Turner, 1992, for its clarity; but especially Scaff, 1989, and Kasler, 1988, for their historical insight and originality; and Kalberg, 1994, and Ringer, 1997, for the significance and distinctiveness of Weber's theoretical and methodological strategy. Collins, 1986, offers quite an original perspective on Weber's political writings, as (superbly) does Hennis, 1988 and (indispensably) Mommsen, 1974, 1985 and 1989.

2   This is from Simmel's essay 'Soziologie der Sinne' (1907), and is cited in Frisby, 1985: 55.

3   For a more detailed discussion of this idea, see the essay 'How is society possible?', in Simmel, 1971.

4   For discussion of these interests, see the essay, 'Sociability', in Simmel, 1971.

5   Simmel argues that 'the impulse to sociability distils, as it were, out of the realities of social life the pure essence of association, of the associative process as a value and a satisfaction' (1971: 128).

6   For a more detailed discussion of this connection, see Hennis, 1988: 87–8.

7   For an explanation of the distinction between ideal types and descriptive types, see Giddens, 1971: 142–3.

8   For an example of Weber's range, see Weber, 1961.

9   As Giddens notes, double-entry bookkeeping 'constitutes the most integral expression of what makes the modern type of capitalist production dissimilar to prior sorts of capitalistic activity such as usury or adventurers' capitalism' (1971: 179).

10   For example, see Featherstone, 1990, and Featherstone, Lash and Robertson, 1995.

11   As Collins notes, a 'Weberian theory of politics . . . implies that internal politics is intimately connected with external geopolitics' (1986: 147). Weber's approach is taken up in Theda Skocpol's structural analysis of the three major social revolutions in France, China and Russia (Skocpol, 1978). Giddens's analysis of the emergence of the modern nation-state and the process of globalization also draws closely on Weber, arguing that 'we cannot interpret what the meaning of "internal" compared to "external" influences *is* without an analysis of the consolidation of the modern state as a political form' (1985: 167, Giddens's emphasis).

12   This argument has undoubtedly proved to be controversial. For a rounded discussion, see Hennis, 'Max Weber's theme: "personality and life orders"', in Hennis, 1988. The specific passage in which Weber writes on the physical and spiritual qualities of the nation comes from 'Die deutschen Landarbeiter', in *Bericht über die Verhandlungen des 5 Evangelisch – sozialen Kongress* (1894), and is cited in Hennis, 1988: 83.

13   The study is reproduced in translation in Weber, 1979.

14   For an excellent summary and discussion of this study, see Tribe, 1979.

15   For a rounded discussion of these influences, see Riesebrodt, 1986: 484–5 and 499 n11; and Hennis's essay, 'Max Weber's theme', in Hennis, 1988. For a somewhat different emphasis, see Tribe, 1979: 175–6.

16   For an example of this particular line, see Weinstein and Weinstein, 1989.

17   Simmel argues that the freedom to use money for so many different ends 'may be compared with the fate of the insecure person who has foresworn his Gods and whose newly acquired "freedom" only provides the opportunity for mak-

ing an idol out of any fleeting value' (1990: 402).

18   This is an expression sufficiently powerful, according to Levine, as to convey in Simmel a 'devotion to the principle of individuality' (introduction to Simmel, 1971: xlii).

19   This is from Simmel's essay, 'Die Grossstädte und das Geistesleben' (1903) and is cited in Frisby, 1992a: 112–13. The essay is reproduced in translation as 'The metropolis and mental life' in Simmel, 1964.

20   For further discussion of Simmel's arguments on space, see Lechner, 1991.

21   It is worth consulting the argument developed in Simmel, 1991, in this context.

22   This is from an essay published by Simmel under the pseudonym of Paul Liesegang, 'Infelices possidentes' (1893), and is cited in Frisby, 1992a: 127.

23   For a fuller discussion of this distinction, see Brubaker, 1984: 106. For further discussion of Weber's conceptualization of reason, see Lash and Whimster, 1986.

24   For an explanation of this point, see Giddens, 1971: 167.

25   Some commentators have argued that Weber was committed to German nationalism, for example Mommsen, 1974 and 1985. But even Mommsen emphasizes the complexity of Weber's political views (see 1989, part 1). As he states in the preface, 'Max Weber never followed narrow party lines' (p. viii). Hennis contends that Weber merely sought 'a break with the preoccupations implicit in the values of a past world, without at the same time falling under the influence of the contemporary belief in progress' (1988: 64). This would suggest that Weber was more of a reluctant modernist, or realist, than anything else.

26   For a discussion of this, see Hennis, 1988: 117–20.

27   This distinction is discussed in Goldman, 1988: 14.

28   This argument is contained in Weber's essay, 'Science as a vocation', see Weber, 1991.

29   This is the line taken in Frisby, 1992a: 170.

30   Those seeking further material on Simmel's methodology should consult Simmel, 1980. For discussion, see Lichtblau, 1991.

31   For a rich exploration of this idea, see Zelizer, 1994.

32   Much on this can be found in Frisby, 1992b; see the 'Afterword' in particular.

33   For a discussion of these and other affinities between the work of Simmel and Weber, see Fraught, 1991.

34   For an explanation of this, see Scaff, 1989: 149.

35   For an example of this argument, see Hennis, 1988: 171.

36   These points are thoroughly discussed in Huff, 1984; Kasler, 1988; Kalberg, 1994; Oakes, 1991; and Ringer, 1997.

37   I am indebted to the argument in Jagd, 1998, and to discussions with its author, for my interpretation of these points.

38   Weber himself puts it in the following way: 'An ideal type is formed by the one-sided *accentuation* of one or more points of view and by the synthesis of a great many diffuse, discrete, more or less present and occasionally absent *concrete individual* phenomena, which are arranged according to those one-sidedly emphasized viewpoints into a unified *analytical* construct. In its conceptual purity, this mental construct cannot be found empirically anywhere in reality' (1969: 90, Weber's emphasis).

39   For example, commonality seems more likely to be present in the ideal-types which address complex systems or patterns of development, than in those which address only individual phenomena. For an explanation of these distinctions, see Burger, 1987.

40   For a discussion of this, see Turner, 1992, ch. 9.

41   For a clear examination of this, see Anderson, 1992: 192.

42   The notion of 'violent abstraction' is explored further in Sayer, 1987.

43   This is an argument advanced most intriguingly, from a modernist stance, in Gellner, 1992.

Chapter 3   A Critique of Reason

1   Arato and Gebhardt, 1978, remains just about the most comprehensive collection of Frankfurt School writings. For more specific selections relating to the theorists discussed in this chapter, see Adorno, 1990, which suggests a slightly more affirmative interpretation of his approach to the culture industry than the one I advance in this chapter; and also Adorno, 1998a; Horkheimer, 1972, which contains key texts including the comparison between traditional and critical theory; Horkheimer, 1995, which contains some of his earliest writings; Marcuse, 1968 and 1970, for most of his key articles and essays; and Marcuse, 1998, which marks the beginning of what should turn out to be a full series of his papers. For critical summaries: Held, 1980, and Jay, 1973, remain unrivalled for their clarity and historical insight, respectively. But Wiggershaus's extensive history of the Frankfurt School in Wiggershaus, 1994, repays close reading. Jay's short book on Adorno (Jay, 1984a) is excellent. And for a fresh slant on Horkheimer, consult Benhabib et al., 1993.

2   This essay is reproduced in Horkheimer, 1972.

3   Although for reasons why the designation 'school' is at least partly justified, see Wiggershaus, 1994: 2; and Held, 1980: 14–15. The Frankfurt theorists can be divided into central and peripheral groups. At the centre were Max Horkheimer, Theodor Adorno, Herbert Marcuse, Leo Lowenthal, Friedrich Pollock, Eric Fromm, and Carl Grünberg. As for peripheral members, we can identify Franz Neumann, Otto Kirchheimer, Henryck Grossman, Arkadij Gurland, and Walter Benjamin. The term 'Frankfurt School' derives from the close connections of the Critical Theorists with the Frankfurt Institute for Social Research, founded in 1923 as a department of Frankfurt University, although privately funded. The Critical Theorists – who were almost all Jewish – sought exile from Germany in 1933 and scattered: some to Geneva, others to Paris and Oxford, and the most influential members, Adorno and Horkheimer, to the USA, where they were joined by Fromm, Marcuse and Lowenthal. The Institute was re-established in Frankfurt by 1953, with Adorno and Horkheimer still its leading figures.

4   As Jay writes of Adorno: 'whereas Marx lived at a time when a disunited, "backward" Germany sought to realize the promises of greatness contained in the ambitious systems of its idealist metaphysicians, Adorno was alive when a much chastened philosophy had to make sense as best it could of the monstrous failure of that attempt' (1984a: 56).

5 For a more detailed account of this argument, see in particular Marcuse, 'Industrialization and capitalism in the work of Max Weber', in Marcuse, 1968. In order to grasp more clearly the difference between Weber's position and the Frankfurt theorists' approach, it is worth noting the distinction drawn by Giddens between attributions of the 'failure of sweet reason' to *design faults* on the one hand and *operator failure* on the other: see Giddens, 1990: 151–2. Cast in these terms, the Frankfurt theorists attribute design faults *to* operator failure in the sense that the so-called operators have failed to recognize the true character of reason itself. This view is important to Adorno's concept of 'non-identity' thinking, which I shall discuss later on.

6 Grossman agrees with Marx that a crisis of capitalism is 'objectively necessary'. Adorno and Horkheimer incorporate elements of Freudian psychoanalysis into the Marxist framework placing greater emphasis on the superstructure. Pollock argues that while the tensions and contradictions underlying capitalism in 1930s Germany are broadly the same as those that characterized liberal capitalism in the form analysed by Marx, the features that are meant to lead to the formation of a 'class for itself' are absent, i.e. a decline in the skilled working-class population due to the rationalization of production methods, see Arato and Gebhardt, 1978: 16. Pollock focuses increasingly on the state, inviting parallels with the work of Habermas later on, particularly in Habermas, 1976.

7 For a clear discussion of this basic division, see Held, 1980: 52–3.

8 This is from Pollock's essay, 'Die gegenwärtige Lage des Kapitalismus und die Aussichten einer planwirtschaftlichen Neuordnung' (1932), and is cited in Held, 1980: 57–8.

9 For an explanation of these connections, see Held, 1980: 41–2.

10 This is from Horkheimer's essay, 'Autorität und Familie', see the translation in Horkheimer, 1972.

11 A useful discussion of these historical changes can be found in Zolberg, 1990.

12 According to Adorno and Horkheimer, 'culture monopolies are weak and dependent' in comparison to the 'most powerful sectors of industry' such as steel and chemicals. In short, the process of interlocking between finance, industry and culture tends to be one-sided: 'The dependence of the most powerful broadcasting company on the electrical industry, or of the motion picture industry on the banks, is characteristic of the whole sphere, whose individual branches are themselves interwoven' (1979: 123).

13 See his various entries in Adorno et al., 1980: 100–41.

14 I refer to vulgar Marxism simply because there is plenty of evidence from Marx's own writings to suggest that he himself would not have advanced such a simplistic concept of ideology.

15 It should be noted that the Frankfurt theorists do not refer to 'positivism' as a single approach but as several. These include the logical positivism of the Vienna circle (Carnap and others), logical empiricism, realism, logical atomism and the early work of Wittgenstein (Arato and Gebhardt, 1978: 373).

16 Adorno, 'On the logic of the social sciences', in Adorno et al., 1976: 115.

17 Marcuse, 'Some social implications of modern technology', in Marcuse, 1968: 431. According to Marcuse, private power relationships 'appear not only as relationships between objective things but also as the rule of rationality itself' (1968: 154). The essay can also be found in Marcuse, 1998. The arguments are

laid out more extensively in the indispensable Marcuse, 1991.

18   For essays on these and other subjects, see Adorno, 1957, 1974 and 1994. See also Adorno, 1975.

19   For an explanation of this, see Adorno, 1978.

20   As McCarthy notes, while the approach of Adorno and Horkheimer 'does not abstractly negate ideas of reason', it does seek to 'appropriate them and to enlist them in the struggle for a better world' (Hoy and McCarthy, 1994: 20).

21   For his arguments on and interpretation of instrumental reason, see Horkheimer, 1974a and 1974b.

22   This probably represents the gist of Horkheimer's position during the 1930s. In the essay, 'Zum Rationalismusstreit in der gegenwärtigen Philosophie' (1934), he argues that 'the value of a theory is decided by its connection with the tasks, which in the particular historical moment are taken up by progressive social forces' (cited in Held, 1980: 192). As Held observes (p. 195), there are echoes of Lukács when Horkheimer aligns theory explicitly with the 'mental and materialistic situation . . . of a particular social class', although Horkheimer defends the interests of a broader cross-section of society than would be expected within the parameters of orthodox Marxism. (He uses the term *Allgemeinheit*, which Held translates as the 'general public'.) Over time, however, Horkheimer moves closer to Adorno's position, suggesting in an article published in 1941 that social theory must 'reflect the actual rift between the social reality and the values it posits' (1941: 122). And his outlook becomes progressively more bleak, not least in the continuing absence of genuine radicalism among the working classes in Europe and the United States. As Held notes, Horkheimer 'became more and more concerned to preserve a past in danger of being forgotten – the history of struggles for emancipation – and maintain a capacity for independent, critical, thinking' (1980: 198). Much of that capacity, he later argued, must be derived from theology.

23   Adorno writes: 'It lies in the definition of negative dialectics that it will not come to rest in itself, as if it were total' (1973b: 406).

24   For his arguments on revolution, see Marcuse, 1960, 1969 and 1972.

25   Freud's argument can be found in 'Civilization and its discontents', and is reprinted with other relevant articles in Freud, 1985.

26   This is from his introduction to part 3 of Arato and Gebhardt, in 1978: 391.

27   See Gebhardt in Arato and Gebhardt, 1978: 403.

28   Contrary to the views of some critics, Adorno and Horkheimer do not place a negative value on popularity, or even necessarily on populism. Nor do they confine their critique to the technical qualities of art works. Their argument focuses on the relationship between the popularization of culture and the economic organization of the culture industry, and draws directly on Marx's notion of commodity fetishism: 'The use value of art, its mode of being, is treated as a fetish; and the fetish, the work's social rating (misinterpreted as its artistic status) becomes its use value – the only quality which is enjoyed' (Adorno and Horkheimer, 1979: 158).

29   Witness Adorno, in a letter to Benjamin: 'the idea that a reactionary is turned into a member of the avant-garde by expert knowledge of Chaplin's films strikes me as out-and-out romanticization' (from Adorno et al., 1980: 123).

30   This is from the essay, 'The work of art in the era of mechanical reproduction'.

The quotation can be found in Benjamin, 1968: 234.

31   It is worth consulting Adorno, 1973c on these questions.

32   For a more detailed discussion, see Adorno, 1984. It is worth adding that the autonomous work of art must also contain some unresolved elements: 'That factor in a work of art which enables it to transcend reality . . . is to be found in those features in which discrepancy appears: in the necessary failure of the passionate striving for identity' (Adorno and Horkheimer, 1979: 131).

33   Adorno maintains that 'sociology should not question how music functions, but how it stands towards fundamental social antinomies, whether it sets about to master them or let them remain or even hide them, and this question leads only to what is immanent in the form of the work in itself' (cited in Jay, 1984a: 135).

34   Briefly and simplistically, Schönberg's serial technique rests on the principle of sounding each note of the twelve-note chromatic scale which makes up the musical octave in a particular order without any specific note taking precedence over the others, i.e. being sounded more often. This contrasts starkly with conventional harmony, where the music proceeds through a series of 'keys', each derived from a particular collection of notes. Although just a handful of Schönberg's works genuinely adopt this principle, Adorno applauds both the rationalism and egalitarianism of serial music.

35   For a much more detailed understanding of Adorno's arguments on modern music, see Adorno, 1973a and 1973d. His writings on Beethoven are now available as Adorno, 1998b.

36   Adorno goes so far as to suggest that the 'real interests of the individuals are still strong enough, at the margins, to resist total control' (cited in Jay, 1984a: 128). It is debatable, however, whether this represents a softening of Adorno's earlier position or a clarification of the difficulties already inherent in that position. According to Jay, 'perhaps the best that can be said is that it reflected a long overdue abandonment of his assumption of a tacit identity between American popular culture and its fascist counterpart' (ibid.).

37   This point is discussed clearly by Thompson, 1984: 269.

38   Adorno is referring primarily to the concept of the death instinct.

39   For a rounded discussion of this, see Jay, 1973: 109 and 104.

40   This is explained in Adorno, 1967b: 87.

41   Adorno and Horkheimer led a series of studies of the 'authoritarian personality' from around 1945. See, for example, Adorno, 1946 and 1951; Adorno et al., 1950; Lowenthal, 1987; and Massing, 1949. In *Dialectic of Enlightenment*, Adorno and Horkheimer argue that the individual who is caught up in the contradictory forces of modern society is bound to seek some outlet whereby 'impulses which are normally taboo and conflict with the requirements of the prevailing form of labour are transformed into conforming idiosyncrasies' (1979: 185). Anti-Semitism provides one such outlet because it enables the passive, weakened ego to be inverted. Fascism therefore 'defines a psychological area which can be successfully exploited by the forces which promote it for entirely nonpsychological reasons of self-interest' (Adorno, 1951: 135).

42   For a clear explanation of this problem, see Held, 1980: 388.

43   As Jay notes, there are two aspects to this. First, the work of art must imitate social reality (*immanence*), particularly its contradictions. Second, the work of

art should contain elements of natural reality, some reflection of the ideal of natural beauty (*transcendence*). Art would thereby serve a transcendent function because it implies 'a prefiguration of a possible restoration of that condition in the future'. Only then can art be said to achieve 'progressive liberation from the mythic, cultic, ritualized context out of which it emerged' (Jay, 1984a: 156–7).

44 As Jay notes, 'a vague hope for the sudden collapse of the system as a whole provides little real impetus to political action of any kind either now or in the future.' Theoretically, to conceive of the system as a totality suggests a combination of 'an increasingly gloomy analysis of the totality on the macrological level with a call for theoretical and artistic resistance to it on the micrological' (1984b: 264–5).

45 While conceding that 'it has been one of the principal tenets of the critical theory of society . . . to refrain from what might be reasonably called utopian speculation,' Marcuse argues that 'this restrictive conception must be revised' because such revision 'is suggested, and even necessitated, by the actual evolution of contemporary societies' (1969: 3). The central question for critical theory is no longer 'how can the individual satisfy his needs without hurting others, but rather: how can he satisfy his needs without hurting himself, without reproducing . . . his dependence on an exploitative apparatus which . . . perpetuates his servitude?' (1969: 4). For the ramifications of these questions in an aesthetic context, see Marcuse, 1979.

Chapter 4 Reason and Power

1 There are no entirely satisfying collections of Foucault's writing, although Foucault, 1984, is reasonably comprehensive. The interviews contained in Foucault, 1977a, 1980 and 1988a may well be as good a starting-point as any. Merquior provides a wonderfully concise and incisive summary of Foucault's work in Merquior, 1991, although for a more sympathetic and arguably more balanced account, see McNay, 1994, and Cousins and Hussain, 1984. There are many essay collections on Foucault's work, some of which could serve as a reasonable overall introduction. These include Hoy, 1986b; Ramazanoğlu, 1993; Caputo and Yount, 1993; Diamond and Quinby, 1988; and Gane and Johnson, 1993. For an angle on Foucault's later writing, consult Bernaeur and Rasmussen, 1988.

2 Merquior likens the episteme to Kuhn's concept of the paradigm (see Kuhn, 1970). There are two basic similarities: first, different epistemes are incommensurable; and second, change from one episteme to another stems from something like a cultural sea-change rather than the straightforward existence of contrary evidence. Merquior defines the episteme as 'a basement . . . of thought, a mental infrastructure underlying all strands of knowledge (on man) at a given age, a conceptual "grid" . . . that amounts to an "historical *a priori*"' (1991: 38). There are also important differences, though: unlike the paradigm, the episteme cuts across various sciences, and the episteme is less consciously prescriptive than the paradigm, which is like a theory or model.

3 Foucault points out four main differences between archaeology and the his-

tory of ideas (1972: 138–40). First, the archaeologist is not interested in what documents reveal about ideas but in the structure of documents themselves. Second, the archaeologist does not seek to trace where ideas come from and where they lead, but investigates only ideas for themselves. Third, the archaeologist does not seek to establish sociological or psychological causes of intellectual events or trends. Fourth, the archaeologist is not searching for the 'essence' of ideas, nor for the original intentions of their author.

4   Foucault argues in *The Archaeology of Knowledge* that there has been an 'epistemological mutation' in historiography which can be traced back to Marx. In the history of events, questions of causality have been replaced by a concern with classification which emphasizes continuity (1972: 3). In the history of ideas, the opposite has happened (p. 4). According to Foucault, these contrasting tendencies have a single underlying cause, namely, a transformation in the relationship between documents and monuments as historical sources. Whereas traditional history 'undertook to "memorize" the *monuments* of the past, transform them into *documents*', modern history 'transforms *documents* into *monuments*' (p.7, Foucault's emphasis). This transformation in the relationship between events and texts has three main consequences for historiography (pp. 8–10). First, the notion of discontinuity has assumed a major role in all historical disciplines. Second, the notion of 'total' history has been replaced by an idea of 'general' history. Third, the historian faces new methodological questions, for example, whether to treat a body of texts as 'exhausted or inexhaustible'.

5   As Merquior writes: 'His point is, showing the strangeness of the worlds we have lost compels us moderns to take stock of our cultural identity through a realization of our distance from older forms of life and thought' (1991: 72).

6   As Hoy notes, the idea of human nature tends to be regarded as 'the lowest common denominator throughout all historical change' (1986a: 133).

7   For a fuller account of this argument, see 'Nietzsche, genealogy, history', which is published both as Foucault, 1977c, and in Foucault, 1984.

8   As Foucault argues, 'we cannot exercise power except through the production of truth' (1980: 98).

9   Foucault writes that 'it is already one of the prime effects of power that certain bodies, certain gestures, certain discourses, certain desires, come to be identified and constituted as individuals' (1980: 98).

10   This earlier argument is contained in Foucault, 1987.

11   As Foucault remarks: 'It is for the other world that the madman sets sail in his fools' boat; it is from the other world that he comes when he disembarks' (1971: 11).

12   For the analysis in full, see Foucault, 1973.

13   Merquior describes these apparatuses as 'motley ensembles made of discourses, institutions, laws, administrative measures, scientific statements, philanthropic initiatives, etc.' (1991: 123).

14   For these arguments, see in particular, Foucault, 1985 and 1986.

15   Foucault defines the aesthetics of existence as 'those intentional and voluntary actions by which men not only set themselves rules of conduct, but also seek to transform themselves, to change themselves in their singular being, and to make their life into an *oeuvre* that carries certain aesthetic values and meets certain stylistic criteria' (1985: 10–11). Some of these arguments can also be

found in Foucault, 1988b.

16 This is taken from an article by Foucault published in the *London Review of Books*, 21 May–3 June 1981. The passage here is cited at length in Merquior, 1991: 123.

17 Oliver argues that the concept of resistance implies support for a form of 'fractal politics', which is likened to chaos theory: 'small changes can cascade upward' because the 'geometry' of a situation is altered by an initial event. This process creates patterns 'which repeat, with slight differences, on different levels'. Change is therefore 'amplified on larger and larger scales throughout the system' (1991: 189). In Foucault's terms, this idea is translated in the following way: 'Local instability allows small interventions which in turn are amplified exponentially on level after level until the very character of the system is changed' (Oliver, 1991: 192). Oliver argues, further, that Foucault's analysis demonstrates that 'placing our hopes on an overthrow of state power is more hopelessly utopian than encouraging individual resistance on all levels' (p. 183).

18 As Gordon notes, 'genealogical narration is an inverse, a post-mortem, a satire of the Enlightenment's prospectuses of progress' (1993: 25).

19 With regard to the shift of emphasis in the second and third volumes of *The History of Sexuality*, for example, see O'Farrell, 1989, and Ferry and Renaut, 1990.

20 This argument is summarized in Davidson, 1986: 230.

21 For another three-stage description of Foucault's output, see Poster, 1993: 64.

22 This is Merquior's preferred interpretation of Foucault's overtly political writings, where he defines the work of intellectuals simply as the struggle 'for undermining and capturing authority'. On this basis, Merquior contrasts the Marxist 'conflation' of theory into praxis with a Foucauldian 'collapse': 'Praxis ceases to have a theoretical ballast: each social practice runs its own show, and "theoretical practice" – the intellectuals' job – would just be one of them, were it not for the fact that, in a sense, it is bound to be an unhappy practice, doomed to self-suspicion and bad consciousness' (1991: 85).

23 The interview was with Jean-Louis Ézine, and was published in *Nouvelles Littéraires*, 17–23 March 1975. The citation here is from Merquior, 1991: 118.

24 The distinction is drawn in Fraser, 1985: 180.

25 For an explanation and discussion of this problem, see Fraser, 1992a: 68.

26 This, at least, is the view advanced forcefully by Merquior, 1991: 151.

27 Fuss defines essentialism as 'the idea that men and women . . . are identified as such on the basis of transhistorical, eternal, immutable essences' (1990: xi).

28 For a full summary of this perspective, see Bartky, 1988.

29 This is the view advanced, for example, in Butler, 1990: 93.

30 For example, O'Brien argues that Foucault's analysis of the body in his work on the prison is slanted unreasonably towards the experiences of men. There were important differences between categories of crime for which men and women tended to be imprisoned during the nineteenth century in France. Moreover, there was a distinctive explanatory discourse surrounding women's crime which 'at its most extreme was that all menstruating, lactating, ovulating, pregnant, newly delivered, newly sexually initiated and menopausal women were prone to crime' (1982: 68). Giddens argues that Foucault fails to

analyse the way in which discursive techniques relate specifically to women: after all, most of his analyses concern total institutions such as the prison and the asylum (see Giddens, 1992: 18–36, 168–72).

31 For a fuller explanation of this, see Benhabib, 1991a: 229; Ransom, 1993.

32 For analyses of this, see McNay, 1992: 42; Willis, 1988; Smith-Rosernberg, 1986.

33 This point is well made in Dews, 1987: 188.

34 Foucault goes to considerable lengths in denying this, referring to 'certain half-witted "commentators" [who] persist in labelling me "structuralist" ' (1970: xiv). But as Merquior notes, a study 'which speaks of perceptual codes and structures, describes the "spatializations of the pathological", and insists on a non-linear rendering of intellectual history . . . was bound to be compared' to structuralism (1991: 33). Foucault offers at least tacit agreement when he remarks that, in his study of the clinic, there is 'frequent recourse to structural analysis' which threatens to bypass 'the level proper to archaeology' (1972: 16).

35 Michael Mann addresses this problem when outlining 'networks' of power, where he writes memorably of particular causal relationships being 'too complex to theorize', see Mann, 1986: 29.

36 For this particular argument, see Merquior, 1991: 115.

Chapter 5   The Potential of Reason

1 For a selection of writings by Habermas, see Habermas, 1996b. For an authoritative account of the philosophical background to and genesis of Habermas's earlier ideas, see McCarthy, 1978; and for his later arguments, White, 1988, and the introduction to White, 1995b. Ingram, 1987, provides another comprehensive survey of Habermas's ideas up to and including the publication of *The Theory of Communicative Action*. In addition, one could do far worse for an introduction than consult the illuminating interviews in Habermas, 1986 and 1994. Of the more accessible textbooks on Habermas's work, I would recommend Outhwaite, 1994; Rassmussen, 1990; and Brand, 1990. And for a well-researched survey of specific debates between Habermas and other philosophers and social theorists, including the debate with Gadamer, see Holub, 1991. Of the many collections of essays on Habermas's work, Thompson and Held, 1982, Bernstein 1985, and Honneth and Joas, 1991, provide a representative selection of the debates surrounding *The Theory of Communicative Action*, while White, 1995b, covers the arguments arising from the publication of *Between Facts and Norms*. For more specialized articles on communicative ethics, see Benhabib and Dallmayr, 1990; on the transformation of the public sphere, Calhoun, 1992; and on the project of modernity, d'Entrèves and Benhabib, 1996.

2 Habermas argues that 'a precise analysis of the first part of the *German Ideology* reveals that Marx does not actually explicate the interrelationship of interaction and labour, but instead, under the unspecific title of social praxis, reduces one to the other' (1988: 168–9; see Marx, 1965).

3 See Kohlberg, 1981: 409. For Habermas's discussion, see Habermas, 1990: 116–94; 1993: 113–32.

4   This is explained more fully in Habermas, 1990: 161.

5   For an explanation of this, see Mead, 1981: 284.

6   For Parsons's own account of this approach, see Parsons, 1952, 1967, 1976 and 1977; Parsons and Smelser, 1957.

7   The article can be found in Parsons, 1967.

8   Specifically, Habermas argues that power cannot be measured like money; that it is more restricted than money in its 'circulation'; that power cannot be deposited with the same freedom as money; that the 'value' of power depends on its holder more than money; that the analogy between banking and elections is unrealistic; and that the 'inflation' or 'deflation' of power is much more difficult to quantify (1987c: 268–70). For other perspectives on, and a summary of, Parsons and economic life, see Holton, 1986, and Savage, 1977. On the specific subject of money, it is worth consulting Ganßmann, 1988, and Dodd, 1994, ch. 4.

9   These points are laid out in Habermas, 1987c: 368. See also Habermas, 1976 and 1987d.

10 There are, of course, other influences, such as the work of Charles Peirce and Wilhelm Dilthey. For a more detailed discussion of Habermas's sources, see McCarthy,1978; Held, 1980, ch.11; and Thompson, 1981: 71–111.

11 For a fuller discussion of this connection, see Wittgenstein, 1967, sec. 23; and Thompson, 1981: 19.

12 Habermas does criticize Wittgenstein's approach, however, for failing to distinguish between the skills involved in particular language games and those needed for a basic level of competence in general speech. The notion of general linguistic competence is a vital part of Habermas's argument. For a discussion of this, see Dallmayr and McCarthy, 1977: 335–63.

13 The speech-act has three main components: the locutionary act, i.e. the act of speaking itself; the illocutionary act, i.e. the act performed in speaking; and the perlocutionary act, i.e. the act performed by speaking, see Thompson, 1981: 19.

14 As Habermas argues: 'Every process of reaching understanding takes place against a background of a culturally ingrained preunderstanding . . . For both parties the interpretive task consists in incorporating the other's interpretation of the situation into one's own in such a way that in the revised version "his" external world and "my" external world can – against the background of "our" lifeworld – be relativized in relation to "the" world' (1984: 100).

15 The term 'prejudgement' is a translation of *Voruteil*, which can also be translated as 'prejudice'.

16 The disagreement sparked a debate which ranged much more widely than it is possible to explain here. For fuller summaries and discussion, see Bubner, 1975, and commentaries by Blakey, McCarthy and Gadamer in the same volume; Giddens, 1979: 135–64; How, 1980; Hoy, 1978: 117–30; Ingram, 1983; Jay, 1982; McCarthy, 1978: 169–93; Mendelson, 1979; Misgeld, 1977; and Holub, 1991, ch. 3.

17 Habermas's argument has been diluted to some extent as his theory has developed. The idea that knowledge is 'driven' by deep-rooted collective interests of this kind seems to be less and less palatable to him. For an explanation, see Habermas, 1987a: 351–86; and his introduction to Habermas, 1988: 1–40. More generally, see Habermas, 1989c and 1992a. For critical comment, Ingram, 1987: 15.

18 Habermas argues that *'the critique of ideology,* as well, moreover, as *psycho-analysis,* take into account that information about lawlike connections sets off a process of reflection in the consciousness of those whom the laws are about' (1987a: 310, Habermas's emphasis). He likens distorted, i.e. non-rational, communication to repression, and suggests that 'the relation of theory to therapy is just as constitutive for Freudian theory as the relation of theory to praxis is for Marxist theory' (1988: 9). It should be emphasized, however, that he does not intend to suggest that society is merely an expanded version of the human subject. As he makes clear later on, the analogy between critical theory and psychoanalysis centres around 'methodological structures and basic concepts'. Unlike the therapeutic client, society is no 'addressee' whose eyes can be opened by the social theorist: 'In a process of enlightenment, there are only participants' (1994: 102).

19 For this reason, Habermas's concept of the 'ideal speech situation' – i.e. the form of dialogue in which all four validity-claims are advanced and fulfilled – can be misleading. The conditions outlined by this concept are threefold: first, that nobody should be excluded from dialogue; second, that all participants have the right to advance arguments and to question the arguments advanced by others; and third, that only questions which are in the general interest can be raised. This can easily seem utopian, and perhaps it is. But Habermas's point is that these conditions are already implicit in communication, not plucked out of the sky. If anything, they should be thought of as a 'counterfactual ideal', i.e. something against which we can evaluate political dialogue as it actually occurs, not something that we might actually attain. But, for Habermas, this is an 'ideal' only in the sense that it consists of 'normative contents that are *encountered* in practice, which we cannot do without, since language, together with the idealizations it demands of speakers, is simply constitutive for socio-cultural forms of life' (1994: 102, Habermas's emphasis). See also Habermas, 1993. For a more practical application of these ideas in a range of contexts, see the interviews in Habermas, 1994; and in the specific context of a united Europe and a reunified Germany, respectively, see Habermas, 1992b and 1997.

20 See in particular, Misgeld, 1985; Zelizer, 1994; and Dodd, 1994.

21 These arguments are contained in Habermas, 1996a.

22 For an explanation of this, see Baynes, 1995: 201.

23 Habermas counters this criticism by maintaining that while 'we can at any time decide to manipulate others . . . in fact not everyone could behave in this way at any time' (1994: 102). In other words, if we all – simultaneously – decided to subvert the principles of communication as he characterizes them, communication would not be possible at all. This seems a little like the old adage about the population of China jumping up and down simultaneously and causing a tidal wave. It might well be true, but does not seem to be terribly useful to know.

24 Habermas makes these points in response to criticisms from Wellmer, 1979. For a discussion, see Habermas, 1990.

25 For a discussion of these questions in respect of gender differences, see Fraser, 1992b, and more extensively Fraser, 1989. These criticisms are also expressed in the literature addressing Habermas's account of the transformation of the public sphere. From a feminist perspective, see Landes, 1988, who argues that

Habermas ignores the importance of women's role in the 'salon culture' which existed before the public sphere as he defines it, just as much as he ignores the absence of women in the public sphere itself; Ryan, 1990, who suggests that Habermas has overlooked the existence of competing, non-bourgeois public spheres in the seventeenth century; and Eley, 1992, who maintains that, in any case, Habermas has underestimated the degree of conflict within the public sphere itself.

26 Benhabib proposes a way out of these difficulties. Briefly, it involves outlining a more concrete notion of communicative reason, one which is embedded in the real lives and background of the members of a political community. Alongside the generalized other, she envisages a concrete other. Whereas the former emphasizes our commonality, the latter focuses on our individuality, and 'requires us to view each and every rational being as an individual with a concrete history, identity and affective-emotional constitution' (1991a: 159). The point, according to Benhabib, is that we should be able to express our differences *through* dialogue, not set them aside before it even begins.

27 This comes from Dews' introduction to Habermas, 1986: 1. From the opposite corner, Hoy suggests that there is nothing wrong with seeking out a series of local agreements within a community without expecting this to lead to a 'single, universal solidarity' (Hoy and McCarthy, 1994: 262).

28 For a somewhat singular view of these matters, consult Scruton's concise and clear account of modernity, modernism and postmodernism in Scruton, 1996: 500–4.

Chapter 6 Reality in Retreat

1 For a reasonably comprehensive selection of Baudrillard's writings which includes excerpts from the important book on symbolic exchange and death, see Baudrillard, 1988c. The interviews contained in Baudrillard, 1993c, are also a very useful source for summaries and explanations of some of his basic arguments and ideas. For further extracts, it is worth consulting Baudrillard, 1989. For a collection of Lyotard's writing, see Lyotard, 1989c; and for his more directly political work, see Lyotard, 1993a and 1998. Gane is probably the most sympathetic, albeit not uncritical, commentator on Baudrillard, so consult Gane, 1991a and 1991b, in the first instance, and also his fine introduction to Baudrillard, 1993c. For a rather more hostile interpretation of Baudrillard's work, which is nevertheless useful because it comes from the territory of critical theory, see Kellner, 1989. There is no genuinely reliable and accessible introduction to Lyotard's work, but Dews, 1987, offers a challenging and critical account of the relationship between Lyotard's arguments and the tradition of critical theory. The essays and articles contained in A. Benjamin, 1992, provide a reasonable alternative overview, although they are written mostly from a philosophical and aesthetic orientation. The debates surrounding Baudrillard's work vary widely in quality and depth, although Rojek and Turner, 1993, is worth consulting for its sociological emphasis.

2 Of course, it is open to question whether such views contradict the notion of postmodern society itself. As a result, some postmodern theorists appear in-

creasingly reluctant to employ the concept of postmodernity without qualification; although such reluctance may also have something to do with standing out from the crowd.

3   Lyotard makes this statement in Lyotard, 1991: 24–5. One is tempted to ask what he thought he was doing when he wrote a book with the title, *The Postmodern Condition.* But he later implies that his use of the concept of postmodernity had been a provocation: 'Postmodernity is not a new age, but the rewriting of some of the features claimed by modernity, and first of all modernity's claim to ground its legitimacy on the project of liberating humanity as a whole through science and technology' (1991: 34).

4   Baudrillard approvingly writes of America, for example, as living in 'perpetual simulation, in a perpetual present of signs' (1988a: 76).

5   The concept of postmodern*ism* has a range of applications, most of them aesthetic (Giddens, 1990: 45). For example, we can refer to the architecture of a shopping precinct as postmodern; or similarly to a novel, a piece of furniture, and a planned urban environment. As a collection of articles and essays on the aesthetic implications of postmodernism, Foster, 1985, is unrivalled. For a history of the concept of the postmodern, see Bertens, 1995.

6   For analyses of these concepts, see Lyon, 1988 and 1994; Bell, 1979; and Amin, 1994. For an accessible overview of arguments and debates surrounding the concept of the information society – and which usefully ties this in with the work of Habermas, Giddens and the postmodernists – consult Webster, 1995.

7   For Bell's account of post-industrialism, see Bell, 1974; for its cultural ramifications, Bell, 1976; for his interpretation of the information society, Bell, 1979; and for shorter essays which summarize his arguments, Bell, 1980.

8   A summary of these points can be found in Bell, 1976: 14.

9   The gist of the case against Bell is that he has really only diagnosed developments which have long been underway in industrial society. As Kumar argues: 'Beneath the post-industrial gloss, old, scarred problems rear their heads: alienation and control in the workplaces of the service economy; scrutiny and supervision of the operations of private and public bureaucracies, especially as they come to be meshed in with technical and scientific expertise' (1978: 230–1).

10 Habermas, for example, labels Bell's analysis 'neoconservative', see Habermas, 1989b.

11 These arguments are laid out in Gorz, 1982 and 1985.

12 To summarize some basic criticisms of Gorz's position: he has probably misunderstood the socioeconomic impact of automation, and his analysis of the apparent decline in working-class occupations is both exaggerated and, in its details, reliant on an ambiguous notion of the service economy. See, for example, Giddens, 1987: 275–96.

13 Their basic position is set out in Lash and Urry, 1987, and developed further in Lash and Urry, 1993. For more on Lash's arguments specifically, see his contribution to Beck et al., 1994, and Lash, 1993.

14 This theme was anticipated in the earlier work of Bell on the end of ideology, see Bell, 1960. Here, he argues that contemporary Western societies, led by the United States, have reached a stage at which ideology is superseded by a technocratic consensus. Intriguingly, however, in his later work on the cultural

contradictions of capitalism, Bell argues that culture is in crisis because of its preoccupation with materialist values, which he interprets as hedonism: 'It is the tensions between the norms of . . . three realms – efficiency and bureaucracy, equality and rights, self-fulfilment and the desire for novelty – that form the contradictions of the modern world, contradictions that are enhanced under capitalism, since the techno-economic realm is geared to promote not economic necessities but the cultural wants of a hedonistic world' (1980: 329–30). See also Bell, 1976.

15 Fukuyama draws on Kojève's treatment of Hegel's philosophy of spirit – especially its translation into a full-blown philosophy of history – in order to argue that the combination of liberal democracy and market capitalism which marks the end-point of history is logically inevitable. From Hegel, Fukuyama emphasizes the importance of the liberal constitutional state, especially its commitment to human freedom, and also the optimistic tenor of Hegel's sense of resolution in his account of the passage of spirit through time, see Fukuyama, 1992: 199–205.

16 This analysis is extended in Fukuyama's more recent work, *Trust*, 1995.

17 For a discussion of the main themes and arguments outlined by Fukuyama, see H. Williams et al., 1997.

18 For clarification of this point, see Lyotard, 1984: 79. It is also worth consulting Lyotard, 1989a.

19 For examples of Lyotard's writing on aesthetics, see Lyotard, 1989b and 1993b. See also chapter 6 of Sarup, 1993.

20 According to Ashley, the relationship between the work of Lyotard and Baudrillard can be viewed as a division of labour in which Lyotard 'concentrates on the metacritique of modern philosophy and social theory while Baudrillard elaborates (perhaps to an extreme) the consequences of postmodernization' (1994: 57). But this seems to be a suspiciously tidy formulation.

21 It seems inappropriate, however, to write of the 'development' of Baudrillard's work in so far as he rejects the narrative form. Baudrillard's position in this respect has been expressed by his publication of diaries (see 1988a, 1990a, 1996a and 1997). There is something about the form of the diary, consisting as it does of a series of fragments, which is well suited to the postmodern critique of linear narratives. As Gane observes, the diaries 'do not attempt to reproduce a linear story of a life', but instead 'present impressions, fugitive reflections, paradoxes, poetic play, short accounts of people, encounters, events and theoretical exploration, experimentation' (introduction to Baudrillard, 1993c: 7).

22 He therefore likens his project to that of Marx himself, who 'thought it necessary to clear the path to the critique of political economy with a critique of the philosophy of law'; likewise, for Baudrillard, the critique of political economy, now 'completed', must be replaced by 'the critique of the metaphysic of the signifier and the code, in all its current ideological content' (excerpt from Baudrillard, 1975, as cited in Baudrillard, 1988c: 116).

23 This point is made in Baudrillard, 1981: 136. For more detailed discussion, see Baudrillard, 1998a.

24 These ideas are contained in Saussure, 1974.

25 Baudrillard uses the concept of simulation as an extension of the earlier argu-

ment that there is an arbitrary relation between the signifier and what it is meant to signify. This means that conventional modes of representation have broken down: 'truth, reference and objective causes have ceased to exist' (1983b: 6).

26 These ideas are laid out in McLuhan, 1973, and Benjamin, 1968, respectively.

27 The concept derives from Baudrillard's conception of the ecstatic qualities of media images, particularly of experiencing them subjectively. Thus he describes the hyperreal as an 'ecstatic form of the real' (1990c: 71). See also Baudrillard, 1988b.

28 Baudrillard explains this in more detail in Baudrillard, 1993b: 8–9.

29 This point is clarified and discussed in Baudrillard, 1993c: 69.

30 This idea is explored in Baudrillard, 1983b: 55.

31 However, Baudrillard does not agree that the media industry therefore envelopes the mass. On the contrary, he argues that *'the masses are a stronger medium than all the media*, that it is the former who envelop and absorb the latter – or at least there is no priority of one over the other. The mass and the media are one single process' (1983a: 44, Baudrillard's emphasis).

32 These articles are contained in Baudrillard, 1991a, 1991b, 1991c and 1991d; and the argument as a whole summarized in Baudrillard, 1995.

33 This interpretation would certainly be consistent with much of Baudrillard's work on the media, and with the consequences of this work for our capacity even to begin to represent reality. His basic argument has been crisply summarized by Mark Poster: 'the media generate a world of simulations which is immune to rationalist critique, whether Marxist or liberal. The media present an excess of information, and they do so in a manner that precludes response by the recipient. This simulated reality has no referent, no ground, no course. It operates outside the logic of representation' (see Poster's introduction to Baudrillard, 1988c: 7).

34 Rojek suggests that Baudrillard *'wants* to be accused of talking nonsense in order to compel critics to confront the nonsense which lies behind their own assumptions and proposals' (1993: 111). But the logic of this is difficult to follow. In what sense exactly does being accused of talking nonsense *compel* one's accusers re-examine their own assumptions?

35 The temptation to interpret Baudrillard's writing in this way seems irresistible even to those who seek to explicate, rather than offhandedly dismiss, his work. Rojek and Turner, for example, note how Baudrillard 'could be found . . . predicting that the Gulf War was impossible . . . because the phoney war has already been fought by the communications industry' (see the introduction to Rojek and Turner, 1993: xi).

36 For a further example of Baudrillard's approach to military events, see his writing on Sarajevo in Baudrillard, 1996c. Some sense of what he might be driving at can also be gained from his discussion of the relationship between knowledge and an event: 'Today, knowledge about an event is only the degraded form of this event . . . When knowledge, through its models, anticipates the event, in other words, when the event (or opinion) is preceded by its degraded form (or its simulated form) its energy is entirely absorbed into the void' (1990c: 91).

37 As Baudrillard explains in Baudrillard, 1983b.

38   For examples of this approach, see Baudrillard, 1988a, 1990a, 1996a and 1997.

39   Three essays in *The Transparency of Evil* reflect this proposition in their titles: 'Transaesthetics', 'Transsexuality', and 'Transeconomics' (1993a: 14–35).

40   As Baudrillard remarks in an interview: 'There is no "reality" with respect to which theory could become dissident or heretical, pursuing its fate other than in the objectivity of things. Rather, it's the objectivity of things we must question' (1993c: 123).

41   In Baudrillard, 1998b, he seems to be saying that we are 'beyond' the end already in so far as we are no longer marking time in terms of some past origin but counting down towards the end of the millennium.

42   In more literal terms, Lyotard recommends that the government of Quebec democratize access to computerized information (1984: 67).

43   Lyotard explains this idea in Lyotard, 1993a: 9–10, and explores it in Lyotard, 1988.

44   Lyotard argues that foundationalism in philosophy, and the claim that knowledge can be universally true, 'is, understood in terms of drives, a mark of the destruction of personal identities' (cited in Dews, 1987: 211).

45   This is how Baudrillard puts it: 'At the precise point that its *psychical* reality principle merges into its *psychoanalytical* reality principle, the unconscious, like political economy, also becomes a model of simulation' (1993b: 3, Baudrillard's emphasis). See also Baudrillard, 1996b.

46   For a more extensive discussion of the concept of seduction, see Baudrillard, 1990b.

47   As Baudrillard notes: 'Seduction is dual: I cannot seduce if I am not already seduced, no one can seduce me if he is not already seduced' (1990c: 105). Love, by contrast, can always go unrequited.

48   This conviction dominates the argument throughout Baudrillard, 1990c.

49   Baudrillard also uses the concepts of ironic strategy and banal strategy. The former captures more closely the sense in which seduction is playful, while the latter seems to reflect the character of silence as he defines it. But Baudrillard maintains that these two forms of strategy are versions of, not deviations from, the fatal strategy: 'Banality – that of the masses, of silent majorities – all that is our ambience . . . For me it is however a fatal strategy . . . It is there at the heart of the system, at a strategic point in the system, at its point of inertia, at its blind spot. That is my definition (there isn't any other) of the fatal' (1993c: 50).

50   There is a faintly Foucauldian sense to this notion of resistance, but as Baudrillard remarks, Foucault 'doesn't talk in terms of the mass' but in terms of 'a power which infiltrates everywhere' (1993c: 89). Foucault therefore would not regard inertia as a strategy.

51   As with seduction and silence, so with death. Today, death tends either to be concealed – made to disappear – or subjected to industrial prolongation. This is characteristic of a society in which life itself 'is no longer anything but a doleful, defensive book-keeping, locking every risk into its sarcophagus' (1983a: 178). Death is therefore the ultimate reversal for the political economy of industrialism: 'If political economy is the most rigorous attempt to put an end to death, it is clear that only death can put an end to political economy' (1983a: 187). Death puts a stop to accumulation, progress and development.

52   The basic ingredients of this criticism are set out in Keane, 1992.

53 See also Benhabib, 1991b. However, Steuerman (1992) argues that Lyotard's arguments represent a radicalization of the project of modernity, not its abandonment.
54 The dilemma is explained with particular clarity in Dews, 1987: 216.
55 This is explained in Lyotard and Thébaud, 1985: 5.
56 These observations come mainly from Dews, 1987: 220.
57 Jameson's interpretation is based largely on the appendix to *The Postmodern Condition*, 'Answering the question: what is postmodernism?' (Lyotard 1984: 71–82).
58 The point is echoed forcefully in Dews, 1987: 218.
59 This comes from his contribution to Thompson and Held, 1982: 195.
60 Turner agrees that Baudrillard is unsuccessful in his challenge. Empirically, his descriptions of contemporary society do not venture much further than Bell on post-industrial society and McLuhan on the media. Theoretically, Baudrillard's writing is 'striking', but arguments 'which depend on allusion, allegory and similar rhetorical devices are decorative but . . . not necessarily powerful' (Turner, 1993: 82). Perhaps Turner is too generous anyway in describing Baudrillard's work as a challenge. Rojek prefers the term provocation, and suggests that Baudrillard seeks to be provocative for its own sake (Rojek, 1993). According to Turner, Baudrillard's approach 'is successful because it simulates the condition it wishes to convey rather than producing a critical style in opposition to postmodern culture' (Turner, 1993: 85). Baudrillard seems to confirm Turner's interpretation when he suggests that, in a simulated society, theory 'can only tear concepts from their critical zone of reference and force them beyond a point of no-return (it too is moving into the hyperspace of simulation), a process whereby it loses all "objective" validity but gains substantially in *real affinity with the present system*' (1994: 2–3, my emphasis).
61 Baudrillard argues that, besides military power, America's greatest weapon is information, i.e. 'the electronic bombardment of the rest of the world' (1988a: 49). For Baudrillard, European culture can only be fully understood in contradistinction with America: 'the key to Europe is not to be found in its past history, but in this crazy, periodic anticipation that is the New World' (1988a: 104). Smart asks why Baudrillard fails to consider the question of America's apparent decline as an economic and military hegemon, and suggests that the decline is not only economic but cultural (1993: 65–6).
62 Smart suggests that in his work on America Baudrillard temporarily abandons the distinction between modernity and postmodernity for a distinction between modernity and radical modernity, although he also warns of the 'risk of organizing and systematizing comments and observations that are singularly lacking such qualities' (1993: 60–1). Rojek suggests that Baudrillard is actually modernist in so far as he 'traces the dispersal' of modernist projects concerned with replacing 'the existing set of politico-economic conditions with a state of affairs that is judged to be superior on rational or moral grounds', rather than 'acting as the harbinger of a new postmodern state of affairs' (1993: 23). One is entitled to wonder exactly what this state of affairs might be.
63 These seems to be one of the major complaints advanced by Kellner against Baudrillard, see in particular Kellner, 1989: 149.

64 For a fuller discussion of this concept, see Baudrillard, 1990c.

65 As Baudrillard notes, rather confusingly perhaps: 'There is perhaps but one fatal strategy and only one: theory' (1990c: 181).

66 There is some confusion here. On the one hand, seduction seems to appeal to Baudrillard by virtue of its power to negate. On the other, he argues that seduction already characterizes our relationship with electronic media. As Kellner notes, Baudrillard therefore appears to be saying both that 'seduction describes how society works' and that 'seduction is our destiny' (1989: 149). However, most critics focus on what they regard as Baudrillard's unpalatable call for passivity. Kellner accuses him of 'capitulation to the hegemony of the Right and a secret complicity with aristocratic conservatism' (1989: 215). Lash refers to Baudrillard's work as an 'uncritical and irresponsible celebration' (1990: 2). And Bauman rejects Baudrillard's position because it amounts to saying 'that bovine immobility . . . is the best form of activity that we have, and that . . . doing nothing is the most excellent form of resistance' (1992b: 153).

Chapter 7 Society under Suspicion

1 There is no truly representative collection of writings available for either of these theorists. However, the essays contained in Bauman, 1992b and 1995 provide a succinct survey of his basic arguments and ideas; likewise, the essays contained in Rorty, 1989. Of the two volumes of essays published by Rorty in the early 1990s – Rorty, 1991a and 1991b – the former is most relevant to the discussion in this chapter. Those seeking a general survey and introduction to the work of Rorty, as well as a rounded summary of the debates arising from his work in the various branches of philosophy, could do no better than consult Malachowski, 1990b: the quality of the Introduction, and the chapters which follow, is consistently high. Hall, 1994, provides a rather more slanted interpretation of Rorty's work, but is still worth reading. Rorty's most recent philosophical engagements are collected in Rorty, 1998b, while his political arguments are brought to fruition in Rorty, 1998a. Bauman's arguments on ethics are summarized concisely in Bauman, 1994, while the arguments contained in Bauman, 1992a suggest a novel means of understanding how he interprets the distinction between modernity and postmodernity, dealing as they do with society's treatment of the dying and the dead. A special issue of *Theory, Culture and Society* devoted to Bauman's work was published in 1998: the articles by Bauman, 1998b, D. Smith, 1998, and from the perspective of critical theory, Kellner, 1998, provide a reasonably accessible overview of his most recent arguments.

2 Bauman argues that the 'theory of postmodernity must be free of the metaphor of progress' because 'its temporal record cannot be linearly represented' (1992b: 189).

3 This theme is explored extensively in Bauman, 1997.

4 For a sparkling analysis of the ideological ramifications of the idea of the market – and above all of market freedom – see Jameson, 1991: 260–78.

5 These arguments are discussed extensively in Bauman, 1998b.

6 Malachowski offers a clear summary of the central points in Rorty's argu-

ment, particularly of why it has been called anti-foundationalist. As Malachowski notes, Rorty's basic position is that 'reason cannot *justify*, or in any other strong sense "legitimate", our established ways of knowing.' More specifically, anti-foundationalism refers to the argument that 'there is nothing upon which reason can build the appropriate theoretical edifice' for our knowledge about ourselves and the world (1990a: 142, Malachowski's emphasis).

7   For a wonderfully pithy summary of these alternatives and their implications for philosophy, see Williams, 1990: 27.

8   See his *Structure of Scientific Revolutions* (1970). In the postscript to this second edition, Kuhn examines some of the questions arising from his earlier treatment of the concept of the scientific paradigm; and also, incidentally, undertakes what may well be a significant U-turn in his basic position regarding the progress of scientific knowledge.

9   Rorty suggests that it is quite easy to imagine how one might conflate specific sentences with the world itself: for example, the sentence 'the butler did it' can be assessed as true or false according to an actual sequence of events in the world. But this should not justify running together 'the truth that the world sometimes causes sentences to be true or false, with the falsehood that what causes the sentence to be true is, somehow, itself true, that the world splits up, on its own initiative, into sentence-shaped chunks called facts' (1986a: 3).

10   This is from Rorty, 1980, and is cited in Williams, 1990: 30.

11   For an extended and illuminating discussion of this point, see Clark, 1990.

12   Although this assertion depends on precisely what is meant by relativism. Perhaps it might be helpful here to distinguish in a very basic way between 'strong' and 'weak' relativism. Strong relativism suggests that there is no such thing as independent reality, that reality effectively *is* what we want to describe it to be. Weak relativism, on the other hand, suggests that, although there is a world which is independent of our descriptions, we have no access to it other than *through* our descriptions, and therefore no means of evaluating those descriptions. In basic terms, this second definition of relativism is probably the closest we can get to describing the position held by most postmodern theorists. The normative implications of relativism concern the relationship between language and objective truth. Significantly, strong relativism requires the kind of philosophical argument that the postmodernists would prefer watered down. This is because strong relativism implies an *absolute* position. As Scruton suggests, 'in asserting that relativism is true for *him*, the relativist asserts that it is true for him absolutely. He is committed to absolute truth by the very practice of assertion' (1996: 33, Scruton's emphasis). Compared to this, weak relativism is agnostic. It seems most reasonable to place Rorty's argument in this category.

13   For an explanation of this, see Bauman, 1993b: 43–4. Bauman here alludes to a distinction between philosophy and sociology, and this closely corresponds to the distinction he draws elsewhere, between *legislators* – whose authority 'involved the right to command the rules the social world was to obey' and legitimized this right by reference to 'a superior knowledge guaranteed by the proper method of its production' – and *interpreters*, for whom 'knowledge has no extralinguistic standards of correctness and can be grasped only inside the

communicatively supported, shared stock of knowledge of the members' (1992b: 11, 22; see also Bauman, 1987).

14   This argument is reiterated in Bauman, 1993a: 44–7.

15   This argument is extended in Bauman, 1998b, where he writes approvingly of the theories of Knud Løgstrup and Emanuel Levinas: both, for Bauman, emphasize that the plurality of moral choices we face in the present day is a precondition for extending, not a threat to, our moral lives.

16   In this vein, Bauman characterizes postmodernity as '*modernity without illusions* (the obverse of which is that modernity is postmodernity refusing to accept its own truth' (1993a: 32, Bauman's emphasis).

17   The concept of relativization suggests that there has been a significant change in our culture, marked by declining belief in the idea of a central, orthodox system of belief and thought, for example rationalism or a religious doctrine. Subsequently, we are unable or unwilling to arbitrate between various or competing beliefs. This attitude is spelled out by Rorty, for example, when he suggests that 'a belief can still regulate action, can still be thought worth dying for, among people who are quite aware that this belief is caused by nothing deeper than contingent historical circumstance' (1989: 189). Rorty therefore seems to be advocating, not just describing, the relativization of values and beliefs.

18   It is important to note, however, that Bauman resists any notion of globalization as simply going on above our heads. In Bauman, 1998a, he emphasizes the local impact of globalization, and also the uneven nature of its consequences as far as individuals are concerned.

19   For a full account of this argument, see Maffesoli, 1995.

20   These correspond to the chapters which make up part I of Rorty's *Contingency, Irony, and Solidarity*, and also to the titles of his three Northcliffe lectures – 'The contingency of language', 'The contingency of selfhood' and 'The contingency of community' – which were published in *London Review of Books* during 1986.

21   Irony is defined as 'a figure of speech in which the intended meaning is the opposite of that expressed by the words used' (*OED*).

22   One might say that an important difference between the arguments of Rorty and Lyotard is provided by the spectre of violence. Where Lyotard sees competitive games within and between vocabularies, Rorty fears war and oppression.

23   For a clear summary of this argument, see Malachowski, 1990a.

24   This argument is laid out in Rorty, 1989: 6.

25   This distinction between common, or public, purpose and private purpose is vital to Rorty's critique of Habermas: 'I want to see freely arrived at agreement as agreement on how to accomplish common purposes . . . but I want to see these common purposes against the background of an increasing sense of the radical diversity of private purposes' (1989: 67).

26   Rorty does concede that his argument that 'one is at liberty to rig up a model of the self to suit oneself . . . presupposes that there is no "objective truth" about what the human self is *really* like'; and that this 'seems a claim that could be justified only on the basis of a metaphysical-epistemological view of the traditional sort'. But characteristically, his response to this potential difficulty consists of a rather deft side-step: he contends that the exercise of tracing his argument back to first principles, or even asking what kinds of reasons he *can*

offer for such an argument, is merely 'pointless and sterile' (1990: 292–3; also in 1991a: 192–3).

27 In an interview, Rorty explains the popularity of so-called high theory by suggesting that 'it's easier and more fun' to theorize rather than organize. The interview is with Scott Stossel in *The Atlantic Monthly*, April 1998.

28 For an explanation and discussion of this basic distinction, see 'Movements and campaigns' in Rorty, 1998a. The argument is also laid out in an essay of the same title, published in *Dissent* during 1995.

29 Fischer likens it to 'a pre-school playroom rather than . . . a restrained conversation' (1990: 235), and argues that the metaphor is inappropriate because 'literary critics speak a more stable vocabulary and heed firmer rules than Rorty supposes' (p. 237). Hollis defends Rorty's approach on the grounds that he emphasizes human creativity. Literature is a more positive model for politics because it helps to sever the link between philosophy and ethics. After all, philosophers are 'better at disciplining the mind than at understanding its *activity* in creating knowledge' (1990: 252, Hollis's emphasis). But according to Fischer, Rorty actually misrepresents philosophy anyway by portraying it as 'imprecise, capricious and methodologically dishevelled' (Fischer, 1990: 241). Taylor agrees: Rorty wrongly characterizes analytic philosophers as 'Raving Platonists' (Taylor, 1990: 269). Taylor argues that Rorty rejects one extreme argument, that 'our thoughts don't correspond to things-in-themselves', in favour of another, that 'they don't correspond to anything at all' (p. 271). Rorty has also been criticized as slapdash in his approach to the history of philosophy and the work of his contemporaries. Bernard Williams writes of how Rorty displays an irritating tendency 'to parade lists of great names and of turning points in the history of philosophy' (1990: 27).

30 Hollis argues, further, that to focus on the political means, i.e. a 'continuing conversation', while refusing to consider political ends adds up to a vacuous argument, for 'without the goal the activity is unintelligible.' According to Hollis, the political framework envisaged by Rorty resembles 'diplomatic cocktail parties' where 'one perhaps passes the platitudes for the sake of passing them.' He argues that it 'takes a special sort of conversation to encourage a broadening franchise, one with rules of discourse which have this effect'. Such rules nevertheless can be argued for on pragmatic rather than philosophical grounds, emphasizing their 'advantages for civilized living and . . . for including someone (anyone) in the fellowship of rational persons' (Hollis, 1990: 250–2).

31 Rorty argues, in any case, that even the collapse of liberal democracy 'would not, in itself, provide much evidence for the claim that human societies cannot survive without widely shared opinions on matters of ultimate importance . . . any more than it would show that human societies require kings or an established religion' (1990: 295; also in 1991a: 195–6). He associates this viewpoint with communitarianism, an approach which is closely associated with the work of philosophers such as Robert Bellah, Alasdair MacIntyre, Michael Sandel and Charles Taylor. For an account of this approach, see Bellah et al., 1985. Rorty's main disagreement with the communitarianist argument seems to be that 'the social theory of the liberal state rests on false philosophical presuppositions' (1990: 293; also in 1991a: 194). For Rorty's discussion of Taylor, see Rorty, 1998b, ch. 4.

32   It is worth noting that the concept of 'vocabulary' is not clearly defined by
Rorty. He uses terms like 'jargon' and 'idiom' interchangeably with vocabulary (see Sorell, 1990: 18–19). The lack of clarity causes problems for Rorty's
analysis of the relationship between scientific knowledge and the natural world,
and his argument that science 'progresses' not because it helps us gain a truer
picture of the world but because it is 'paying its way' (cited in Williams, 1990:
30). Rorty tries to clarify his argument in the following way: 'Incommensurability entails irreducibility but not incompatibility, so the failure to "reduce"
. . . various vocabularies to that of "bottom-level" atoms-and-the-void science
casts no doubt upon their cognitive status' (1980: 387–8).

33   Similarly, Burrows argues that Rorty will only interpret an argument on its
own terms 'if it fits in with [his] liberal outlook': all other arguments are described as 'metaphysical scaremongering' or as 'ideologically unsound' (1990:
332–3).

34   The argument is extended in Rorty, 1998b, ch. 11.

35   An important corollary of this argument seems to be Rorty's scepticism towards notions of 'total' or revolutionary change. For example, he is at pains to
describe the feminist movement as reformist, not revolutionary: as 'more analogous to eighteenth-century abolitionism than to nineteenth-century communism'. The argument is laid out in Rorty, 1993. For an earlier but more extensive
discussion, see Rorty, 1991c.

36   For a fuller, and quite stunning, discussion of this connection, see Bauman,
1989.

37   But, as I have already said, to refer to the fragmentation of values makes it
quite difficult to avoid normative questions. On the one hand, we might simply describe a process in which Western societies become increasingly
multicultural and therefore less geared towards a core value system. At the
same time, however, even to describe this process begs the question as to
whether the truth-claims of rival value systems are *in fact* equivalent, i.e.
whether they genuinely do have an equal claim on our attention and credulity.

Chapter 8   Modernity Renewed

1   For a reasonably comprehensive selection of Giddens's writing, see Giddens,
1993. The essays contained in Giddens, 1987, present a good summary of many
of his key arguments and positions, while Giddens, 1990, provides the clearest
statement of his ideas about globalization, postmodern social theory and reflexive modernization. No representative collection of writings exists in the
case of Beck, but some of the essays in Beck, 1995a and 1998, provide a clear
and useful survey of his basic ideas. For a collection of short essays dealing
with the broad ramifications of the most recent ideas of Giddens and Beck, see
Franklin, 1998. For those seeking a critical survey of Giddens's arguments –
from his earliest work on the rules of sociological method, through structuration
theory, to his recent work on reflexive modernization – the mammoth Bryant
and Jay, 1996, presents the most obvious port of call, although Held and
Thompson, 1989, is still worth consulting, not least for Thompson's succinct

summary and appraisal of structuration theory. A bleakly critical interpretation of Giddens's work can be found in Mestrovic, 1998. For a crisp summary of Giddens's political ideas, see Giddens, 1998, although Giddens, 1994, locates these ideas more securely in relation to social theory. The series of conversations collected in Giddens and Pierson, 1998, also provides an accessible introduction to his recent ideas. Finally, the essays contained in Beck, Giddens and Lash, 1994, provide perhaps the most convenient source for discovering what they each mean by reflexive modernization.

2 A later, and slightly easier, formulation holds that reflexivity refers to 'the use of information about the conditions of activity as a means of regularly reordering and redefining what that activity is' (Giddens, 1994: 86).

3 Giddens defines the problem in the following way: 'What is at issue is how the concepts of action, meaning and subjectivity should be specified and how they might relate to notions of structure and constraint. If interpretative sociologies are founded, as it were, upon an imperialism of the subject, functionalism and structuralism propose an imperialism of the social object' (1984: 2).

4 Giddens characterizes this idea in the following terms: 'Repetitive activities, located in one context of time and space, have regularized consequences, unintended by those who engage in those activities, in more or less "distant" time-space contexts. What happens in this second series of contexts then, directly or indirectly, influences the further conditions of action in the original context . . . The unintended consequences are regularly "distributed" as a by-product of regularized behaviour reflexively sustained by its participants' (1984: 14).

5 This is explained in Giddens, 1984: 257.

6 Giddens is careful to avoid overemphasizing the degree of continuity here: 'The current period of globalization is not simply a continuation of the expansion of capitalism and of the West. If one wanted to fix its specific point of origin, it would be the first successful broadcast transmission made via satellite' (1994: 80). There are some important agreements between Giddens's analysis of the so-called local/global axis and the argument laid out in Bauman, 1998a. But for a critical survey of the concept of globalization, see Scott, 1997; and for those in search of even greater scepticism, Hirst and Thompson, 1996. See also Bradshaw and Wallace, 1996.

7 On the specific connections between these arguments, see Giddens, 1985.

8 Giddens expresses the point in the following way: 'The spread of modern institutions across the world was originally a Western phenomenon and was affected by all four institutional dimensions . . . The combination of all these factors made Western expansion seemingly irresistible' (1990: 62–3).

9 These ideas are explained more fully in Giddens, 1990: 17–45, 53–4.

10 Some of these arguments are summarized in Beck, 1992b.

11 Beck suggests, however, that both forms of modernization are present in the contemporary world. If geopolitical conflict exists, it will be cast in these terms: between countries still in the midst of primary modernization, or industrialization, and 'those that are attempting to relativize and reform this project self-critically' (1998: 31).

12 In a similar way, Giddens distinguishes between simple and reflexive modernization. Simple modernization consisted of industrialization and the growth

of capitalism, and was relatively predictable. Reflexive modernization is wrapped up in the way individuals and institutions monitor what they do: 'they refract back to start to reshape modernization at its points of origin' (1994: 80).

13 There are five main strands to this argument (see Beck, 1992a: 13–14; and 1995a: 37–62). First, industrial society has declined as a class society. Social classes depend on traditions which are in decline. Second, the nuclear family is disintegrating. The role of women in the workplace and home is being transformed. Rising divorce rates are one important side-effect of this transformation. Third, the boundary between work and non-work has shifted. There has been a dramatic rise in the number of individuals who are neither employed nor unemployed but simply underemployed. Fourth, the legitimacy of science has been undermined by widespread scepticism which concerns not only the outcome of scientific research but, increasingly, its epistemological assumptions. Fifth, parliamentary democracy has come under threat from a new form of subpolitics which consists of specialists making technical decisions beyond the auspices of the state and without political scrutiny.

14 This might be taken to suggest that the kind of reflexivity talked about by Giddens is not so different from the reflexive monitoring which characterizes every kind of society, traditional or modern, and therefore raises a number of questions about the relationship between the definition of reflexivity we find in structuration theory, and Giddens's use of the concept later on to characterize what is distinctive in late modern society. If reflexive monitoring describes the way that *any* society reproduces itself, how can it also be something which is unique to late modern society? Giddens answers this by suggesting that, while 'reflexivity is a defining characteristic of all human action' (1990: 36), it is its institutionalization which distinguishes late modern society: 'It is introduced into the very basis of system reproduction, such that thought and action are constantly refracted back upon one another' (1990: 38). This is fancy footwork, at least.

15 For a fuller explanation of this, see Giddens's contribution to Beck et al., 1994.

16 As Giddens argues, these are not usually the kinds of risk which are in the forefront of our minds. They remain largely implicit and unarticulated: 'When I go out of the house and get into a car, I enter settings which are thoroughly permeated by expert knowledge – involving the design and construction of automobiles, highways, intersections, traffic lights, and many other items . . . In choosing to go out in the car, I accept that risk, but rely on the aforesaid expertise to guarantee that it is minimized as far as possible' (1990: 28).

17 Giddens explains the key difference between natural and manufactured risk, in so far as it affects our lives, in the following way: 'in a situation in which many aspects of modernity have become globalized . . . no one can completely opt out of the abstract systems involved in modern institutions . . . Individuals in pre-modern settings, in principle and in practice, could ignore the pronouncements of priests, sages, and sorcerers and get on with the routines of daily activity. But this is not the case in the modern world, in respect of expert knowledge' (1990: 84).

18 This also means that the claim of science 'to be able to investigate objectively the hazardousness of a risk permanently refutes itself' (Beck, 1992a: 29).

19 For these arguments, see also Beck, 1996a. It is also worth consulting Beck, 1996b.

20 According to Giddens, this process confronts us with four basic kinds of dilemma (1991: 187–201): first, between unification and fragmentation, where our remoteness from events is intensified as we know more about them; second, between powerlessness and appropriation, where our apparent helplessness in the face of expert systems is combined with the opportunities they provide to appropriate new knowledge; third, between authority and uncertainty, where the decline of traditional orthodoxy may generate greater levels of insecurity; and fourth, between personalized and commodified experience, where personal life choices are available in an increasingly commodified form.

21 For a fuller discussion of both arguments, see Giddens, 1991: 181–208; and Beck, 1998: 122–40.

22 This is spelled out in Giddens, 1990: 149.

23 Giddens argues that 'late modernity produces a situation in which humankind in some respects becomes a "we", facing problems and opportunities where there are no "others"' (1991: 27).

24 Giddens draws a distinction between 'romantic love' and 'confluent love'. Whereas the former seeks out a shared history with another person, the latter is a more active and contingent love which 'jars with the "for-ever", "one-and-only" qualities of . . . romantic love' (1992: 61). Reflexive monitoring – scrutinizing a relationship against an ideal rather than taking it for granted, and ending it if it fails to live up to that ideal – accounts for this difference.

25 The empowerment of women stems from an increasing equality – both sexual and emotional – within what Giddens calls the pure relationship and confluent love (1992: 184–204).

26 For detailed discussion of the broad ramifications of these changes, see Beck and Beck-Gernsheim, 1995; and Beck-Gernsheim, 1995.

27 See Giddens, 1990, for Giddens's critique of the concept of cultural impoverishment (pp. 144–5) and of Lasch (pp. 171–80). For a first-hand account of Lasch's arguments, see Lasch, 1980 and 1985.

28 Giddens likens this process to reskilling.

29 Beck suggests that it is not difficult to imagine that 'the next generation, or the one after that, will no longer be upset at pictures of birth defects, like those of tumour-covered fish and birds that now circulate around the world' (1992a: 83). For further discussion of the relationship between nature and society, see Eder, 1996.

30 Somewhat extravagantly, Beck claims that the theory of reflexive modernization is different from *any* alternative approach to social theory. Unlike theories of crisis such as Marxism, it claims that 'the pressing questions are the expression of triumphs, not crises, of industrialism.' Unlike functionalism, it suggests that modern society is 'denormalizing' itself. Unlike postmodern theory, it argues that modernization in its fullest sense has only just begun. And unlike theories of the social and ecological limitations of modern society, 'it points to the transformation of the premises and the coordinate system of industrial modernity' (1998: 29).

31 As Giddens notes, in the post-traditional order, traditions 'have to explain themselves, to become open to interrogation and discourse' (1994: 5). Similarly, Beck

argues that 'traditional social forms are scarcities in the systemic innovation that is subverting them. They are picked apart with one hand and upheld and coddled with the other' (1995a: 46).

32 For a discussion of the concept of individualization as it is used by Beck – or what he calls 'the withering away of solidarity' – see Beck, 1998: 32–8.

33 Beck maintains that fatalism characterizes the thinking of those who are critical of, just as much as those who seek to justify, the process of industrialization: 'Industrial fatalism is not only not a contrast to a radical critique of progress, it is actually its origin and star witness. Apologizing for progress and criticizing it are the opposing voices in the duet of industrial fatalism' (1995a: 83).

34 For a full discussion of socialism and reflexive modernization, see Giddens, 1994: 51–77.

35 According to Beck, this presumes 'a repoliticization of municipal policy, indeed a rediscovery and redefinition of it by mobilizing programmes, ideas and people to make the incomprehensible and impossible real and possible, step by step' (1998: 16).

36 For Beck's analysis of the political significance of microelectronics, see Beck, 1995a: 42–3.

37 For Fukuyama's position, see Fukuyama, 1992; and Williams et al., 1977. For their criticisms, see Beck, 1995a: 151; and Giddens, 1994: 104–10.

38 The concept of deliberative democracy is discussed in Miller, 1992.

39 This is discussed in Giddens, 1994: 117–24.

40 See for example Giddens, 1990: 52–3.

References

Adorno, T. 1946: Anti-Semitism and Fascist propaganda. In E. Simmel (ed.), *Anti-Semitism: A Social Disease*, New York: International Universities Press.
—— 1951: Freudian theory and the pattern of fascist propaganda. In G. Roheim (ed.), *Psychoanalysis and the Social Sciences*, New York: International Universities Press.
—— 1956: Modern music is growing old. *The Score*, nos 16–17.
—— 1957: Television and the patterns of mass culture. In B. Rosen and D. M. White (eds), *Mass Culture: The Popular Arts in America*, Glencoe, Ill.: Free Press.
—— 1967a: *Prisms*. London: Neville Spearman.
—— 1967b: Sociology and psychology. *New Left Review*, 46.
—— 1973a: *Introduction to the Sociology of Music*. New York: Seabury Press.
—— 1973b: *Negative Dialectics*, trans. E. B. Ashton. New York: Seabury Press.
—— 1973c: *Jargon of Authenticity*, trans. K. Tarnowski and F. Will. London: Routledge and Kegan Paul.
—— 1973d: *Philosophy of Modern Music*, trans. A. G. Mitchell and W. V. Blomster. London: Sheed and Ward.
——1974: The stars down to earth: the Los Angeles Times astrology column. *Telos*, 19, pp. 11–89.
——1975: Culture industry reconsidered. *New German Critique*, 6, 12–19.
—— 1978: On the fetish-character in music and the regression of listening. In A. Arato and E. Gebhardt (eds), *The Essential Frankfurt School Reader*, Oxford: Blackwell.
—— 1984: *Aesthetic Theory*. London: Routledge and Kegan Paul.
—— 1990: *The Culture Industry: Selected Essays on Mass Culture*. London: Routledge.
—— 1994: *The Stars Down to Earth and Other Essays on the Irrational in Culture*. London: Routledge.
—— 1998a: *Critical Models: Interventions and Catchwords*. New York: Columbia University Press.
—— 1998b: *Beethoven: The Philosophy of Music*, trans. E. Jephcott. Cambridge: Polity Press.

Adorno, T. and Horkheimer, M. 1979: *Dialectic of Enlightenment*. London: Verso.

Adorno, T., Frenkel-Brunswick, E., Levinson, D. J. and Sanford, R. N. 1950: *The Authoritarian Personality*. New York: Harper.

Adorno, T., Albert, H., Dahrendorf, R., Habermas, J., Pilot, H. and Popper, K. R. 1976: *The Positivist Dispute in German Sociology*, trans. G. Adey and D. Frisby. New York: Harper Torchbooks.

Adorno, T., Benjamin, W., Bloch, E., Brecht, B. and Lukács, G. 1980: *Aesthetics and Politics*, ed. R. Taylor. London: Verso,

Amin, A. (ed.) 1994: *Post-Fordism: A Reader*. Oxford: Blackwell.

Anderson, P. 1992: *A Zone of Engagement*. London: Verso.

Appignanesi, L. (ed.) 1989: *Postmodernism: ICA Documents*. London: Free Association Books.

Arato, A. and Gebhardt, E. (eds) 1978: *The Essential Frankfurt School Reader*. Oxford: Blackwell.

Ashley, D. 1994: Postmodernism and antifoundationalism. In D. R. Dickens and A. Fontana (eds), *Postmodernism and Social Inquiry*, London: UCL Press.

Avineri, S. 1968: *The Social and Political Thought of Karl Marx*. Cambridge: Cambridge University Press.

Barnes, B. 1995: *The Elements of Social Theory*. London: UCL Press.

Bartky, S. 1988: Foucault, femininity and the modernisation of patriarchal power. In I. Diamond and L. Quinby (eds), *Feminism and Foucault: Reflections on Resistance*, Boston: Northeastern University Press.

Baudrillard, J. 1975: *The Mirror of Production*. St Louis: Telos.

—— 1981: *For a Critique of the Political Economy of the Sign*. St Louis: Telos.

—— 1983a: *In the Shadow of the Silent Majorities*. New York: Semiotext(e).

—— 1983b: *Simulations*. New York: Semiotext(e).

—— 1988a: *America*. London: Verso.

—— 1988b: *The Ecstasy of Communication*. New York: Semiotext(e).

—— 1988c: *Jean Baudrillard: Selected Writings*, ed. M. Poster. Cambridge: Polity Press.

—— 1989: *The Revenge of the Crystal: A Baudrillard Reader*, ed. M. Carter. London: Pluto Press.

—— 1990a: *Cool Memories*. London: Verso.

—— 1990b: *Seduction*. London: Macmillan.

—— 1990c: *Fatal Strategies*. London: Pluto Press.

—— 1991a: La Guerre du Golfe n'aura pas lieu. *Libération*, 4 Jan., p. 5.

—— 1991b: La Guerre du Golfe a-t-elle vraiment lieu? *Libération*, 6 Feb., p. 10.

—— 1991c: La Guerre du Golfe n'a pas eu lieu. *Libération*, 29 Mar., p. 6.

—— 1991d: The reality gulf. *Guardian*, 11 Jan., p. 25.

—— 1993a: *The Transparency of Evil: Essays on Extreme Phenomena*. London: Verso.

—— 1993b: *Symbolic Exchange and Death*. London: Sage.

—— 1993c:*Baudrillard Live: Selected Interviews*, ed. M. Gane. London: Routledge.

—— 1994: *The Illusion of the End*. Cambridge: Polity Press.

—— 1995: *The Gulf War Did Not Take Place*. Bloomington: Indiana University Press.

—— 1996a: *Cool Memories II*. Cambridge: Polity Press.

—— 1996b:*The System of Objects*. London: Verso.

—— 1996c:*The Perfect Crime*. London: Verso.

—— 1997: *Cool Memories III, 1991–95*. London: Verso.

—— 1998a: *The Consumer Society: Myths and Structures*. London: Sage.

—— 1998b: The end of the millennium, or the countdown *Theory, Culture and Society*, 15, 1–10.

Bauman, Z. 1987: *Legislators and Interpreters: On Modernity, Post-Modernity and Intellectuals*. Cambridge: Polity Press.

—— 1989: *Modernity and the Holocaust*. Cambridge: Polity Press.

—— 1991: *Modernity and Ambivalence*. Cambridge: Polity Press.

—— 1992a: *Mortality, Immortality and Other Life Strategies*. Cambridge: Polity Press.

—— 1992b: *Intimations of Postmodernity*. London: Routledge.

—— 1993a:*Postmodern Ethics*. Oxford: Blackwell.

—— 1993b: The sweet scent of decomposition. In C. Rojek and B. Turner (eds), *Forget Baudrillard?* London: Routledge, 1993.

—— 1994: *Alone Again: Ethics after Certainty*. London: Demos.

—— 1995: *Life in Fragments: Essays in Postmodern Morality*. Oxford: Blackwell.

—— 1997: *Postmodernity and its Discontents*. Cambridge: Polity Press.

—— 1998a: *Globalization: The Human Consequences*. Cambridge: Polity Press.

—— 1998b: What prospects of morality in times of uncertainty? *Theory, Culture and Society*, 15, 11–22.

Baynes, K. 1995: 'Democracy and the *Rechtsstaat*: Habermas's *Faktizität und Geltung*'. In S. K. White (ed.), *The Cambridge Companion to Habermas*, Cambridge: Cambridge University Press.

Beck, U. 1992a: *Risk Society: Towards a New Modernity*. London: Sage.

—— 1992b: From industrial society to the risk society: questions of survival, social structure and ecological enlightenment. *Theory, Culture and Society*, 9, 97–123.

—— 1995a: *Ecological Enlightenment: Essays on the Politics of the Risk Society*. Atlantic Highlands, N.J.: Humanities Press.

—— 1995b: *Ecological Politics in an Age of Risk*. Cambridge: Polity Press.

—— 1996a: *The Reinvention of Politics*. Cambridge: Polity Press.

—— 1996b: Risk society and the provident state. In S. Lash, B. Szerszynski and B. Wynne (eds), *Risk, Environment and Modernity: Towards a New Ecology*, London: Sage.

—— 1998: *Democracy without Enemies*. Cambridge: Polity Press.

Beck, U. and Beck-Gernsheim, E. 1995: *The Normal Chaos of Love*. Cambridge: Polity Press.

Beck, U., Giddens, A. and Lash, S. 1994: *Reflexive Modernization: Politics, Tradition and Aesthetics in the New Modern Order*. Cambridge: Polity Press.

Beck-Gernsheim, E. 1995: Life as a planning project. In S. Lash, B. Szerszynski and B. Wynne (eds), *Risk, Environment and Modernity: Towards a New Ecology*, London: Sage.

Bell, D. 1960: *The End of Ideology*. Glencoe, Ill.: Free Press.

—— 1974: *The Coming of Post-Industrial Society: A Venture in Social Forecasting*, London: Heinemann.

—— 1976: *The Cultural Contradictions of Capitalism*. New York: Basic Books.

—— 1979: The social framework of the information society. In M. L. Dertouzos and J. Moses (eds), *The Computer Age: A Twenty Year View*, Cambridge, Mass.: MIT Press.

—— 1980: *Sociological Journeys: Essays 1960–1980*. London: Heinemann.

Bellah, R., Madsen, R., Sullivan, R., Swidler, A. and Tipton, S. 1985: *Habits of the*

Heart: Individualism and Commitment in American Life. Berkeley: University of California Press.

Benhabib, S. 1984: Epistemologies of postmodernism: a rejoinder to Jean-François Lyotard. *New German Critique*, 33, 103–27.

—— 1991a: *Situating the Self*. Cambridge: Polity Press.

—— 1991b: Feminism and postmodernism: an uneasy alliance. *Praxis International*, 11, 137–49.

Benhabib, S. and Cornell, D. (eds) 1987: *Feminism as Critique*. Cambridge: Polity Press.

Benhabib, S. and Dallmayr, F. (eds) 1990: *The Communicative Ethics Controversy*. Cambridge, Mass.: MIT Press.

Benhabib, S., Bonss, W. and McCole, J. (eds) 1993: *On Max Horkheimer: New Perspectives*. Cambridge, Mass.: MIT Press.

Benjamin, A. (ed.) 1992: *Judging Lyotard*. London: Routledge.

Benjamin, W. 1968: *Illuminations*, ed. H. Arendt. London: Fontana.

Bernaeur, J. and Rasmussen, D. (eds) 1988: *The Final Foucault*. Cambridge, Mass.: MIT Press.

Bernstein, R. (ed.) 1985: *Habermas and Modernity*. Cambridge: Polity Press.

Bertens, H. 1995: *The Idea of the Postmodern: A History*. London: Routledge.

Blau, P. (ed.) 1976: *Approaches to the Study of Social Action*. London: Open Books.

Bottomore, T. (ed.) 1991: *A Dictionary of Marxist Thought*. Oxford: Blackwell.

Bradshaw, Y. W. and Wallace, M. 1996: *Global Inequalities*. Thousand Oaks, Calif.: Pine Forge Press.

Brand, A. 1990: *The Force of Reason: An Introduction to Habermas's 'Theory of Communicative Action'*. Sydney: Allen and Unwin.

Brubaker, R. 1984: *The Limits of Rationality: An Essay on the Social and Moral Thought of Max Weber*. London: Allen and Unwin.

Bryant, C. G. A. and Jary, D. (eds) 1996: *Anthony Giddens: Critical Assessments* (4 vols). London: Routledge.

Bubner, R. 1975: Theory and practice in the light of the hermeneutic-criticist controversy. *Cultural Hermeneutics*, 2, 337–52.

Burger, T. 1987: *Max Weber's Theory of Concept Formation*. Durham, N.C.: Duke University Press.

Burrows, J. 1990: Conversational politics: Rorty's pragmatist apology for liberalism. In A. R. Malachowski (ed.), *Reading Rorty: Critical Responses to Philosophy and the Mirror of Nature (and Beyond)*, Oxford: Blackwell.

Butler, J. 1990: *Gender Trouble: Feminism and the Subversion of Identity*. London: Routledge.

Calhoun, C. (ed.) 1992: *Habermas and the Public Sphere*. Cambridge: Polity Press.

Caputo, J. and Yount. M. (eds) 1993: *Foucault and the Critique of Institutions*. University Park, Pa.: Pennsylvania State University Press.

Clark, M. 1990: Fact and fiction. In A. R. Malachowski (ed.), *Reading Rorty: Critical Responses to Philosophy and the Mirror of Nature (and Beyond)*. Oxford: Blackwell.

Cohen, G. A. 1978: *Karl Marx's Theory of History: A Defence*. Oxford: Clarendon Press.

Collins, R. 1986: *Weberian Sociological Theory*. Cambridge: Cambridge University Press.

Cousins, M. and Hussain, A. 1984: *Michel Foucault*. London: Macmillan.

Dallmayr, F. and McCarthy, T. (eds) 1977: *Understanding and Social Enquiry*. Notre Dame: University of Notre Dame Press.

Davidson, A. I. 1986: Archaeology, geneaology, ethics. In D. C. Hoy (ed.), *Foucault: A Critical Reader*, Oxford: Blackwell.

de Lauretis, T. (ed.) 1986: *Feminist Studies/Critical Studies*. Bloomington: Indiana University Press.

d'Entrèves, M. P. and Benhabib, S. (eds) 1996: *Habermas and the Unfinished Project of Modernity: Critical Essays on 'The Philosophical Discourse of Modernity'*. Cambridge: Polity Press.

Dertouzos, M. L. and Moses, J. (eds) 1979: *The Computer Age: A Twenty Year View*. Cambridge, Mass.: MIT Press.

Dews, P. 1987: *Logics of Disintegration: Post-Structuralist Thought and the Claims of Critical Theory*. London: Verso.

Diamond, I. and Quinby, L. (eds) 1988: *Feminism and Foucault: Reflections on Resistance*. Boston: Northeastern University Press.

Dickens, D. R. and Fontana, A. (eds) 1994: *Postmodernism and Social Inquiry*. London: UCL Press.

Dodd, N. 1994: *The Sociology of Money: Economics, Reason and Contemporary Society*. Cambridge: Polity Press.

Dreyfus, H. L. and Rabinow, P. 1986: What is maturity? Habermas and Foucault on 'What is enlightenment?' In D. C. Hoy (ed.), *Foucault: A Critical Reader*, Oxford: Blackwell.

Durkheim, E. 1952: *Suicide: A Study in Sociology*, ed. G. Simpson. London: Free Press.

—— 1953: *Sociology and Philosophy*, trans. D. F. Pocock. London: Cohen and West.

—— 1972: *Selected Writings*, ed. A. Giddens. Cambridge: Cambridge University Press.

—— 1973:*Émile Durkheim on Morality and Society: Selected Writings*, ed. R. N. Bellah. Chicago: University of Chicago Press.

—— 1975: *Durkheim on Religion: A Selection of Readings with Bibliographies*, ed. W. S. F. Pickering. London: Routledge and Kegan Paul.

—— 1976: *The Elementary Forms of the Religious Life*. London: Allen and Unwin.

—— 1979: *Durkheim: Essays on Morals and Education*, ed. W. S. F. Pickering. London: Routledge and Kegan Paul.

—— 1982: *The Rules of Sociological Method and Selected Texts on Sociology and its Method*, ed. S. Lukes. London: Macmillan.

—— 1984: *The Division of Labour in Society*. Basingstoke: Macmillan.

—— 1985: *Readings from Émile Durkheim*, ed. K. Thompson. London: Routledge.

—— 1986: *Durkheim on Politics and the State*, ed. A. Giddens. Cambridge: Polity Press.

—— 1992: *Professional Ethics and Civic Morals*. London: Routledge.

—— 1994: *Émile Durkheim on Institutional Analysis*, ed. M. Traugott. Chicago: University of Chicago Press.

Eder, K. 1996: *The Social Construction of Nature*. London: Sage.

Eley, G. 1992: Nations, publics, and political cultures: placing Habermas in the nineteenth century. In C. Calhoun (ed.), *Habermas and the Public Sphere*, Cambridge: Polity Press.

Elster, J. 1985: *Making Sense of Marx*. Cambridge: Cambridge University Press.

Featherstone, M. (ed.) 1990: *Global Culture: Nationalism, Globalization and Modernity*. London: Sage.

Featherstone, M., Lash, S. and Robertson, R. (eds) 1995: *Global Modernities*. London: Sage.

Ferry, L. and Renaut, A. 1990: *French Philosophy of the Sixties: An Essay on Antihumanism*. Amherst: University of Massachusetts Press.

Fine, B. 1984: *Marx's Capital*, 2nd edn. London: Macmillan.

Fine, B. and Harris, L. 1979: *Rereading 'Capital'*. London: Macmillan.

Fischer, M. 1990: Redefining philosophy as literature: Richard Rorty's 'defence' of literary culture. In A. R. Malachowski (ed.), *Reading Rorty: Critical Responses to Philosophy and the Mirror of Nature (and Beyond)*, Oxford: Blackwell.

Foster, H. (ed.) 1985: *Postmodern Culture*. London: Pluto Press.

Foucault, M. 1970: *The Order of Things: An Archaeology of the Human Sciences*. London: Tavistock.

—— 1971: *Madness and Civilization: A History of Insanity in the Age of Reason*. London: Tavistock.

—— 1972: *The Archaeology of Knowledge*. London: Tavistock.

—— 1973: *The Birth of the Clinic: An Archaeology of Medical Perception*. New York: Vintage Books.

—— 1977a: *Language, Counter-Memory, Practice: Selected Essays and Interviews*, ed. D. F. Bouchard. Ithaca, N.Y.: Cornell University Press.

—— 1977b: *Discipline and Punish*. New York: Pantheon.

—— 1977c: Nietzsche, genealogy, history. In M. Foucault, *Language, Counter-Memory, Practice: Selected Essays and Interviews*, ed. D. F. Bouchard. Ithaca, N.Y.: Cornell University Press.

—— 1978: *The History of Sexuality, Volume I: An Introduction*. New York: Pantheon.

—— 1980: *Power/Knowledge: Selected Interviews and Other Writings, 1972–1977*, ed. C. Gordon et al. Brighton: Harvester Press.

—— 1985:*The History of Sexuality, Volume II: The Use of Pleasure*. Harmondsworth: Penguin Books.

—— 1986:*The History of Sexuality, Volume III: Care of the Self*. Harmondsworth: Penguin Books.

—— 1987: *Mental Illness and Psychology*. New York: University of California Press.

—— 1988a: *Politics, Philosophy, Culture: Interviews and Other Writings, 1977–1984*, ed. L. D. Kritzman. London: Routledge.

—— 1988b: The ethic of the care for the self as a practice of freedom. In J. Bernauer and D. Rasmussen (eds), *The Final Foucault*, Cambridge, Mass.: MIT Press.

Franklin, J. (ed.) 1998: *The Politics of Risk Society*. Cambridge: Polity Press.

Fraser, N. 1985: Michel Foucault: a 'Young Conservative'? *Ethics*, 96, 165–84.

—— 1989: *Unruly Practices: Power, Discourse and Gender in Contemporary Social Theory*. Cambridge: Polity Press.

—— 1990: Solidarity or singularity? Richard Rorty between romanticism and technocracy. In A. R. Malachowski (ed.), *Reading Rorty: Critical Responses to Philosophy and the Mirror of Nature (and Beyond)*, Oxford: Blackwell (also in *Praxis International*, 8 (1988), 257–72).

—— 1992a: The uses and abuses of French discourse theories for feminist politics. *Theory, Culture and Society*, 9, 51–71.

—— 1992b: Rethinking the public sphere: a contribution to the critique of actually existing democracy. In C. Calhoun (ed.), *Habermas and the Public Sphere*, Cambridge: Polity Press.

Fraught, F. 1991: Neglected affinities: Max Weber and Georg Simmel. In P. Hamilton (ed.), *Max Weber: Critical Assessments*, London: Routledge.

Freud, S. 1985: *Civilization, Society and Religion*, vol. 12 of the Pelican Freud Library. Harmondsworth: Penguin Books.

Frisby, D. 1985: *Fragments of Modernity*. Cambridge: Polity Press.

—— 1992a: *Simmel and Since*. London: Routledge.

—— 1992b: *Sociological Impressionism: A Reassessment of Georg Simmel's Social Theory*, 2nd edn. London: Routledge.

Fukuyama, F. 1992: *The End of History and the Last Man*. London: Hamish Hamilton.

—— 1995: *Trust: The Social Virtues and the Creation of Prosperity*. London: Hamish Hamilton.

Fuss, D. 1990: *Essentially Speaking: Feminism, Nature and Difference*. London: Routledge.

Gadamer, H.-G. 1989: *Truth and Method*. London: Sheed and Ward.

Gane, M. 1991a: *Baudrillard: Critical and Fatal Theory*. London: Routledge.

—— 1991b: *Baudrillard's Bestiary: Baudrillard and Culture*. London: Routledge.

Gane, M. and Johnson, T. (eds) 1993: *Foucault's New Domains*. London: Routledge.

Ganßmann, H. 1988: Money – a symbolically generalized medium of communication? On the concept of money in recent sociology. *Economy and Society*, 17, 285–316.

Garfinkel, H. 1984: *Studies in Ethnomethodology*. Cambridge: Polity Press.

Gellner, E. 1992: *Postmodernism, Reason and Religion*. London: Routledge.

Giddens, A. 1971: *Capitalism and Modern Social Theory*. Cambridge: Cambridge University Press.

—— 1978: *Durkheim*. London: Fontana Press.

—— 1979: *Studies in Social and Political Theory*. London: Hutchinson.

—— 1982: Historical materialism today: an interview with Anthony Giddens. *Theory, Culture and Society*, 1, 63–77.

—— 1984: *The Constitution of Society*. Cambridge: Polity Press.

—— 1985: *The Nation-State and Violence*. Cambridge: Polity Press.

—— 1987: *Social Theory and Modern Sociology*. Cambridge: Polity Press.

—— 1990: *The Consequences of Modernity*. Cambridge: Polity Press.

—— 1991: *Modernity and Self-Identity*. Cambridge: Polity Press.

—— 1992: *The Transformation of Intimacy: Sexuality, Love and Eroticism in Modern Societies*. Cambridge: Polity Press.

—— 1993: *The Giddens Reader*, ed. P. Cassell. Basingstoke: Macmillan.

—— 1994: *Beyond Left and Right*. Cambridge: Polity Press.

—— 1998: *The Third Way: The Renewal of Social Democracy*. Cambridge: Polity Press.

Giddens, A. and Pierson, C. 1998: *Conversations with Anthony Giddens: Making Sense of Modernity*. Cambridge: Polity Press.

Goldman, H. 1988: *Max Weber and Thomas Mann: Calling and the Shaping of the Self*. Berkeley: University of California Press.

Gordon, C. 1993: Question, ethos, event: Foucault on Kant and Enlightenment. In M. Gane and T. Johnson (eds), *Foucault's New Domains*, London: Routledge.

Gorz, A. 1982: *Farewell to the Working Class: An Essay on Post-Industrial Socialism*. London: Pluto Press.

—— 1985: *Paths to Paradise: On the Liberation from Work*. London: Pluto Press.

Grossberg, L. and Nelson, C. (eds) 1988: *Marxism and the Interpretation of Culture.* London: Macmillan.

Habermas, J. 1976: *Legitimation Crisis.* London: Heinemann.

—— 1979: *Communication and the Evolution of Society.* London: Heinemann.

—— 1981: Modernity versus postmodernity. *New German Critique*, 22, 3–14.

—— 1984: *The Theory of Communicative Action*, vol. 1: *Reason and the Rationalization of Society.* London: Heinemann.

—— 1986: *Autonomy and Solidarity: Interviews*, ed. P. Dews. London: Verso.

—— 1987a: *Knowledge and Human Interests.* Cambridge: Polity Press.

—— 1987b: *The Philosophical Discourse of Modernity: Twelve Lectures.* Cambridge: Polity Press.

—— 1987c: *The Theory of Communicative Action*, vol. 2: *A Critique of Functionalist Reason.* Cambridge: Polity Press.

—— 1987d: *Toward a Rational Society: Student Protest, Science, and Politics.* Cambridge: Polity Press.

—— 1988: *Theory and Practice.* Cambridge: Polity Press.

—— 1989a: *The Structural Transformation of the Public Sphere: An Inquiry into a Category of Bourgeois Society.* Cambridge: Polity Press.

—— 1989b: *The New Conservativism: Cultural Criticism and the Historians' Debate.* Cambridge: Polity Press.

—— 1989c: *On the Logic of the Social Sciences.* Cambridge, Mass.: MIT Press.

—— 1990: *Moral Consciousness and Communicative Action.* Cambridge: Polity Press.

—— 1992a: *Postmetaphysical Thinking: Philosophical Essays.* Cambridge: Polity Press.

—— 1992b: Citizenship and national identity: some reflections on the future of Europe. *Praxis International*, 12, 1–19.

—— 1993: *Justification and Application: Remarks on Discourse Ethics.* Cambridge: Polity Press.

—— 1994: *The Past as Future: Jürgen Habermas interviewed by Michael Haller*, ed. M. Pensky. Cambridge: Polity Press.

—— 1996a: *Between Facts and Norms: Contributions to a Discourse Theory of Law and Democracy.* Cambridge: Polity Press.

—— 1996b: *The Habermas Reader*, ed. W. Outhwaite. Cambridge: Polity Press.

—— 1997: *A Berlin Republic: Writings on Germany.* Lincoln: University of Nebraska Press.

Hall, D. L. 1994: *Richard Rorty: Prophet and Poet of the New Pragmatism.* Albany: State University of New York Press.

Hamilton, P. (ed.) 1991: *Max Weber: Critical Assessments* (4 vols). London: Routledge.

Held, D. 1980: *Introduction to Critical Theory: Horkheimer to Habermas.* Cambridge: Polity Press.

—— (ed.) 1992: *Prospects for Democracy.* Special issue, *Political Studies*, 40.

Held, D. and Thompson, J. B. 1989: *Social Theory of Modern Societies: Anthony Giddens and his Critics.* Cambridge: Cambridge University Press.

Hennis, W. 1988: *Max Weber: Essays in Reconstruction.* London: Allen and Unwin.

Hindess, B. (ed.) 1977: *Sociological Theories of the Economy.* London: Macmillan.

Hirst, P. and Thompson, G. 1996: *Globalization in Question.* Cambridge: Polity Press.

Hohendahl, P. U. 1985: The Dialectic of Enlightenment revisited: Habermas' critique of the Frankfurt School. *New German Critique*, 35, 3–26.

Hollis, M. 1990: The poetics of personhood. In A. R. Malachowski (ed.), *Reading*

Rorty: Critical Responses to Philosophy and the Mirror of Nature (and Beyond), Oxford: Blackwell.

Holton, R. J. 1986: Talcott Parsons and the theory of economy and society. In R. J. Holton and B. S. Turner (eds), *Talcott Parsons on Economy and Society*, London: Routledge.

Holton, R. J. and Turner, B. S. (eds) 1986: *Talcott Parsons on Economy and Society*. London: Routledge.

Holub, R. 1991: *Jürgen Habermas: Critic in the Public Sphere*. London: Routledge.

Honneth, A. and Joas, H. (eds) 1991: *Communicative Action: Essays on Jürgen Habermas' 'The Theory of Communicative Action'* Cambridge: Polity Press.

Horkheimer, M. 1941: Notes on Institute activities. *Studies in Philosophy and Social Science*, 9(1).

—— 1972: *Critical Theory: Selected Essays*, trans. M. J. O'Connell. New York: Herder and Herder.

—— 1974a: *Critique of Instrumental Reason*, trans. M. J. O'Connell. New York: Seabury Press, .

—— 1974b: *Eclipse of Reason*. New York: Seabury Press.

—— 1995: *Between Philosophy and Social Science: Selected Early Writings*. Cambridge, Mass.: MIT Press.

How, A. R. 1980: Dialogue as productive limitation in social theory: the Habermas–Gadamer debate. *Journal of the British Society for Phenomenology*, 11, 131–43.

Hoy, D. C. 1978: *The Critical Circle: Literature, History and Philosophical Hermeneutics*. Berkeley: University of California Press.

—— (ed.) 1986b: *Foucault: A Critical Reader*. Oxford: Blackwell.

—— 1986a: Power, repression, progress: Foucault, Lukes, and the Frankfurt School. In D. C. Hoy (ed.), *Foucault: A Critical Reader*, Oxford: Blackwell.

Hoy, D. C. and McCarthy, T. 1994: *Critical Theory*. Oxford: Blackwell.

Huff, T. 1984: *Max Weber and the Methodology of the Social Sciences*. London: Transaction Books.

Hughes, J. A., Martin, P. J. and Sharrock. W. W. 1995: *Understanding Classical Sociology: Marx, Weber, Durkheim*. London: Sage.

Ingram, D. 1983: The historical genesis of the Gadamer–Habermas controversy. *Auslegung*, 10, 86–151.

—— 1987: *Habermas and the Dialectic of Reason*. New Haven: Yale University Press.

Jagd, S. 1998: Max Weber and the division of labour between economic theory and economic sociology. Paper presented at the First Portuguese Congress on Economic Sociology, Lisbon, 4–6 Mar. 1998. Søren Jagd, Department of Social Sciences, Roskilde University, Denmark.

Jameson, F. 1991: *Postmodernism, or, The Cultural Logic of Late Capitalism*. London: Verso.

Jay, M. 1973: *The Dialectical Imagination: A History of the Frankfurt School and the Institute of Social Research, 1923–1950*. Boston: Little, Brown.

—— 1982. Should intellectual history take a linguistic turn? Reflections on the Habermas–Gadamer debate. In D. LaCapra and S. L. Kaplan (eds), *Modern European Intellectual History: Reappraisals and New Perspectives*, Ithaca, N.Y.: Cornell University Press.

—— 1984a: *Adorno*. Cambridge, Mass.: Harvard University Press.

—— 1984b: *Marxism and Totality: The Adventures of a Concept from Lukács to Habermas*.

Berkeley: University of California Press.

Kalberg, S. 1994: *Max Weber's Comparative-Historical Sociology*. Cambridge: Polity Press.

Kasler, D. 1988: *Max Weber: An Introduction to his Life and Work*. Cambridge: Polity Press.

Keane, J. 1992: The modern democratic revolution: reflections on Lyotard's *The Postmodern Condition*. In A. Benjamin (ed.), *Judging Lyotard*, London: Routledge.

Kellner, D. 1988: Postmodernism as social theory: some challenges and problems. *Theory, Culture and Society*, 5, 239–270.

—— 1989: *Jean Baudrillard: From Marxism to Postmodernism and Beyond*. Cambridge: Polity Press.

—— 1998: Zygmunt Bauman's postmodern turn. *Theory, Culture and Society*, 15, 73–86.

Kohlberg, L. 1981: *The Philosophy of Moral Development: Moral Stages and the Idea of Justice*. San Francisco: Harper and Row.

Kuhn, T. 1970: *The Structure of Scientific Revolutions*, 2nd edn. London: University of Chicago Press.

Kumar, K. 1978: *Prophecy and Progress: The Sociology of Industrial and Post-Industrial Society*. Harmondsworth: Penguin Books.

LaCapra, D. and Kaplan, S. L. (eds) 1982: *Modern European Intellectual History: Reappraisals and New Perspectives*. Ithaca, N.Y.: Cornell University Press.

Landes, J. 1988: *Women and the Public Sphere in the Age of the French Revolution*. Ithaca, N.Y.: Cornell University Press.

Lasch, C. 1980: *The Culture of Narcissism*, London: Abacus.

—— 1985: *The Minimal Self*. London: Picador.

Lash, S. 1990: *Sociology of Postmodernism*. London: Routledge.

—— 1993: Reflexive modernization: the aesthetic dimension. *Theory, Culture and Society*, 10, 1–23.

Lash, S. and Urry, J. 1987: *The End of Organized Capitalism*. Cambridge: Polity Press.

—— 1993: *Economies of Signs and Space*. London: Sage.

Lash, S. and Whimster, S. 1986: *Max Weber, Rationality and Modernity*. London: Allen and Unwin.

Lash, S., Szerszynski, B. and Wynne, B. (eds.) 1996: *Risk, Environment and Modernity: Towards a New Ecology*. London: Sage.

Lechner, F. J. 1991: Simmel on social space. *Theory, Culture and Society*, 8, 195–201.

Lichtblau, K. 1991: Causality or interaction? Simmel, Weber and interpretive sociology. *Theory, Culture and Society*, 8, 33–62.

Lowenthal, L. 1987: *False Prophets: Studies on Authoritarianism*. New Brunswick: Transaction Books.

Lukes, S. 1975: *Émile Durkheim*. Harmondsworth: Penguin Books.

Lyon, D. 1988: *The Information Society: Issues and Illusions*. Cambridge: Polity Press.

—— 1994: *The Electronic Eye: The Rise of Surveillance Society*. Cambridge: Polity Press.

Lyotard, J.-F. 1984: *The Postmodern Condition: A Report on Knowledge*. Manchester: Manchester University Press.

—— 1988: *The Differend: Phrases in Dispute*. Minneapolis: University of Minnesota Press.

—— 1989a: Defining the postmodern. In L. Appignanesi (ed.), *Postmodernism: ICA Documents*, London: Free Association Books.

—— 1989b: Complexity and the sublime. In L. Appignanesi (ed.), *Postmodernism: ICA Documents*, London: Free Association Books.

—— 1989c: *The Lyotard Reader*, ed. A. Benjamin. Oxford: Blackwell.

—— 1991: *The Inhuman: Reflections on Time*. Cambridge: Polity Press.

—— 1993a: *Political Writings*, trans. B. Readings and K. P. Geiman. London: UCL Press.

—— 1993b: *Libidinal Economy*. London: Athlone Press.

—— 1998: *The Politics of Jean-François Lyotard*, ed. C. Rojek and B. S. Turner. London: Routledge.

Lyotard, J.-F. and Thébaud, J. L. 1985: *Just Gaming*. Manchester: Manchester University Press.

McCarthy, T. 1978: *The Critical Theory of Jürgen Habermas*. London: Hutchinson.

—— 1985: Complexity and democracy, or, the seducements of systems theory. *New German Critique*, 35, 27–53.

McLellan, D. 1995: *The Thought of Karl Marx: An Introduction*, 3rd edn. London: Papermac.

McLuhan, M. 1973: *Understanding Media*. London: Abacus Books.

McNay, L. 1992: *Foucault and Feminism*. Cambridge: Polity Press.

—— 1994: *Foucault: A Critical Introduction*. Cambridge: Polity Press.

Maffesoli, M. 1995: *Time of the Tribes: The Decline of Individualism in Mass Society*. London: Sage.

Malachowski, A. R. 1990a: Deep epistemology without foundations (in language). In A. R. Malachowski (ed.), *Reading Rorty: Critical Responses to Philosophy and the Mirror of Nature (and Beyond)*, Oxford: Blackwell.

—— (ed.) 1990b: *Reading Rorty: Critical Responses to Philosophy and the Mirror of Nature (And Beyond)*. Oxford: Blackwell.

Mann, M. 1986: *The Sources of Social Power*, vol. 1: *A History of Power from the Beginning to AD 1760*. Cambridge: Cambridge University Press.

Marcuse, H. 1960: *Reason and Revolution: Hegel and the Rise of Social Theory*. Boston: Beacon Press.

—— 1966: *Eros and Civilization: A Philosophical Inquiry into Freud*, 2nd edn. Boston: Beacon Press.

—— 1968: *Negations: Essays in Critical Theory*. Boston: Beacon Press.

—— 1969: *An Essay on Liberation*. Boston: Beacon Press.

—— 1970: *Five Lectures: Psychoanalysis, Politics and Utopia*, trans. J. J. Shapiro and S. M. Weber. Boston: Beacon Press.

—— 1972: *Counterrevolution and Revolt*. Boston: Beacon Press.

—— 1979: *The Aesthetic Dimension: Toward a Critique of Marxist Aesthetics*. London: Macmillan.

—— 1991: *One-Dimensional Man: Studies in the Ideology of Advanced Industrial Society*, , 2nd edn. London: Routledge.

—— 1998: *Technology, War and Fascism*, collected papers of Herbert Marcuse, vol. 1, ed. D. Kellner. London: Routledge.

Marx, K. 1956: *Capital*, vol. 2. London: Lawrence and Wishart.

—— 1959: *Capital*, vol. 3. London: Lawrence and Wishart.

—— 1965: *The German Ideology*. London: Lawrence and Wishart.

—— 1970: *The Economic and Philosophical Manuscripts of 1844*. London: Lawrence and Wishart.

—— 1977: *Selected Writings*, ed. D. McLellan. Oxford: Oxford University Press.

—— 1981: *A Contribution to the Critique of Political Economy*. London: Lawrence and Wishart.

—— 1982: *Capital*, vol. 1. Harmondsworth: Penguin Books.

—— 1986: *Karl Marx: A Reader*, ed. J. Elster. Cambridge: Cambridge University Press.

Marx, K. and Engels, F. 1992: *The Communist Manifesto*, ed. D. McLellan. Oxford: Oxford University Press.

Massing, P. 1949: *Rehearsal for Destruction: A Study of Political Anti-Semitism in Imperial Germany*. New York: Harper.

Mead, G. H. 1981: *Selected Writings*, ed. A. J. Reck. Chicago: University of Chicago Press.

Mendelson, J. 1979: The Habermas–Gadamer debate. *New German Critique*, 18, 44–73.

Merquior, J. G. 1991: *Foucault*, 2nd edn. London: Fontana Press.

Mestrovic, S. 1998: *Anthony Giddens: The Last Modernist*. London: Routledge.

Miller, D. 1992: Deliberative democracy and public choice. In D. Held (ed.), *Prospects for Democracy*. Special issue, *Political Studies*, 40.

Misgeld, D. 1977: Discourse and conversation: the theory of communicative competence and hermeneutics in the light of the debate between Habermas and Gadamer. *Cultural Hermeneutics*, 4, 321–44.

—— 1985: Critical hermeneutics versus neoparsonianism? *New German Critique*, 35, 55–82.

Mommsen, W. J. 1974: *The Age of Bureaucracy: Perspectives on the Political Sociology of Max Weber*. Oxford: Blackwell.

—— 1985: *Max Weber and German Politics, 1890–1920*. Chicago: University of Chicago Press.

—— 1989: *Political and Social Theory of Max Weber*. Cambridge: Polity Press.

Oakes, G. 1991: The Verstehen thesis and the foundations of Max Weber's methodology. In P. Hamilton (ed.), *Max Weber: Critical Assessments*, London: Routledge.

O'Brien, P. 1982: *The Promise of Punishment: Prisons in Nineteenth Century France*. Princeton: Princeton University Press.

O'Farrell, C. 1989: *Foucault: Historian or Philosopher?* London: Macmillan.

Oliver, K. 1991: Fractal politics: how to use 'the subject'. *Praxis International*, 11, 178–94.

Outhwaite, W. 1994: *Habermas: A Critical Introduction*. Cambridge: Polity Press.

Parsons, T. 1952: *The Social System*. London: Tavistock.

—— 1967: *Sociological Theory and Modern Society*. New York: Free Press.

—— 1976: Social structure and the symbolic media of interaction. In P. Blau (ed.), *Approaches to the Study of Social Action*, London: Open Books.

—— 1977: *Social Systems and the Evolution of Action Theory*. New York: Free Press.

Parsons, T. and Smelser, N. 1957: *Economy and Society*. London: Routledge.

Poggi, G. 1983: *Calvinism and the Capitalist Spirit: Max Weber's Protestant Ethic*. London: Macmillan.

—— 1993: *Money and the Modern Mind: Georg Simmel's 'Philosophy of Money'*. Berkeley: University of California Press.

Poster, M. 1993: Foucault and the problem of self-constitution. In J. Caputo and

M. Yount (eds), *Foucault and the Critique of Institutions*, University Park, Pa.: Pennsylvania State University Press.

Ransom, J. 1993: Feminism, difference and discourse: the limits of discursive analysis for feminism. In C. Ramazanoğlu (ed.), *Up Against Foucault*, London: Routledge.

Ramazanoğlu, C. (ed.) 1993: *Up Against Foucault*. London: Routledge.

Rasmussen, D. M. 1990: *Reading Habermas*. Oxford: Blackwell.

Riesebrodt, M. 1986: From patriarchalism to capitalism: the theoretical context of Max Weber's agrarian studies (1892–93). *Economy and Society*, 15, 476–502.

Ringer, F. 1997: *Max Weber's Methodology: The Unification of the Cultural and Social Sciences*. Cambridge, Mass.: Harvard University Press.

Roheim, G. (ed.) 1951: *Psychoanalysis and the Social Sciences*. New York: International Universities Press.

Rojek, C. 1993: Baudrillard and politics. In C. Rojek and B. Turner (eds), *Forget Baudrillard?* London: Routledge.

Rojek, C. and Turner, B. (eds) 1993: *Forget Baudrillard?* London: Routledge.

Rorty, R. 1980: *Philosophy and the Mirror of Nature*. Oxford: Blackwell.

—— 1983: Postmodernist bourgeois liberalism. *Journal of Philosophy*, 80, 583–9.

—— 1986a: The contingency of language. *London Review of Books*, 17 Apr.

—— 1986b: The contingency of selfhood. *London Review of Books*, 8 May.

—— 1986c: The contingency of community. *London Review of Books*, 24 July.

—— 1989: *Contingency, Irony and Solidarity*. Cambridge: Cambridge University Press.

—— 1990: The priority of democracy to philosophy. In A. R. Malachowski (ed.), *Reading Rorty: Critical Responses to Philosophy and the Mirror of Nature (and Beyond)*, Oxford: Blackwell.

—— 1991a: *Objectivity, Relativism and Truth: Philosophical Papers, Volume 1*. Cambridge: Cambridge University Press.

—— 1991b: *Essays on Heidegger and Others: Philosophical Papers, Volume 2*. Cambridge: Cambridge University Press.

—— 1991c: Feminism and Pragmatism. *Michigan Quarterly Review*, 30, 231–58.

—— 1993: Feminism, ideology, and deconstruction: a pragmatist view. *Hypatia*, 8.

—— 1998a: *Achieving our Country: Leftist Thought in Twentieth-Century America*. Cambridge, Mass.: Harvard University Press.

—— 1998b: *Truth and Progress: Philosophical Papers, Volume 3*. Cambridge: Cambridge University Press.

Rosen, B. and White, D. M. (eds) 1957: *Mass Culture: The Popular Arts in America*. Glencoe, Ill.: Free Press.

Ryan, M. P. 1990: *Women in Public: Between Banners and Ballots, 1825–1880*. Baltimore: Johns Hopkins University Press.

Sarup, M. 1993: *Post-Structuralism and Postmodernism*, 2nd edn. New York: Harvester Wheatsheaf.

Saussure, F. de 1974: *Course in General Linguistics*. London: Fontana/Collins.

Savage, S. P. 1977: Talcott Parsons and the structural-functionalist theory of the economy. In B. Hindess (ed.), *Sociological Theories of the Economy*, London: Macmillan.

Sayer, D. 1987: *The Violence of Abstraction: The Analytic Foundations of Historical Materialism*. Oxford: Blackwell.

—— 1990: *Capitalism and Modernity: An Excursus on Marx and Weber*. London: Routledge.

Scaff, L. A. 1989: *Fleeing the Iron Cage: Culture, Politics and Modernity in the Thought of Max Weber*. Berkeley: University of California Press.

Scott, A. (ed.) 1997: *The Limits of Globalization: Cases and Arguments*. London: Routledge.

Scruton, R. 1996: *Modern Philosophy: An Introduction and Survey*. London: Mandarin.

Simmel, E. (ed.) 1946: *Anti-Semitism: A Social Disease*. New York: International Universities Press.

Simmel, G. 1964: *The Sociology of Georg Simmel*, ed. K. H. Wolff. Glencoe, Ill.: Free Press.

—— 1971: *On Individuality and Social Forms: Selected Writings*, ed. D. Levine. Chicago: University of Chicago Press.

—— 1978: *The Philosophy of Money*, 1st edn. London: Routledge.

—— 1980: *Essays on Interpretation in Social Science*, ed. G. Oakes. Totowa, N.J.: Rowman and Littlefield.

—— 1990: *The Philosophy of Money*, 2nd edn. London: Routledge.

—— 1991: The problem of style. *Theory, Culture and Society*, 8, 63–71.

—— 1997: *Simmel on Culture: Selected Writings*, ed. D. Frisby and M. Featherstone. London: Sage.

Skocpol, T. 1978: *The Structure of Social Revolutions*. Cambridge: Cambridge University Press.

Smart, B. 1993: Europe/America: Baudrillard's fatal comparison. In C. Rojek and B. Turner (eds), *Forget Baudrillard?* London: Routledge.

Smith, A. 1986: *The Wealth of Nations*. Harmondsworth: Penguin Books.

Smith, D. 1998: Zygmunt Bauman: how to be a successful outsider. *Theory, Culture and Society*, 15, 39–46.

Smith-Rosernberg, C. 1986: Writing history: language, class and gender. In T. de Lauretis (ed.), *Feminist Studies/Critical Studies*, Bloomington: Indiana University Press.

Sorell, T. 1990: The world from its own point of view. In A. R. Malachowski (ed.), *Reading Rorty: Critical Responses to Philosophy and the Mirror of Nature (and Beyond)*, Oxford: Blackwell.

Stauth, G. and Turner, B. 1988: *Nietzsche's Dance*. Oxford: Blackwell.

Steuerman, E. 1992: Habermas vs Lyotard: modernity vs postmodernity? In A. Benjamin (ed.), *Judging Lyotard*, London: Routledge.

Swedberg, R. 1987: *Economic Sociology: Past and Present*. Special issue, *Current Sociology*, 35.

Taylor, C. 1990: Rorty in the epistemological tradition. In A. R. Malachowski (ed.), *Reading Rorty: Critical Responses to Philosophy and the Mirror of Nature (and Beyond)*, Oxford: Blackwell.

Thompson, J. B. 1981: *Critical Hermeneutics: A Study in the Thought of Paul Ricoeur and Jürgen Habermas*. Cambridge: Cambridge University Press.

—— 1984: *Studies in the Theory of Ideology*. Cambridge: Polity Press.

—— 1990: *Ideology and Modern Culture: Critical Social Theory in the Era of Mass Communication*. Cambridge: Polity Press.

Thompson, J. B. and Held. D. (eds) 1982: *Habermas: Critical Debates*. London: Macmillan.

Touraine, A. 1971: *The Post-Industrial Society*. New York: Random House.

Tribe, K. 1979: Introduction to Weber. *Economy and Society*, 8, 172–6.

Turner, B. S. (ed.) 1989: *Theories of Modernity and Postmodernity*. London: Sage.

—— 1992: *Max Weber: From History to Modernity*. London: Routledge.

—— 1993: Baudrillard for sociologists. In C. Rojek and B. Turner (eds), *Forget Baudrillard?* London: Routledge.

Weber, M. 1930: *The Protestant Ethic and the Spirit of Capitalism*. London: Allen and Unwin.

—— 1961: *General Economic History*. London: Collier-Macmillan.

—— 1969: *On the Methodology of the Social Sciences*, trans. E. A. Shils and H. A. Finch. New York: Free Press.

—— 1978a: *Economy and Society* (2 vols: vol. 1, pp. 1–640; vol. 2, p. 641 on). Berkeley: University of California Press.

—— 1978b: *Max Weber: Selections in Translation*, ed. W. G. Runciman. Cambridge: Cambridge University Press.

—— 1979: Developmental tendencies in the situation of East Elbian rural labourers. *Economy and Society*, 8, 177–205.

—— 1991: *From Max Weber: Essays in Sociology*, ed. H. H. Girth and C. Wright Mills. London: Routledge.

Webster, F. 1995: *Theories of the Information Society*. London: Routledge.

Weinstein, D. and Weinstein, M. A. 1989: Simmel and the theory of postmodern society. In B. Turner (ed.), *Theories of Modernity and Postmodernity*, London: Sage.

Wellmer, A. 1979: *Praktische Philosophie und Theorie der Gesellschaft*. Konstanz: Universitätsverlag.

White, S. K. 1988: *The Recent Work of Jürgen Habermas*. Cambridge: Cambridge University Press.

—— 1995a: Reason, modernity, and democracy. In S. K. White (ed.), *The Cambridge Companion to Habermas*, Cambridge: Cambridge University Press.

—— (ed.) 1995b: *The Cambridge Companion to Habermas*. Cambridge: Cambridge University Press.

Wiggershaus, R. 1994: *The Frankfurt School: Its History, Theories, and Political Significance*. Cambridge: Polity Press.

Williams, B. 1990: Auto-da-fé: consequences of pragmatism. In A. R. Malachowski (ed.), *Reading Rorty: Critical Responses to Philosophy and the Mirror of Nature (and Beyond)*, Oxford: Blackwell.

Williams, H., Sullivan, D. and Matthews, G. 1997: *Francis Fukuyama and the End of History*. Cardiff: University of Wales Press.

Willis, E. 1988: Comment. In L. Grossberg and C. Nelson (eds), *Marxism and the Interpretation of Culture*, London: Macmillan.

Wittgenstein, L. 1967: *Philosophical Investigations*. Oxford: Blackwell.

Young, I. 1987: Impartiality and the civic public: some implications of feminist critiques of moral and political theory. In S. Benhabib and D. Cornell (eds), *Feminism as Critique*, Cambridge: Polity Press.

Zelizer, V. 1994: *The Social Meaning of Money*. New York: Basic Books.

Zolberg, V. L. 1990: *Constructing a Sociology of the Arts*. Cambridge: Cambridge University Press.

Index